BYZANTIUM
A HISTORY

BYZANTIUM

A HISTORY

John Haldon

TEMPUS

First published 2000

PUBLISHED IN THE UNITED KINGDOM BY:

Tempus Publishing Ltd
The Mill, Brimscombe Port
Stroud, Gloucestershire GL5 2QG

PUBLISHED IN THE UNITED STATES OF AMERICA BY:

Arcadia Publishing Inc.
A division of Tempus Publishing Inc.
2 Cumberland Street
Charleston, SC 29401
(Tel: 1-888-313-2665)

Tempus books are available in France, Germany and Belgium
from the following addresses:

Tempus Publishing Group	Tempus Publishing Group	Tempus Publishing Group
21 Avenue de la République	Gustav-Adolf-Straße 3	Place de L'Alma 4/5
37300 Joué-lès-Tours	99084 Erfurt	1200 Brussels
FRANCE	GERMANY	BELGIUM

British Library Cataloguing in Publication Data.
A catalogue record for this book is available from the British Library.

ISBN 0 7524 1777 0

Typesetting and origination by Tempus Publishing.
PRINTED AND BOUND IN GREAT BRITAIN.

Contents

List of maps

Foreword

Many people, both friends and colleagues in the field of Byzantine Studies as well as in other fields, have contributed in one way or another to the present brief introduction to Byzantium. Perhaps most important have been the students, especially the undergraduate students, whom I have had the pleasure to teach over the last twenty years, since this book is aimed chiefly at them and at members of the general public who are looking for more than the usual romanticizing political history, or catalogue of Byzantine art and architecture, as an introduction to the history of the medieval East Roman Empire. I should like to thank all of them here, in particular James Morris and Rosemary Morris, who kindly read the manuscript in draft and offered many valuable criticisms and comments. If I have not been able to incorporate all their suggestions for improvement of the book, I can only plead the constraints of time and publishers' word limits! Finally, I owe an especial debt of thanks to Anthony Bryer, who first opened my eyes to Byzantium and who helped me to ask some of the right questions. He has always been keen and able to make Byzantium accessible to more than just the specialist, and the present contribution is intended as a recognition both of that aim and of his own contribution.

John Haldon
Birmingham, March 2000

A note on names and transliteration

All books dealing with the Byzantine world begin with a note on the transliteration of Greek words, for the simple reason that there are several different systems in use. I have decided to use the simplest: Greek terms will be transliterated as literally as possible, but without employing macrons on long vowels (thus no ê or ô for the letters eta and omega), or the phonetic rendering of certain letters (thus b will be kept as 'b' rather than 'v', for example, which is the way it would have been pronounced in most contexts). There are a few concessions towards standard modern Greek phonetic transliterations – thus Thessaloniki, rather than Thessalonike – because these are now the common form, but not many.

In addition, while Greek was the language of culture and government from the later sixth and seventh centuries, both Greek and Latin were employed before that time, and indeed the empire included at various times considerable areas where Latin was the main or only language – parts of Italy, parts of the northern Balkan region and central and western North Africa. To Latinize Greek names of the medieval period looks odd, just as Hellenizing earlier Latin names and terms appears unreasonable or confusing. I have, inevitably, had to compromise. Technical terms and names will, therefore, be presented usually in their Latin form for the period before the year AD 600, and in their Greek form thereafter. This leaves many contradictions, but is the best that can be done. Where standard English versions of technical terms, personal names or placenames exist, I have used them (thus Constantine rather than Konstantinos).

Introduction

The name 'Byzantium' is a convenient convention, coined by French scholars during the seventeenth century to describe the Roman Empire in the east after the fifth and sixth centuries AD. Consecrated in 330, Constantinople was the ancient city of Byzantion, in origin a colony of Megara in Attica, which was renamed the 'city of Constantine' by the first Christian emperor of the Roman world. He made it his capital in an effort to establish a new strategic focus for the vast Roman State, as well as to distance himself from the politics of the previous centuries. By the middle of the fifth century, the western parts of the Roman Empire were already undergoing the process of transformation which was to produce the barbarian successor kingdoms, such as those of the Franks, Visigoths and Ostrogoths, and the Burgundians, while the eastern parts remained largely unaffected by these changes. When exactly 'Byzantine' begins and 'late Roman' ends is a moot point. Some prefer to use 'Byzantine' for the eastern part of the Roman Empire from the time of Constantine I, that is to say, from the 320s and 330s; others apply it to the Eastern Empire from the later fifth or sixth century, especially from the reign of Justinian (527-565). In either case, the term 'Byzantine' legitimately covers the period from the late Roman era on, and is used to describe the history of the politics, society and culture of the medieval East Roman Empire until its demise at the hands of the Ottomans in the fifteenth century.

The 'Byzantines' actually called themselves Romans – *Romaioi* – and if they did use the word 'Byzantium' or 'Byzantine', it was used (an illustration of the connections which learned Byzantines drew between their own culture and that of the ancient world) to describe the capital city of their empire: Constantinople, ancient Byzantion. The hallmarks of this culture were that it was Christian, that the language of the state and the dominant elite was Greek, and that its political ideology was founded on its identity with the Christian Roman Empire of Constantine the Great. Much more importantly from the perspective of cultural self-identity, the literate Byzantine elite from the later eighth and ninth centuries located its roots in the late Roman world, and regarded the classical inheritance in learning and literature – naturally in a suitably Christian guise – as its own. The elite used this cultural identity to differentiate itself both from the foreigner, barbarian or outsider and, within Byzantine society, from the semi-literate or illiterate masses of rural and townsfolk.

Byzantium was a society of contrasts: a mass of provincial peasant producers, perhaps 90% of the total population for most of its history, and a few major urban centres. Constantinople – the Queen of Cities, the second Rome – was by far the largest and wealthiest. It was the seat of emperors, the focal point of literacy and elite culture. The Byzantine empire was a sophisticated state, with a complex fiscal system supporting an army, navy and administrative bureaucracy, able to preserve the basic forms of the late ancient state well into the late middle ages. It was also the heartland of the Orthodox Church; from the ninth century it became the centre of a far-flung Christian cultural commonwealth and of a network of imitative polities

9

stretching from the Balkans to the Russian principalities. The empire functioned through a complex political-theological system, in which the emperor was an autocratic ruler whose power derived directly from God, and whose task was to maintain order and harmony in imitation of the heavenly realm. In consequence, ceremony and ritual were fundamental components both of court life – which itself was felt to act as an exemplar for the rest of society and the barbarian world – and of Byzantine understanding of the world. Emperors were appointed by God; but emperors could be overthrown, and a successful usurper must, it was reasoned, have the support of God (even if people were unable at first to grasp the logic of His choice!) otherwise he could not have met with success. God's choice of a bad ruler and, by the same token, the occurrence of natural calamities and phenomena of all kinds, including defeats in battle or enemy attacks, were interpreted as signs from God, usually of His displeasure. A seventh-century story records that the abbot of a monastery near Constantinople had a dream in which he was able to ask God if all rulers and tyrants were appointed by divine choice. The answer was in the affirmative. 'Then why, O Lord', replied the abbot, 'did you send the wicked tyrant Phocas to rule over the Romans?' 'Because I could find no-one worse,' came the reply.

Plagues, earthquakes, comets, wars and other such phenomena were thus part of the relationship between the human and the divine, and were acted upon accordingly. Disasters or political calamities were frequently taken as warnings that the Chosen People – the Christian Romans – had strayed from the path of righteousness and were to be brought back to it by appropriate action, so that the search for a reason, or a scapegoat, usually followed. Such logic underlay many important imperial initiatives, even if there were longer-term social and economic factors at work which determined the choice of a particular form of action or response. Such motives also lay behind the stress on Orthodoxy ('correct belief', that is, correct interpretation of the Scriptures and the writings of the Fathers of the Church), so that many of the ecclesio-political conflicts within the Byzantine world, and thus between the Byzantine Church or government and the papacy, for example, were set off by conflicts begun over the issue of whether or not a particular imperial policy was accepted as 'Orthodox' or not.

Given the length of its existence, it is not surprising that considerable changes in state organization, as well as in social and cultural values, took place over time, so that, while there are enough constants and continuities to make the use of one term for the whole social and political formation entirely legitimate, it is also true to say that in several respects the state and society of the fifteenth century bear little relationship to those of the sixth. This is particularly true of the social and economic relationships in Byzantine society and the vocabulary through which they were understood; it is even more so in the case of many of the state's key administrative apparatuses.

In 1869 the historian William Lecky wrote:

> Of that Byzantine empire, the universal verdict of history is that it constitutes, without a single exception, the most thoroughly base and despicable form that civilization has yet assumed. There has been no other enduring civilization so absolutely destitute of all forms and elements of greatness, and none to which the epithet *mean* may be so emphatically applied...The history of the empire is

a monotonous story of the intrigues of priests, eunuchs, and women, of poisonings, of conspiracies, of uniform ingratitude.[1]

This image, which nicely reflects the morality and prejudices of the mid-Victorian world, has been remarkably resilient. Indeed, it lives on in some popular ideas about the Byzantine world, a combination of Victorian moralizing with Crusaders' prejudices; and in the use of the adjective 'Byzantine' in a pejorative sense. And there are some modern writers – for the most part, not professional historians – who have, consciously or not, transferred these prejudices to the world of contemporary scholarship, if not in respect of the 'corrupt' Byzantine court, then in terms of a romantic, 'orientalist' image of Byzantium which merely contributes to the continued obfuscation of the true nature of Byzantine society and civilization. In the light of the evidence in the written sources and the material record, the Byzantine court was certainly no more corrupt, venal or conspiracy-ridden than any other medieval court in the West or East. But it has taken a long time to deconstruct these attitudes. Historians working within the Western European tradition have been particular victims in this respect of the nationalist and Eurocentric propaganda which first arose in the seventeenth and eighteenth centuries, in the context of the evolving nationalist and rationalist attitudes of the age. Northern and Western European culture was credited with an integrity, sense of honour and straightforwardness which the corrupt 'orientalized' Byzantine world (and that of Islam) had lost.

Like any other political system, the East Roman Empire struggled throughout its existence to maintain its territorial integrity. Its greatest problem was posed by its geographical situation, for it was always surrounded by potential or actual enemies: in the east, the Sassanid Persian empire until the 620s, then the Islamic Caliphates, and finally the Seljuk and Ottoman Turks; in the north, various groups of immigrant Slavs (6th-7th century), along with nomadic peoples such as the Avars, Bulgars, Chazars, Hungarians [Magyars] and Pechenegs; and in Italy and the western coastal region of the Balkans the Lombards and Franks, and later both Saracens (from North Africa and Spain) and Normans (later 10th to mid-12th century). Finally, from the twelfth century, Italian maritime powers vied to maximize their influence over Byzantine emperors and their territory. Over-ambitious (although sometimes initially very successful) plans to recover former imperial lands, and a limited and relatively inflexible budgetary system, were key structural constraints which affected the history of the empire. From the 11th century the empire's economy was gradually overtaken by the rapidly expanding economies of Western Europe and the Italian peninsula. The capture and sack of Constantinople by the Fourth Crusade in 1204, and the partition of its territory among a variety of Latin principalities and a Latin 'empire' – a rump of the former Byzantine state – spelled the end of Byzantium as a serious international power. In spite of the re-establishment of an imperial state at Constantinople in 1261, the growth of Balkan powers such as the Serbian empire in the 14th century, and the Ottomans in both Anatolia and the Balkans thereafter, were to prevent any reassertion of Byzantine power in the region. By the time of its final absorption into the Ottoman state, the 'empire' consisted of little more than Constantinople, some Aegean islands, and parts of the southern Peloponnese in Greece.

The history of Byzantium is not just the history of its political fortunes. The evolution of Byzantine society, transformations in economic life, the relationship between urban centres and rural hinterlands, the constantly shifting apparatuses of the state's fiscal and administrative machinery, the nature and development of Byzantine (Roman) law, the growth of ecclesiastical and monastic power – both in economic as well as in ideological terms, developments in forms and styles of visual representation, literature, architecture, the sciences; all these elements are but part of a complex whole described by the term 'Byzantine' which this brief survey will introduce. Beyond description, however, comes explanation, and in the following pages I will try to provide enough information for the uninitiated reader to piece together a picture which will at once describe the course and shape of Byzantine history and also suggest an explanation for them. Byzantine society was just like any other medieval society in the sense that its social relations – based on kinship, private wealth and power, control of natural and man-made resources, and access to political authority and other forms of legitimation – can be analysed and dissected by a careful and painstaking interrogation of the relevant sources. In what follows I will attempt both to demystify the Byzantine world, and at the same time to explain its uniqueness.

There are many approaches one could adopt to introduce the Byzantine world. Two of the most useful are readily available in English, in the form of Cyril Mango's excellent *Byzantium: the empire of New Rome*, and Alexander Kazhdan and Giles Constable's *People and power in Byzantium. An introduction to modern Byzantine Studies*; both of which deal with a series of topics thematically and concentrate primarily on the conceptual, experiential and material-cultural world of Byzantium. The present short volume does not pretend to rival these studies in its coverage or in its approach to the cultural and conceptual universe of the Byzantine world, but to complement them in the form of an introduction to this complex social and cultural formation. Historians of Byzantium have already devoted many volumes to its art and its literature, to the history of its Church and to Orthodox Christianity, and to its cultural evolution in general. These are topics which this volume barely touches upon, still less treats in detail, nor does it set out to present anything like a complete history of the Byzantine world and its complex culture, an undertaking which, modern historians generally agree, is probably too big for an individual to undertake, at least with any hope of doing it properly. Therefore I have tried to present, as concisely as possible, those aspects which I believe will be most helpful to those who want to understand – and who would like to know more about – how the Byzantine state worked, how it was rooted in, and how it actively moulded, the society which supported it.

With this in mind, I have provided for each chapter some further reading, which is intended as a starting point from which readers may follow particular issues in greater detail, where they may find more detailed literature and, more importantly, where they will find more information about the sources for Byzantine history. Every historian comes to his or her material from their own particular perspective, and this perspective unavoidably influences the interpretation which follows. Explaining what that perspective is and how it determines a historical account is important. But in the end the best introduction is the self-image, as reflected unconsciously through different kinds of original source material, of the people who inhabited the past themselves.

PART I

THE LAST ANCIENT STATE

1 The transformation of the Roman world *c*.300-741

The end of the late Roman order

The third century saw the Roman world rent by a series of civil wars and barbarian invasions, which made fundamental administrative changes in both the military as well as the civil apparatus of the state inevitable. A number of features contributed to this. In the first place, the government had to contend with the enormous length of the imperial frontiers, stretching from Britain in the north, along the Rhine and the upper Danube, across the Danube to the northern Balkans and thence to the Black Sea; and in the east from the Black Sea and Caucasus region down through Armenia, Iraq and Mesopotamia to the Sinai peninsula. In Africa, the border stretched along the coastal strip and north of the Atlas mountains to the Atlantic coast and the westernmost province of Tingitania. Even in time of peace, maintaining garrisons and soldiers to police such a frontier incurred huge costs; while in times of war it was virtually impossible to defend if challenged on more than one front at the same time. Unfortunately for Rome, this is precisely what happened during the third century. In the eastern theatre the new Sassanid Persian kingdom – which had replaced the Parthian empire with which Rome had shared Iraq since the late Republic – presented a formidable and dynamic challenge to Roman control and influence in the region. In the north, Germanic immigrant populations pressed against the frontier defences along the Rhine and the Danube, so the eastern front required constant attention. The result was increasing concentrations of troops under provincial commanders whose distance from Rome meant that the central government was unable to exercise any effective authority. The demands of the soldiers for pay and rewards, the burden on the central treasuries, and the bond between soldiers and successful generals on the frontiers provoked rebellions and civil wars, so that the third century saw the empire's very existence threatened by a long series of upheavals. By the end of the century, following a series of successful frontier wars, some semblance of stability was restored; but the system as a whole – which had far outgrown its ability to control and administer such a vast empire – was seriously compromised.

After a number of attempts to introduce the changes necessary to meet the challenges posed by the new situation had proved unsuccessful, the emperor Diocletian resolved to approach the problem from a different perspective. Given the size of the empire and the difficulties of communicating between Rome and the armies on the frontiers, it was decided to divide the empire's military command into four regional groupings. A 'college' of rulers was established, consisting of two senior Augusti, Diocletian and Maximian, the latter in the West, the former in the East, each supported by a junior 'Caesar', Galerius and Constantius respectively. The latter would succeed the senior rulers when their rule ended, appointing two new junior Caesars in their place. This Tetrarchy – 'rule of four' –

worked well initially, but collapsed when Diocletian abdicated in 305, compelling his fellow Augustus, Maximian, to abdicate along with him. Diocletian had formulated policy and directed government in all spheres; and, since the tetrarchic structure applied to the military only (the civil administrative apparatus remained unified), as soon as he resigned, squabbles among his successors resulted in further civil war and disruption. The sons of Maximian, former Augustus in the West, and of Constantius, his Caesar, were passed over in the appointment of new Caesars, the choice falling upon favourites of Galerius: Severus, now appointed in the West under Constantius, and Maximinus Daia in the East under Galerius. When Constantius died his son Constantine was acclaimed emperor by his troops at York; while another claimant to the imperial throne appeared at the same moment, Maxentius the son of Maximian, who – with the support of his father who came out of retirement – was able to force the surrender of Severus, whom he executed. Thus, Maxentius declared himself Augustus.

In the following conflict, which involved a quarrel between Maxentius and Maximian, an alliance between the latter and Constantine, the appointment of Licinius – a client of Galerius – as Caesar in the West, and a second abdication by Maximian, by the year 310 the empire was ruled by no fewer than five Augusti. In 312 Constantine allied himself with Licinius, invaded Italy and defeated Maxentius at the famous battle of the Milvian bridge, during which Constantine's soldiers bore the chi-rho symbol (the first two letters of the name *Christos*) on their shields. Constantine saw his victory as the response to his appeal to the God of the Christians. Once established in Rome, he disbanded the praetorian guard, and in 313 he met with Licinius and agreed an edict of toleration by which Christians would henceforth be entirely free in their worship, and have any property, which has been confiscated during the persecutions of Diocletian and Maximin Daia, restored. Galerius had already recognized the failure of Diocletian's policies which, coming after a period of half a century of toleration of Christianity, were too late to destroy a by now well-established religious organization. The edict of Milan of 313 finalized this recognition. Relations between Constantine and Licinius remained peaceful but uneasy. Finally, in 323 war broke out, and in 324 Constantine was able to defeat Licinius, depose him, and become sole emperor. The empire remained united until the end of the century.

Constantine recognized that the empire as a whole could no longer effectively be ruled from Rome. He moved his capital eastwards, to the site of the ancient Megaran colony of Byzantium, now renamed the 'city of Constantine', Konstantinoupolis. Its strategic position was attractive, for the emperor could remain in contact with both Eastern and Western affairs from its site on the Bosphorus. Roman civic institutions were imported wholesale to the new capital, with the establishment of a senate and of central administrative institutions. The city was expanded, new walls were constructed and the emperor undertook an expensive building programme. Begun in 326, the city was formally consecrated in 330.

Constantine inaugurated a series of important reforms within both the military and civil establishment of the empire. The fiscal system was overhauled and a new gold coin, the *solidus* introduced in a successful effort to stabilize the monetary economy of the state. Military and civil offices were separated; the central administration was restructured and placed under a series of imperially-chosen senior officers directly responsible to the emperor. The armies were reorganized into two major sections: those based in frontier provinces and along the borders, and several field armies of more mobile troops attached directly to the emperor's court as a field reserve, ready to meet any invader who broke through the outer defences. The provincial administration was reformed; more and smaller provincial and intermediate units were established, to permit central control and supervision of fiscal matters. Finally, with the toleration of Christianity and its positive promotion under Constantine at the expense of many of the established non-Christian cults, the Church began to evolve into a powerful social and political force which was, in the course of time, to dominate East Roman society and to vie with the state for authority in many aspects of civil law and justice.

In spite of Constantine's efforts at reform, however, the size of the empire and the different concerns of West and East resulted in a continuation of the principle of a split government, with one ruler in each part, although the tetrarchic system was never revived. Upon Constantine's death in May 337, his three sons inherited his position with the support of the armies. Constantine II, the eldest, was recognized as senior and ruled the West. Constantius ruled in the East and Constans, the youngest, was allotted the central provinces (Africa, Italy and Illyricum). Tension between Constans and Constantine resulted in war in 340 and the defeat and death of the latter, with the result that Constans became ruler of the western regions as well. Following popular discontent among both the civilian population and the army in the West, however, Constans was deposed in 350 and his place taken by a certain Magnentius, a high-ranking officer of barbarian origin. Magnentius was not recognized by Constantius, and he invaded Illyricum. But he was defeated in 351, escaping to Italy where – after further defeats – he took his own life. Constantius ruled the empire alone until his death in 361.

In 355 Constantius had appointed his cousin Julian to represent him in Gaul; in 357, he was given the command against the invading Franks and Alamanni and, following a series of victories, he was acclaimed by his soldiers as Augustus. Constantius was campaigning against the Persian king Shapur who had invaded the eastern provinces in 359, and the acclamation may have been stimulated by the emperor's demand that Julian send him his best troops for the Persian war. Julian marched east, but on the way to meet him Constantius died in 361, naming Julian as his successor. Although a competent general and efficient administrator, Julian was unpopular with many of his soldiers because of his attempts to revive paganism, often at the financial expense of the Church. During the Persian campaign of 363 he was mortally wounded, probably by one of his own men. The troops acclaimed the commander of Julian's guards, a certain Jovian, as emperor. Having made peace with Shapur, Jovian marched back to Constantinople, dying in Bithynia a mere eight months later.

Jovian's successors were Valentinian and Valens, brothers from Pannonia (roughly modern Austria and Croatia), elected by the leading civil and military officers at Constantinople. Valentinian ruled in the West and established his capital at Milan, while Valens had to face a rebellion almost immediately, led by the usurper Procopius and caused by the soldiers loyal to Julian, whose favourite Procopius had been. But the rebellion petered out in 366.

The two new emperors each had substantial military challenges to overcome. In the West Valentinian had to deal with invasions from Franks, Alamanni and Saxons in Gaul, from Picts and Scots in Britain, and from rebellious chieftains in Mauretania. He died in 375 while fighting a Germanic people in Pannonia, the Quadi, and was followed by his chosen successor Gratian. In the east, Valens had to deal with repeated Gothic invasions of Thrace, caused by pressure from the Huns who had destroyed the kingdom of the Ostrogoths (east Goths) in the Ukraine in 373; while he campaigned in Armenia in 371 to recover territories seized by the Persians. In 377 he moved back to Thrace to confront a Gothic invasion, and was disastrously defeated and killed at a battle near Adrianople in Thrace in 378. The Goths overran and plundered Thrace.

Gratian appointed the general Theodosius – son of a successful general of the same name and himself an experienced commander – initially as commander-in-chief and then Augustus, and by a combination of diplomacy and strategy Theodosius was able to make peace with the Goths, permitting them to settle within the empire under their own laws, providing troops for the imperial armies in return for annual food subsidies. Following the death of Gratian in 383 as the result of a coup, and the eventual overthrow of the usurper, Magnus Maximus, by Theodosius in 388, Theodosius became sole ruler. He was, however, the last emperor to hold this position. At his death in 395 his two sons Arcadius (in the East) and Honorius (in the West) ruled jointly. But as minors they were greatly influenced by the chief military and other officers at court. The Germanic generals Stilicho and Gainas were the effective rulers, and although the latter held his position for only a short while at Constantinople, the weakness of the imperial authority was apparent. Even under Stilicho's authority, however, the western half of the empire began to fall apart. The British provinces were abandoned to their own devices in 410 (after further unsuccessful revolts); Rome itself was sacked by the Visigoths in 410; barbarian tribes were increasingly bought off – frequently by near kinsmen in positions of authority within the imperial government – with territorial concessions which effectively established more-or-less autonomous petty chieftainships within Roman territory. And by the 430s whole provinces were under barbarian rule, technically as allies or federates of the Romans, but effectively independent: the Vandals in North Africa, the Suebi in Spain, the Visigoths in southern France and Spain. When the last western emperor was deposed in 476, Italy itself was effectively dominated by Germanic officers, led by the general Odoacer, and occupied by barbarian troops.

The eastern half of the empire survived for a variety of reasons: a healthier economy, more diversified pattern of urban and rural relationships and markets, and a more solid tax-base; for Constantinople had Egypt and the rich provinces of Syria at its disposal. In addition, eastern diplomacy encouraged barbarian leaders to look westward, while at the same time the walls of Constantinople – newly-built on a massive scale under Theodosius II (408-450) – rendered any attempt to take that city fruitless. The *magistri militum* – 'masters of the soldiers' – who commanded the imperial field forces nevertheless remained for the most part of German origin and continued to dominate the court. Only with the appointment of the Emperor Leo I (457-474) was this cycle broken, for Leo – although a candidate promoted by the master of soldiers, Aspar, the 'king-maker' – was able to take the initiative (through using Isaurian mercenaries) and during the last years of his reign rid himself of

Above and right: The fifth-century walls of Constantinople.

Aspar. While the Isaurians, who were involved in factional strife at court and in the provinces, were themselves something of a problem, some stability was thereafter re-established. Leo I was succeeded by his grandson Leo II, the son of a certain Zeno, who had married Leo I's daughter and was commander of the *excubitores*, Leo's Isaurian guards. Leo appointed his father co-emperor, but died in 474, leaving Zeno as sole emperor. After defeating a coup d'état and winning a civil war (which lasted for much of his reign) with the help of Gothic mercenaries, whom he was then able to send to Italy on the pretext of restoring imperial rule there, Zeno died in 491.

His successor was Anastasius (491-518), an able civil official chosen by Zeno's empress Ariadne with the support of the leading officers and court officials. An Isaurian rebellion was crushed in 498, an invasion of Slavs was eventually repulsed, and a campaign against the Persians was finally brought to a successful conclusion in 506. Anastasius' most important act was a reform of the precious-metal coinage of the empire, through which he stabilized the gold coin, the *solidus* (or *nomisma* in Greek) and the relationship between it and its fractions, on the one hand, and the copper coinage, on the other.

Upon his death in 518, Anastasius was succeeded by Justin, who had in turn been commander of the *excubitores*, and who was elected by popular acclaim and with the support of both the garrison troops in Constantinople and leading state officials and senators. His reign saw a stabilization along the eastern front and the consolidation of the political stability won during the reign of his predecessor; when he died in 527 he was succeeded without opposition by his nephew, Justinian. The reign of Justinian was to prove a watershed in the evolution of East Rome – Byzantium – and can be said in many ways properly to mark the beginnings of a medieval East Roman world.

Throughout the period from Constantine's accession, the history of the empire was marked by the fundamental importance of the Christian Church and the development of Christianity itself for its cultural and political evolution. For Constantine, the Christian Church had been a valued political ally in his effort to stabilize the empire and to consolidate his own power. For that reason, it had been essential that the Church remained united; discord and disagreement were politically threatening for an emperor who, while not being baptized until shortly before he died, nevertheless privileged the Christian Church both with the confiscated wealth from pagan temples and formal recognition in his political plans. But, almost immediately, Constantine was forced to deal with a major split within the Church, brought about by the appearance of Arianism, a heresy about the Trinity and the status of Christ. Arius (250-336) was a deacon of the Church at Alexandria. Trained in Greek philosophy, he became an ascetic, and in his attempts to clarify the nature of the Trinity, produced a creed which was for many contemporaries heretical. His philosophical background prevented him from accepting the notion that God could become man: he taught that Jesus was not eternal and co-equal with the father, but created by Him. He was not God, but not human either, rather a kind of demi-God. Arius was excommunicated in 320 by the bishop of Alexandria, and in 325 he was condemned and exiled by the Council of Nicaea, which asserted the equality of Father and Son in eternity, and that Son and Father were 'homoousios', that is to say, 'con-substantial'. Arius returned in 334, but died in 336. The problem was exacerbated by the fact that Constantine himself began eventually to favour the Arian position, and after his death in 337 his son and heir Constantius approved it in the eastern part of the empire. In contrast, in the West, Constans supported the Nicene position. Many synods were held to debate the issue, until in 350 Constans died and the Nicenes were persecuted. But the Arians were themselves split in three factions: those who argued that Father and Son are *unlike*; those who believed that Father and Son are alike, but not consubstantial; and those who thought that Father and Son were of *almost* one substance – a group which eventually accepted the Nicene position. Constantius died in 361, in 362 the Council of Alexandria restored Orthodoxy, and in 381 the ecumenical Council of Constantinople reaffirmed Nicaea.

The early fifth century saw a further Christological split in the form of Nestorianism, which took its name from Nestorius, a monk of Antioch who had studied under Theodore of Mopsuestia. In 428 he was appointed bishop of Constantinopole by Theodosius II, but aroused considerable hostility in Constantinople when he publicly supported the preaching of his chaplain that Mary should not be referred to as the *Theotokos* – 'the God-Bearer'. Demonstrations in the city followed; and the emperor was persuaded to summon the third ecumenical Council after Cyril, bishop of Alexandria (which saw itself as a rival to Constantinople), appealed to Rome, and the Roman Pope Celestine condemned Nestorius. The Nestorians developed a theology in which the divine and human aspects of Christ were seen not as unified in a single person, but operated in conjunction and they referred to the Virgin as *Christotokos*, 'Christ-bearer', to avoid attributing the Divinity with too human a nature. The Nestorians were accused, unfairly, of teaching two persons in Christ, God and man, and thus two distinct sons, human and divine. But the Nestorian position was condemned in 431 (council of Ephesus), and proceeded to secede, formally establishing a separate Church at their own council at Seleucia-Ctesiphon in Persia in 486, whence it established a firm foothold in Persia and was spread across northern India and central Asia as far as China during the following centuries, where it survives today – particularly in northern Iraq – as the Assyrian Orthodox Church.

Although Nestorianism was driven out of the Roman state during the fifth century, the debates it generated contributed to the evolution of a much more significant split within Christianity in the form of the Monophysite movement, which – although only referred to under this name from the seventh century – represented a reaction to some of the Nestorian views. The key problem revolved around the ways in which the divine and the human were combined in the person of Christ, and although two 'schools' of Monophysitism evolved, the more extreme version – elaborated by a certain Eutyches – was that the divine was prior to and dominated the human element; hence the description 'Monophysite': *mono* meaning 'single' and *physis* meaning 'nature'. A council held at Ephesus in 449, which was marred by violence and intimidation on the part of the monks who supported Eutyches, found in favour of the Monophysite position. But at the council of Chalcedon in 451 a larger council rejected it and redefined the traditional creed of Nicaea to make the Christological position clear. The political results of this division can be seen both in the politics of the court at Constantinople and in the regional identities of different provinces of the empire. In Egypt and Syria in particular, Monophysitism became established in the rural populations, and led to occasional – but harsh – persecutions. At court, in contrast, imperial policy varied from reign to reign leaving some confusion within the Church as a whole, and involving persecutions by both sides. The emperor Zeno (474-91) issued a decree of unity – the *Henotikon* – which attempted to paper over the divisions. Anastasius supported a monophysite position, Justin I was 'Chalcedonian', and Justinian, partly influenced by the empress Theodora (d. 548), swung between the two. Theodora lent her support to the Syrian Monophysites by funding the movement led by the bishop Jacob Baradaeus (whose name was afterwards taken to refer to the Syrian 'Jacobite' Church); a similar 'shadow' Church evolved in Egypt, and the Armenian Church also adopted the Monophysite view. In each case, the form of traditional belief may have been one of the most important factors, but it has also been suggested that alienation from the Constantinople regime, especially following the occasional persecutions which took place, also played a role.

These were not the only heretical movements to affect the Church and directly involve the emperors during this period. The 'Donatist' movement, a strictly North African heresy, was led by a puritan sect claiming that the tradition of consecration of bishops of Carthage was improper. Because the Church authorities were supported from Rome, African regional feeling was inflamed, and the heresy flourished – although as a small minority – until the seventh century. Other regional heresies included Messalianism, a Syrian monastic heresy which spread from Mesopotamia to Syria in the 4th century. With a crude and materialistic view of God and sin, it was attacked and finally condemned by the Council of Ephesus in 431. Pelagianism was a largely Western heresy, begun by a British monk, Pelagius, during the later fourth century. It was repeatedly condemned: in 411 and again in 416-48 and, finally, because its chief spokesman Celestius associated himself with Nestorianism, at Ephesus in 431. These local heresies had few longer-term results, but directly involved the emperors on every occasion and cemented the association between the interests of the Church and those of the imperial government.

The forging of Byzantium: Justinian to Leo III (527-741)

Although the western part of the empire had been transformed into a patchwork of barbarian successor states, the emperors at Constantinople continued to view all the lost territories as part of their realm, and in some cases to treat the kings of the successor kingdoms as their legitimate representatives, governing Roman affairs in the provinces in question until Constantinople could re-establish a full administrative and military presence. This is most obviously the case with the (Arian, and therefore heretical) Ostrogoths who – under their leader Theoderic, who had been brought up in Constantinople – had been despatched under Zeno against the usurper Odoacer, who had deposed the last Roman emperor in the West, Romulus Augustulus, and claimed to represent the empire in his stead. Theoderic was successful, and although he ruled nominally in the name of the emperor, he in fact was able to establish a powerful state in Italy. By the same token, Clovis, the leader of the Salian Franks in northern Gaul, had quite deliberately adopted Orthodox Christianity in the last years of the fifth century in

Fifth-century church, Tunisia.

order to gain papal and imperial recognition and support for his rule, where he also claimed, at least nominally, to represent Roman rule, exploiting the fact of his Orthodoxy to justify warfare against his Arian neighbours, the Visigoths in southern Gaul in particular.

Roman emperors thus considered the West not as 'lost', but rather as temporarily outside direct imperial authority. Under Justinian, this point of view was the basis for a series of remarkable reconquests, aimed at restoring the Roman world in its greatness, and re-establishing Rome's power as it had been at its height. Naturally, the plan was too ambitious – in respect of the resources required to carry it out – to have had any real chance of success. But Justinian came very close to achieving a major part of his original aims. The problems which arose after his death and as a result of his policies illustrated their unrealistic aims.

When Theoderic the Ostrogoth died in 526 conflict erupted over the succession, throwing the kingdom into confusion. The same occurred in the Vandal kingdom of North Africa, established during the first half of the fifth century after the Vandals had swept across the Rhine, through Gaul and into Spain, and eventually across the straits of Gibraltar into North Africa. Within a few years their kings had established a powerful kingdom with considerable resources at its disposal, and had also built up a fleet with which they raided Italy, disrupted shipping, and threatened the remaining parts of the empire. The political conflict and civil strife which broke out upon the death of the Vandal king gave Justinian his chance and, in 533, in a lightning campaign, the general Belisarius was able to land with a small force, defeat two Vandal armies and take the capital, Carthage, before finally eradicating Vandal opposition. Encouraged by this success, Sicily and then southern Italy were occupied in 535 on the pretext of intervening in the affairs of the Ostrogoths to stabilize the situation. The Goths felt they could offer no serious resistance: their capital at Ravenna was handed over, their king Witigis was taken prisoner and sent to Constantinople, and the war appeared to be won. At this moment Justinian, who appears to have harboured suspicions about Belisarius' political ambitions, recalled him, partly because a fresh invasion of the new and dynamic Persian king Chosroes I (Khusru) threatened to cause major problems in the East. In 540 Chosroes was able to attack and capture Antioch, one of the richest and most important cities in Syria, and since the Ostrogoths had shortly beforehand sent an embassy to the Persian capital, it is entirely possible that the Persians were working hand-in-glove with the Goths to exploit the Roman preoccupation in the West and to distract them while the Goths attempted to re-establish their situation. For during Belisarius' absence they were able to do exactly that, under a new war leader, the king Totila. Within a short while, they had recovered Rome, Ravenna and most of the peninsula. It took the Romans another ten years of punishing small-scale warfare throughout Italy finally to destroy Ostrogothic opposition, by which time the land was exhausted and barely able to support the burden of the newly re-established imperial bureaucracy.

However, Justinian's ambitions did not end there. He had further expansionist plans, but in the end only the south-eastern regions of Spain were actually recovered from the kings of the Visigoths, also Arians. As part of the realization of his plan to restore Roman greatness, he ordered a codification of Roman law, which produced the Digests and the *Codex Justinianus* and provided the basis for later Byzantine legal developments and codification. He persecuted the last vestiges of paganism in his efforts to play both Roman and Christian ruler, defender of Orthodoxy and of the Church, and he also introduced a large number of administrative reforms and changes in an effort to streamline and bring up-to-date the running of the empire. But his grandiose view of the empire and his own imperial position brought him into conflict with the papacy during the so-called 'Three Chapters' controversy, for example. In 543 the emperor issued an edict against three sets of writings (the 'Three Chapters') of the fourth and fifth centuries, by Theodore of Mopsuestia, Theodore of Cyrrhus and Ibas of Edessa, who had been accused by the Monophysites of being 'pro-Nestorian'. The intention was to conciliate the Monophysites, and required the agreement and support of the Roman Pope Vigilius. The pope did indeed – eventually – accept the edict, but there remained very substantial opposition in the West, and in 553 an ecumenical council at Constantinople condemned the Three Chapters. The Pope was placed under arrest by imperial guards and forced to agree. But the attempt at compromise failed to persuade the Monophysites to accept the 'neo-Chalcedonian' position. Justinian was by no means always popular within the empire, either. In 532, he nearly lost his throne in the great 'Nika' riots, and there were several plots against him during the course of his reign which were uncovered before they came to anything. The historian Procopius, who accompanied Belisarius on his campaigns and kept a record of the reign, wrote a scurrilous 'Secret History' in which he denounced virtually every act of

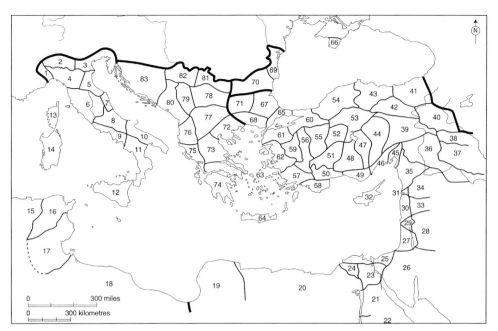

Map 1: Justinianic prefectures and provinces c.565.

Prefecture of Italy

1 Alpes Cottiae
2 Aemilia
3 Venetia
4 Liguria
5 Flaminia
6 Tuscia et Umbria
7 Picenum
8 Samnium
9 Campania
10 Apulia et Calabria
11 Lucania et Bruttium
12 Sicilia

Prefecture of Africa

13 Corsica
14 Sardinia
15 Numidia
16 Zeugitania
17 Byzacena
18 Tripolitania

Prefecture of Oriens

19 Libya Pentapolis
20 Libya Inferior
21 Arcadia
22 Thebais Inferior
23 Augustamnica II
24 Aegyptus I and II
25 Augustamnica I
26 Palaestina III
27 Palaestina I
28 Arabia
29 Palaestina II
30 Phoenice
31 Theodorias
32 Cyprus (in
    quaestura exercitus)
33 Phoenice Libanensis
34 Syria II
35 Syria I
36 Euphratensis
37 Osrhoene
38 Mesopotamia
39 Armenia III
40 Armenia IV
41 Armenia I
42 Armenia II
43 Helenopontus
44 Cappadocia I
45 Cilicia II
46 Cilicia I
47 Cappadocia II
48 Lycaonia
49 Isauria
50 Pamphylia
51 Pisidia
52 Galatia Salutaris
53 Galatia I
54 Paphlagonia
55 Phrygia Salutaris
56 Phrygia Pacatiana
57 Caria (in quaestura
    exercitus)
58 Lycia
59 Lydia
60 Bithynia
61 Hellespontus
62 Asia
63 Insulae (in
    quaestura exercitus)
64 Creta
65 Europa
66 Bosporus
67 Haemimontus
68 Rhodope
69 Scythia (in
    quaestura exercitus)
70 Moesia II (in
    quaestura exercitus)
71 Thracia

Prefecture of Illyricum

72 Macedonia I
73 Thessalia
74 Achaea
75 Epirus vetus
76 Epirus nova
77 Macedonia II
78 Dacia Mediterranea
79 Dardania
80 Praevalitana
81 Dacia ripensis
82 Moesia I
83 Dalmatia

Justinian. Procopius' book is suggestive of the hostility that the emperor's policies and attitude towards particular individuals – in particular Belisarius – seems to have engendered.

Upon his death in 565 Justinian left a vastly expanded but perilously overstretched empire, both in financial as well as in military terms. Justinian had seen himself as the embodiment of Roman imperial power; his successors were faced with the reality of dealing with new enemies, lack of ready cash, and internal discontent over high taxation and constant demands for soldiers and the necessities to support them. Justin II, Justinian's successor and nephew, opened his reign by cancelling the yearly 'subsidy' (in effect, a substantial bribe paid to keep the Persian king at a distance, and regarded by the latter as tribute) to Persia, beginning a costly war in the East. In 568 the Germanic Lombards crossed from their homeland along the western Danube and Drava region into Italy, in their efforts to flee the approaching Avars, a Turkic nomadic power which, like the Huns two centuries earlier, were in the process of establishing a vast steppe empire. While the Lombards rapidly overran Roman defensive positions in the north of the peninsula, soon establishing also a number of independent chiefdoms in the centre and south, the Avars occupied the Lombards' former lands and established themselves as a major challenge to imperial power in the northern Balkan region. Between the mid-570s and the end of the reign of the emperor Maurice (582-602), the empire was able to re-establish a precarious balance in the East. Although the Romans suffered a number of defeats, they were able to stabilize the Danube frontier in the north; the lands over which the campaigning took place, especially in Italy and the Balkans, were increasingly devastated and unable to support prolonged military activity. Maurice cleverly exploited a civil war in Persia in 590-591 by supporting the young, deposed king Chosroes II. When the war ended, with Roman help in the defeat of Chosroes' enemies, the peace arrangements between the two empires rewarded the Romans with the return of swathes of territory and a number of fortresses which had been lost in the previous conflicts.

Maurice was unpopular with the army in the Balkans because of the hard nature of the campaigning there, as well as because of his efforts to maintain some control over the expenses of this constant warfare. This was, rightly or wrongly, perceived as miserly and penny-pinching by the soldiers, and in 602 the Danube army mutinied, marched on Constantinople, and imposed their own candidate as emperor, the centurion Phokas. Maurice's entire family was massacred, and the 'tyranny' of Phokas (602-610) began. While he seems to have been a fairly incompetent politician, his armies seem to have held their own in the Balkans, and against the Persians who, on the pretext of avenging Maurice, had invaded the eastern provinces. Phokas was popular in many regions of the empire, but not all, and in 610 the military governor, or exarch, of Africa, at Carthage – a certain Heraclius – set out with a fleet to depose him, while his cousin Nicetas took a land force across the North African provinces, through Egypt and northwards into Asia Minor. Phokas was deposed with little opposition, and Heraclius was crowned emperor. But some of the troops remained loyal to Phokas, and his deposition was followed by a short period of civil war in Egypt and Asia Minor. But the empire was now unable to maintain its defences intact, and within a few years the Avars and Slavs had overrun much of the Balkans, while the Persians occupied and set up their own provincial governments in Syria

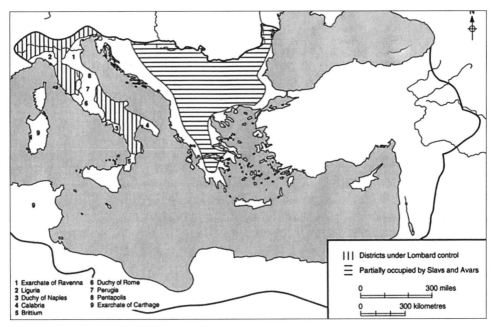

Map 2: The empire c.602.

and Egypt between 614 and 618, and continued to push into Asia Minor. Italy, now divided into a number of military commands isolated from each other by Lombard enclaves, was left to its own devices, encouraging an increasing degree of local autonomy and self-reliance which was eventually to lead to its severance from the empire in all but name. In 626, a combined Persian-Avar siege of Constantinople was defeated (contemporaries attributed the victory to the intercession of the Mother of God), while from 623 Heraclius boldly took the war into Persian territory, invading through Armenia into the Persian heartlands and, in a series of brilliant campaigns, destroyed Chosroes' armies and forced the Persian generals (Chosroes himself having been deposed and murdered) to sue for peace. The *status quo ante* was re-established, and the dominant position of the Roman Empire seemed assured. Although the Danube remained nominally the frontier, the Balkans were, in practice, no longer under imperial authority, except where an army appeared; while the financial situation of the empire, whose resources were quite exhausted by the long wars, was desperate.

The complex ecclesiastical politics of the Church continued to play a crucial role. The disaffection brought about by Constantinopolitan persecution of the Monophysites in particular – under Justin II, for example – rendered some sort of compromise formula an essential for the reincorporation of the territories whose populations had been largely Monophysite and which had been lost to the Persians. Under Heraclius, the patriarch Sergius and his advisers came up with two possible solutions: the first referred to as 'monoenergism' – whereby a single energy was postulated in which both divine and human aspects were unified. At this point, the arrival of Islam on the historical stage made the need for a compromise – which would heal the divisions – even more urgent. Even

Above and below: Byzantine fortresses in eastern Asia Minor.

more importantly, the defeats at the hands of the Arabs will have been interpreted (in keeping with the fundamental assumptions of the era) as a sign of God's displeasure, requiring some sort of action on the part of the Romans, or their guardian and God's representative on earth – the emperor – to make amends. Heraclius and his patriarch, Sergius, undoubtedly framed their proposals for compromise with monophysitism with these considerations in mind. But monoenergism was rejected by several leading Churchmen. The alternative, the doctrine of a single will -'monotheletism' – although initially attracting the support of moderate Monophysites, was eventually rejected by both the hard-line Monophysites and by the majority of the Western Chalcedonian clergy, surviving as an imperial policy which had to be enforced by decree after Heraclius' death in 641. But by this time, of course, the Monophysite lands had been lost to the Arabs and the whole purpose of the compromise was lost.

The origins of Islam lie in the northern Arabian peninsula, where different forms of Christianity and Judaism had competed and co-existed for centuries with indigenous beliefs, in particular in the much-travelled trading and caravan communities of Mecca and Medina. Mohammed was himself a respected and established merchant who had several times accompanied the trade caravans north to Roman Syria. Syria and Palestine already had substantial populations of Arabs, both farmers and herdsmen, as well as mercenary soldiers serving the empire as a buffer against the Persians. Initially reflecting his own synthesis of Judaic, Monophysite Christian and traditional Arab concepts, primarily within a Messianic framework which owed more to Judaism than Christianity, Islam under Mohammed rapidly attained a considerable degree of sophistication and coherence. Although Mohammed's preaching met initially with stiff resistance from his own clan – the Quraysh, who dominated Mecca and its trade (as well as the holy Ka'ba) – by 628-629 he had established his authority over much of the peninsula, made an alliance with the Quraysh, and begun to consider the future direction of the new Islamic community. On his death (traditionally placed, according to the Islamic tradition, in 632, although there is some evidence that he might have lived beyond this date) there followed a brief period of warfare during which his immediate successors had to fight hard to reassert Islamic authority; and there is little doubt that both religious zeal – combined with the desire for glory, booty and new lands – motivated the attacks into both the Persian and Roman lands. A combination of incompetence and apathy, disaffected soldiers and inadequate defensive arrangements resulted in a series of disastrous Roman defeats and the loss of Syria, Palestine, Mesopotamia and Egypt within the short span of 10 years, so that by 642 the empire was reduced to a rump of its former self. The Persian empire was completely overrun and destroyed. The Arab Islamic empire was born.

The most important loss was Egypt. Already during Heraclius' Persian wars, Egypt had been lost to the Persians, albeit briefly, with serious results for the empire, since it was from Egypt that the grain for Constantinople and other cities was drawn. It was a rich source of revenue, and – along with Syria and the other eastern provinces – had provided the bulk of the empire's tax revenue. Constantinople was forced radically to restructure its fiscal apparatus and its priorities, including the way the army was recruited and supported; and the result was, by the later seventh century, an administratively very different state from that which existed a century earlier.

The reduced and impoverished East Roman or Byzantine empire now had to contend not only with an aggressive and extremely successful new foe in the East. It had far fewer resources at its disposal, it had lost effective control in the Balkans, and had no real power in Italy, where the military governor or exarch, based at Ravenna, struggled against increasingly difficult odds to maintain the imperial position. The insistence of the imperial government during the reign of Constans II on enforcing the official Monothelete policy reflected the government's need to maintain imperial authority and the views of those in power that the Romans were being punished for their failure to deal with the divisions within the Church. But it also brought the empire into conflict with the papacy and the Western Church, as well as provoking opposition within the empire, bringing a further degree of political and ideological isolation with it. Through the reigns of Constans II (641-668), Constantine IV (668-685) and Justinian II (685-695), Asia Minor was raided and substantial tracts of territory devastated annually from the early 640s well into the first half of the eighth century, with catastrophic effects on population, on the economy of the regions affected – especially the border zones – and on urban life, which was reduced effectively to fortified garrison towns. A series of sieges and attempts to break Constantinopolitan resistance between 674 and 678 was finally driven back, and a major siege in 717-718 was defeated with great losses on the Arab side. But the situation appeared desperate enough for Constans II to move the imperial court to Sicily in 662. His assassination in 668 brought the experiment to an end, but illustrates the nature of the situation. Justinian II was deposed in 695; a series of short-lived usurpers followed until Justinian II himself recovered his throne in 705. But he was again deposed and killed in 711, and the situation of internal political and military confusion lasted until the seizure of power by the general Leo, who became Leo III (717-741) and, having defeated the Arab besiegers in 717-718, finally re-established some political order.

Arab strategy can be followed through several phases. Until the defeat of the siege of 717-718, Byzantine resistance seems to have been almost entirely passive, limited to holding on to fortified centres and avoiding any open contact. On the few occasions when imperial troops unusually did mark up successes, this was due to the appointment of particularly able commanders. During the Arab civil wars of the late 680s and early 690s, the emperor Justinian II was able to stabilize the situation for a short while; but it was only during the 720s that the empire was able effectively to begin meeting Arab armies in the field and reasserting imperial military control. In the meantime, the Byzantine resistance – focused on fortified key points and a strategy of harassment and avoidance – had at least prevented a permanent Arab presence in Asia Minor, aided of course also by the geography of the region. The Taurus and Anti-Taurus ranges acted as an effective physical barrier, with only a few well-marked passes allowing access and egress, while the climate was in general unsuitable to the sort of economic activity preferred by the invaders.

The Balkan front was also a concern for Constantinople. Technically, the Danube remained the border even in the 660s and 670s. In practice, only the presence of an imperial army could bring the local Slav chieftains to heel, and then only very briefly. In 679, however, the situation was transformed by the arrival of the Turkic Bulgars, a nomadic people who had been forced out of their homelands and pastures around the Volga by the encroachments of the Chazars from the East. Petitioning the emperor

Pamphylia, southern Asia Minor.

Constantine IV for permission to seek refuge and protection south of the Danube on 'Roman' territory (the Danube river itself remained in fact largely under Byzantine control because it was navigable, and the imperial fleet could patrol it), they were refused and, having crossed over, were then met by an imperial army under Constantine himself. Unfortunately, due to poor discipline, a lack of cohesion and mistaken signals, the imperial army fell into panic and was defeated by the Bulgars, who over the next twenty years consolidated their hold over the region and established a loose hegemony over the indigenous Slav and other peoples in the region. By 700, the Bulgar Khanate was an important political and military power threatening Byzantine Thrace, and was to remain so for the next three centuries.

In spite of such failures, the first half of the eighth century saw the reassertion of imperial military strength, the stabilization of the frontier along the Taurus and Anti-Taurus range, and the consolidation of the new fiscal and military administrative arrangements which had evolved out of the crisis of the 640s and after, generally referred to collectively as the 'theme system'. In the final year of his reign Leo issued a brief codification of Roman law, the *Ecloga* ('selection') based on a combination of Justinianic law and strongly Old Testament moral colouring, reflecting the ideological perceptions and assumptions of the times. Under Leo, however, it also saw an increasing alienation between Constantinople and Rome, chiefly over matters of ecclesiastical jurisdiction and imperial taxation policy in Italy, but also over an ideological clash embodied in the imperial adoption of an iconoclastic policy in respect of sacred images. The origins of the debate are no longer clear, but the issue of whether or not Christians were right to employ and pay respect to images of Christ or the Virgin had gradually come to the fore in the later years of the seventh century, and the iconoclasts felt strongly that it was not right. Traditionally – and partly influenced by the iconophile propaganda of the eventual victors

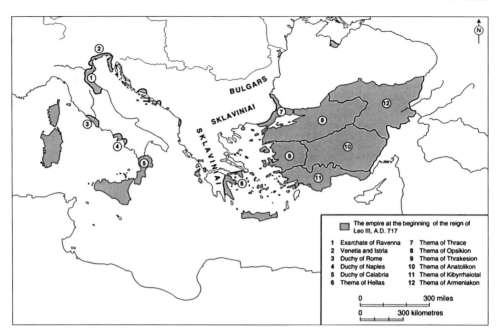

Map 3: The empire at the beginning of the reign of Leo III, c.717

in the conflict during the ninth century – it has been assumed that the sources describing the mass persecution, harassment and death of many iconophiles, as well as the destruction of icons themselves, were more-or-less accurate accounts. In fact, it seems that they have both invented much of their story and exaggerated the rest. Leo III seems to have been a fairly mild critic of the use of images; Constantine V, while theologically more involved, only adopted a strongly iconoclastic policy after the first eight or so years of his reign; and neither seem to have destroyed images. On the contrary, their concern was for images to be removed from those positions in churches, for example, where they would be the object of mistaken veneration.

Whatever the truth of the matter, there is no doubt that it is in the reign of Leo III – a competent general and statesman – that the beginnings of a recovery in the empire's fortunes can be dated. His son, Constantine V, one of the Byzantine empire's most successful generals and a popular hero in his own lifetime, was to use this to re-establish the East Roman Empire as a major power in the east Mediterranean/Balkan region.

2 A medieval empire
*c.*741-1453

The Byzantine commonwealth: Constantine V to Basil II

Leo III was succeeded by his son Constantine V, who almost immediately faced a rebellion from his brother-in-law Artabasdos, one of Leo's closest allies and friends, who may have understood that he should also share in the imperial power upon Leo's death. Although initially deprived of Constantinople and cut off in Asia Minor, Constantine was able, after a campaign of some eighteen months, to defeat Artabasdos and regain his throne. There is no evidence that he set about enforcing his father's iconoclastic policies at this time, contrary to later iconophile assertions; but after an attack of plague had struck Constantinople in the late 740s he appears to have taken the issue up more vocally, calling public meetings to discuss the issue and, in 754, convening a synod at which his theological position was clarified and the arguments against the devotion shown to images were elaborated. This synod, the council of Hiereia, named after the imperial palace on the Bosphorus at which it met, was claimed as the seventh general (ecumenical) council of the Church, although this claim was rejected by the council of 787 at which devotion to and public display of images was re-established. But although Constantine's reputation has been largely determined by his iconoclasm, his importance lies as much in his other achievements: provincial military and administrative changes, the establishment of a small elite imperial field army, the so-called *tagmata* ('the regiments') at Constantinople, changes in the fiscal system, and the establishment of a substantial balance in the imperial treasury. He seems to have been a careful financial manager of state resources; and he employed the resources at his disposal in a series of well-planned military expeditions both against the empire's northern foes, the Bulgars, and in the East. Indeed, his frequent campaigns into the heartland of Bulgarian territory came near to destroying the Bulgar khanate entirely, although the Bulgars offered a tenacious and fierce resistance. In the East, he campaigned against a number of key Arab fortresses, re-establishing military parity between the Roman and Islamic armies, and thus providing the stability economically and politically to permit the devastated provinces to recover from the century and a half of warfare to which they had been subjected.

Constantine's reputation for later generations was entirely associated with his iconoclasm. According to the iconophile tradition, Constantine was fanatical in his hatred of images and monks, and the histories are replete with tales of his persecution and torture of individuals and whole groups of his subjects who opposed his policies. He is accused of burning monasteries as well as images, of turning churches into stables, and similar sacrilegious acts. Yet a careful examination of the evidence suggests that much of this results from propaganda and later misunderstanding. Indeed, the destruction of icons and a generalized persecution of monks is nowhere clearly evidenced in the sources. Neither is there any evidence that the bulk of the population was particularly committed to one point of view or the other. There were certainly

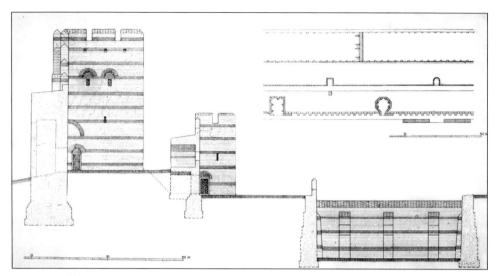

The fifth-century walls of Constantinople, an advanced piece of multi-level defensive engineering.

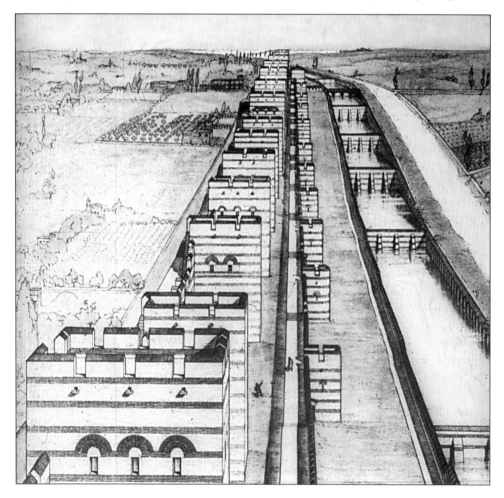

keen proponents of both views – although most were involved either in the state or Church hierarchy at one level or another – and there was also a small but very vocal monastic opposition, although it only appears in the reigns of Leo IV and Eirene and Constantine VI. Be that as it may, there is no doubt that iconoclasm was a convenient vehicle for the politics of the empress Eirene, and it is clear that it was only from the time of the council of 787 that a formal theology of images, so important for later Orthodox doctrine, was first elaborated.

Constantine V died in 775 while on campaign and was succeeded by his son, Leo IV (775-780), who continued his father's policies but did not reign long enough to leave any substantial impact. Upon his death in 780, his empress Eirene became ruler as regent for the young Constantine VI. During her reign, the seventh ecumenical council was convoked and image devotion was restored, with most of the iconoclast clergy accepting the change. But although Eirene seems to have been a reasonably able administrator, the circumstances of her reign, both with her son and after his death in 797 (the result of her own plotting), meant that her rule was not well regarded by many contemporaries. Resurgent Bulgar power produced several military defeats, while the rise of the able Caliph Harun ar-Rashid also led to a number of reverses on the eastern front. Her major achievement was beginning the recovery of the Peloponnese and central Greece, the interior of which had been out of effective imperial control for more than a century. Conversion to Christianity, the establishment of a Church administration and the setting up of a military provincial organization went hand in hand in this process, and was to result by the middle of the ninth century in the complete recovery and reincorporation of these regions into the empire.

Eirene was deposed in 802 and her finance minister Nikephoros became emperor as Nikephoros I. An able administrator, Nikephoros embarked on a series of fiscal and related reforms which set the framework for the administrative changes and improvements introduced by the rulers who followed him. Militarily he held his own, until in 811 he and his army, having penetrated deep into Bulgar territory, were surprised and annihilated at Pliska. The emperor himself and many leading officers were killed. He was succeeded by his son Staurakios who, shortly before he died from his wounds the same year, abdicated in favour of his brother-in-law Michael I Rangabe (811-813). Michael's reign was marked by continued fighting with the Bulgars under their Khan Krum, and in 813, following a defeat at Krum's hands, Michael also abdicated in favour of the general Leo (V: 813-820). A competent general, Leo was able to restore the military position, but also reintroduced imperial iconoclasm, seen as the ideological force behind the victories of Constantine V fifty years earlier. From then until 843 the iconoclastic controversy once more divided Church and state. Under the rule of his successors Michael II (820-829), who deposed Leo, and Theophilos (829-842), his son, the empire continued the slow process of consolidation and recovery inaugurated under Constantine V; and although there were several dramatic set-backs (such as the siege and sack of the fortress city of Amorium in Asia Minor in 838), these were relatively minor events which did not affect the longer term situation.

Imperial iconoclasm, as noted already, seems to have affected chiefly the higher clergy and leading military and civilian officials of the state. The vast majority of the population, if they were affected at all, tacitly continued their traditional practices and followed the official line when and where it mattered. There did evolve a vocal monastic party who organized opposition and propaganda; an opposition which seems to have developed out of

The walls of Constantinople.

the aftermath of the seventh ecumenical council of 787, and which generated a series of myths and legends about the role of monks in opposing Leo III and Constantine V, in order to legitimate its influence and importance thereafter. Monks became a powerful element within the Church from the 840s, and it is to monastic interests in particular that we must ascribe much of the iconophile propaganda of the period which was subsumed by the ninth- and tenth-century historiography of Byzantium. Under the influence of a leading court official, the eunuch Theoktistos, the empress and regent (for the young Michael III, 842-867) agreed to the restoration of sacred images and their public display (on condition that Theophilos not be condemned) at a series of small private meetings in 842-843. The change was made public by a triumphal procession through Constantinople; an event still celebrated in the Orthodox liturgical calendar. It seems to have had few repercussions for the lives of most ordinary people in the empire.

With the outbreak of civil war in the Caliphate in 842 upon the death of the Caliph Mu'tasim, Byzantium was able to take advantage of the situation to begin once again a reassertion of imperial military power on the eastern front. The main enemies in this region were no longer centrally-led Caliphal armies, however, but the forces of the many emirs who governed the frontier fortress towns such as Tarsos in Cilicia or Melitene further east. The struggle was evenly balanced throughout the rest of the century, although the imperial armies were able to achieve several resounding victories and force the Arabs onto the defensive. Under Basil I (867-886), who continued the process of internal consolidation with further fiscal and military reforms and changes, the heretical Paulicians

A Byzantine castle in eastern Asia Minor.

– a dualist sect who had effectively taken over much of eastern Anatolia and actively fought against imperial interests (on occasion with Arab support) – threatened to establish an independent territory. The origins of their sect and its beliefs are obscure, but they appear to have grown in strength and numbers from the seventh century, when they first appear in the sources, and responded to attempts to eliminate their beliefs during the first half of the ninth century by well-organized military action. Basil was able, after several hard campaigns, to defeat them, transferring many by forced relocation to the Balkan provinces.

While the situation on the eastern front was favourable, and relations with the Bulgars were fairly peaceful until the end of the century, the empire's political presence in the central Mediterranean and in Italy had markedly worsened. Ravenna, the last outpost of the Exarchate of Italy, had fallen to the Lombards in 751, and they in their turn had soon come under Frankish domination. The Papacy at Rome had for decades been effectively autonomous and independent, since imperial military support was minimal, and from the 750s, with the tensions caused by the imperial espousal of iconoclasm, the alienation had increased. The Popes forged an alliance with the kings of the Franks, Pepin and then Charlemagne, who now replaced the Eastern emperor as the dominant power in Italy (excluding Sicily); and in 800 the Pope crowned Charlemagne emperor, an act seen in the East as a direct challenge to imperial claims. Diplomacy overcame some of the problems and misunderstandings, but the Byzantine emperors had henceforth to reckon with a 'revived' empire in the West, independent of Constantinople, frequently with contrary interests and potentially also a military opponent. The imperial situation was not helped when in the 820s Arab forces invaded Sicily and Crete, conquering the latter fairly rapidly. Sicily was stoutly defended, but gradually fell, fortress by fortress, to the invaders during a long-drawn-out struggle which lasted until the end of the century. The Cretan Arabs became a major maritime thorn in the flesh of the empire, plundering and devastating coastal regions, and several major expeditions during the ninth century failed to dislodge them. Byzantine power in the central and western Mediterranean was fatally compromised by these developments.

The situation in the Balkans seemed to have improved under Basil I with the conversion to Christianity of the Bulgar Khan Boris, who took the Christian name Michael (852-889) and the title of Tsar (Caesar), and some of his entourage; a strong Christian, pro-Byzantine party developed at the Bulgar court. But during the reign of Symeon (893-927), who was brought up in the imperial court at Constantinople and who had evolved his own imperial pretensions, war broke out once more, a war which – with pauses – lasted until the 920s, and which at one point saw Constantinople besieged by a powerful Bulgar army. When peace was restored, it was through the efforts of the emperor Romanus I, formerly commander of the imperial fleet, who had seized power and who, along with his sons, shared the imperial position with the legitimate heir Constantine VII. The peace lasted into the late 960s under a succession of pro-Byzantine Bulgarian rulers.

One other zone was of constant interest to Byzantine rulers, as it had been to the emperors of the sixth century and before. The steppe region (stretching from the plain of Hungary eastwards through south Russia and north of the Caspian) was the home of many nomadic peoples, mostly of Turkic stock, and it was a fundamental tenet of Byzantine international diplomacy to keep the rulers of these various peoples favourably disposed towards the empire; achieved predominantly through substantial gifts of gold coin, fine silks, and imperial titles and honours. After the collapse of the Avar empire in the 630s, Constantinople had been able to establish good relations with the Chazars whose Khans, although converting to Judaism, remained a faithful ally of most Byzantine emperors, duly exploiting the Byzantine invitation to attack the Bulgars from the north, for example, when war broke out in this region, but serving also to keep the imperial court informed of developments further East. The Chazar empire began to contract during the later ninth century, chiefly under pressure from the various peoples to the east who were set in motion by the expansion of the Pechenegs and allied groups. The Magyars (Hungarians) were established to the north-west and west of the Chazars by the middle of the ninth century, whence they established themselves in what is now Hungary, destroying local Slav kingdoms in the process, by the early tenth century. Both Khazars and Magyars served as mercenaries in Byzantine armies, particularly against the Bulgars, although the establishment by the later tenth century of a christianized Hungarian kingdom on the central Danube posed a potential challenge to Byzantine power in the region, which became especially acute during the twelfth century. The Chazars remained important players in steppe diplomacy until the middle of the tenth century, when the growing power of the Kiev Rus' finally brought about their destruction and replaced them in Byzantine diplomacy. The appearance of the Turkic Pechenegs (Patzinaks) during the late ninth century complicated this well-established bi-polar arrangement: the newcomers clashed with both the Chazars and the Magyars, establishing themselves in the steppe region between the Danube and Don. Their value to the empire as a check on both the Rus' and the Magyars was obvious, particularly in the wars of the later tenth century, but they were a dangerous and frequently unreliable ally. During the middle years of the eleventh century, groups of

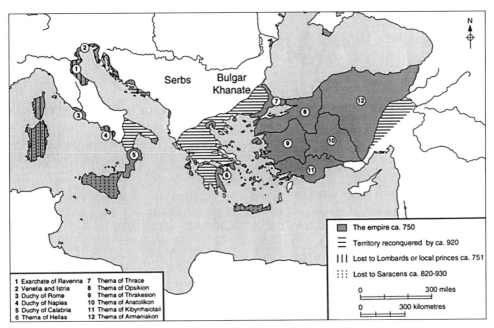

Map 4: The empire in the tenth century.

1 Exarchate of Ravenna 7 Thema of Thrace
2 Venetia and Istria 8 Thema of Opsikion
3 Duchy of Rome 9 Thema of Thrakesion
4 Duchy of Naples 10 Thema of Anatolikon
5 Duchy of Calabria 11 Thema of Kibyrrhaiotaii
6 Thema of Hellas 12 Thema of Armeniakon

The empire ca. 750
Territory reconquered by ca. 920
Lost to Lombards or local princes ca. 751
Lost to Saracens ca. 820-930

Pechenegs began to move into the Balkans, where they clashed with imperial troops. Until the period of civil wars after Manzikert in 1071, however, they were kept more-or-less in check; but thereafter they ravaged and pillaged with little opposition until Alexios I was finally able to crush them in 1091.

The tenth century witnessed a great improvement in Byzantine fortunes, both in terms of cultural developments and, most spectacularly, in terms of the recovery of much formerly Roman territory in the East. Beginning under the direction of a number of able generals during the reigns of Leo VI (886-912) and Constantine VII (912-959), and continuing with the campaigns of the soldier-emperors Nikephoros I Phokas (963-969) and John I Tzimiskes (969-976), the empire was able to expand well into northern Syria, defeat the local emirs of north-west Iraq, reconquer Crete and Cyprus, and occupy substantial tracts around and to the south of Antioch, even threatening to recover Jerusalem. Although beginning his reign with a civil war and military defeat in the Balkans, Basil II (976-1025) continued and consolidated these conquests, re-establishing the Byzantine empire as the paramount power in the region, and took the process a stage further by invading and finally defeating the Bulgars after a long and gruelling war. Their lands were entirely reincorporated into the empire, given their own provincial administration and established as regular imperial provinces. The Danube once more became the imperial frontier in the north; the emirate of Aleppo and its more easterly neighbours became client states of the empire in the East, where the empire now faced the more dynamic military power of the Egyptian Fatimid dynasty, whose interests also lay in control of Syria.

The reigns of the emperors from Romanos I (920-944) onwards were marked also, however, by important developments within Byzantine society. During the eighth and ninth centuries there slowly evolved a social elite of office-holders and landowners who gradually achieved a near monopoly on the senior and middling posts in the military and civil administration of the empire. By the tenth century they were in a position to offer serious opposition to the central government, since it was they whose task it was to realize government policy and apply imperial legislation in the provinces. The tension between these two aspects of the Byzantine state revealed itself most obviously in the efforts of the elite to expand its landholdings, generally at the expense of village communities and small proprietors who were a key element both in the state's fiscal strategy and provided the core of the provincial, or 'thematic', armies. In the 920s a series of natural disasters affected the agriculture of the western Anatolian provinces in particular, giving the wealthy or powerful opportunities to absorb such properties into their estates. The problem for the government lay in the fact that powerful landlords could frequently defy the tax assessors and pay only a minimum, while at the same time they could prevent potential recruits to the army from being called up or presented for duty. The emperors issued a mass of legislation to try to deal with the issue, ultimately with little real success. Instead, and as the leading members of this social elite took on more and more the aspect of a self-conscious aristocracy, the government adopted the tactics of its opponents, turning public land into imperial estates in order to secure the income derived from them.

It was a leading member of one of these clans, Bardas Skleros, who rebelled against Basil II shortly after he had succeeded John I Tzimiskes in 976; and it was another leader of an even more prestigious family, Bardas Phokas, whom the emperor called to his assistance in 978. The rebellion was defeated and Skleros escaped to the Caliphate where he was imprisoned. On his release in 987, however, and with Arab support, he returned and raised an army once more. Bardas Phokas was sent against him, but betrayed the emperor, coming at first to an agreement with Skleros, then imprisoning him and declaring against Basil II himself. The emperor called upon the Russian prince Vladimir for help; an agreement was reached which involved both Vladimir's acceptance of Christianity, and his marriage to Basil's sister Anna; and with a stout body of Norse-Russian troops (known in the Byzantine sources as Varangians), Basil was able to defeat Phokas, who died after a second battle in 989. And although Skleros continued in rebellion for a while, a reconciliation was soon arranged and peace restored. It is significant that on the occasion of all these rebellions the Anatolian soldiery and many of the local elites had no hesitation in supporting the rebels, illustrating the difficulties which the social development of the empire had generated.

By the end of the reign of Basil II the basic elements of what has been dubbed the 'Byzantine commonwealth' were in place. Bulgaria was Christian (although also a breeding ground for a number of heresies); the leading princely families of Kiev had converted or were about to do so. The Balkans to the west and south-west of Bulgarian territory were likewise converts to the Byzantine Church, hence creating a cultural zone that was to be dominated by Byzantine influences not just in ecclesiastical matters, but in every other aspect of social life: attitudes to state and rulership, forms of dress, types of literature, church music, to name but a few. At the same time, the Byzantine empire appeared to be impregnable: rich, with an efficient bureaucracy, a powerful, tried and experienced army which had been victorious on all fronts with few exceptions, and vastly expanded territories in the Balkans and eastern Anatolia. The emperors who followed

Left: The tenth-century church at Chliara, Cappadocia. Right: Detail.

Basil II had no reason to believe that the situation would alter or could alter in any way to their disadvantage. The events of the middle years of the eleventh century were to demonstrate how mistaken this viewpoint was.

Political eclipse, cultural inheritance: Constantine VIII to 1453

The reigns of Basil II's successors are generally compared unfavourably with his own heroic reign. Basil left no children, and his brother Constantine VIII ruled only three years alone before he too died. It was Constantine's elder daughter Zoe whose hand in marriage determined who should become emperor, and in the period from 1028 until 1042 she took successively three husbands who became emperor through her: Romanos III Argyros (1028-1034), Michael IV 'the Paphlagonian' (1034-1041) and Constantine IX Monomachos (1042-1055). Taking for granted the peaceful stability attained by the end of Basil II's reign, and radically reducing investment in the standing army as well as the frontier militias in order to curtail the power and ambition of the 'military' elite of the provinces, the predominantly civilian establishment at Constantinople failed – perhaps quite understandably – to take into account the changing circumstances outside the empire. It is fair to say that the members of the provincial 'military' clans were probably no more aware of these changes, and their concerns focused on their own position within the empire and their relations with the

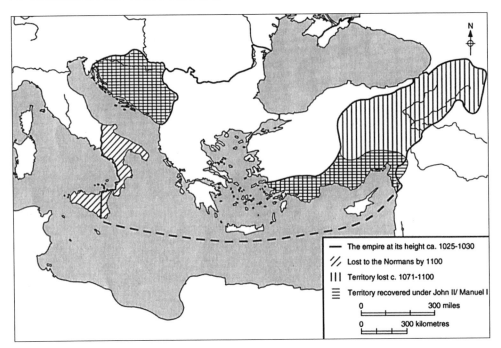

Map 5: The empire 1025-1176.

governing clique and the emperors. Provincial rebellions in Bulgaria in the 1030s and 1040s, a result of misguided fiscal policies as well as political oppression, foreshadowed greater problems. The arrival on the Balkan frontiers of the Pechenegs, a Turkic steppe people, at about the same time, and their first incursions into imperial territory, similarly should have alerted the emperors and their advisers. The rebellion in 1042-1043 led by George Maniakes, commander of the imperial forces in Sicily, while cut short by the death of its leader, indicated that unrest and discontent among leading elements of the elite easily gained military support. The brief reign of the emperor Isaac I Komnenos (1057-1059), a soldier of the Anatolian military clans, indicated the direction of change. And although the empire continued to expand its frontiers in the Caucasus, efforts to re-establish imperial control in Sicily and southern Italy failed, so that by the early 1070s the empire had lost its last foothold there to the aggressively ambitious Normans.

The cultural and economic history of the period presents a number of paradoxes: as the authority and effectiveness of Constantinopolitan power diminished, so the economy of ordinary life – the farming communities of the provinces, small-town merchant activity and local industries (silk-production in particular) – seem to have been flourishing. At the same time, monastic communities thrived, while the establishment of schools under imperial auspices at Constantinople and a revival of interest in the classical world (especially its philosophy) marked the intellectual life of the learned elements of Byzantine society. The empire also faced another variant of dualist heresy, this time in the form of the Bogomil movement, which seems to have owed its origins to the influence of Paulicians who had been transferred to Thrace during the eighth and ninth centuries, although it had a more peaceful aspect than the militant Paulicianism of the time of Basil I. It became especially popular in Bulgaria, and in the later eleventh century attracted some converts from the Byzantine elite. Alexios I moved quickly to crush the heresy, however, and it remained for the most part confined to the central Balkans (with some adherents in Anatolia), where it became also a focus of anti-Byzantine opposition and dissent. It remained an important element in the Balkans until after the Ottoman conquest, and Bogomil preaching played a significant role in the evolution of the Cathar doctrines of southern France.

As well as the Pechenegs in the north, a new and yet more dangerous foe appeared in the 1050s and 1060s in the East, in the form of the Turkic Seljuks, a branch of the Oğuz Turks (called Ouzoi by the Byzantines) who had already established themselves as masters in the Caliphate, and whose energies were now directed northwards from Iraq into the Caucasus and eastern Asia Minor. The emperor Romanos IV Diogenes (1068-1071) made an attempt to stem the flow of raids and incursions, but after some initial success, a combination of treachery and tactical blunders led to his defeat in 1071 at the battle of Manzikert in eastern Anatolia. Losses following the battle were in themselves not great; while the evidence suggests that the strategic situation could have been rescued. But Romanos himself was captured, and although ransomed after a brief period as the guest of the Sultan Alp Arslan, found that he had been deposed. Civil war broke out and the empire's remaining forces exhausted and weakened themselves in the conflict that followed. Asia Minor was simply left open, and Turkic herdsmen with their flocks, families and chattels moved in to the central plateau, ideally suited to their way of life. Further civil conflict ensued, and by the time the general Alexios I Komnenos (1081-1118) seized the throne in 1081, the empire had lost central Asia Minor, while the Balkans were overrun by Pecheneg raiders and the Normans were threatening to invade the empire from the west.

Careful planning, clever diplomacy with the other major elite families of the empire, and good generalship enabled Alexios to stabilize the situation between his accession and 1105. The Pechenegs were soundly beaten and settled within the empire in return for service in the imperial army; the Normans were thrown out of Epirus, that is, north-western Greece; and the Seljuks were held. Part of this success can be ascribed to Alexios' astute use of the armies of the first Crusade, which passed through Byzantine territory in 1097-1098; part to Alexios' administrative reforms; and part to his intelligent alliance with other families of the elite to re-found a coherent central administration and palatine establishment. Under Alexios' son John II (1118-1143) substantial tracts in western Asia Minor were recovered; while under Manuel I (1143-1180) the imperial position in the Balkans was strengthened and the imperial armies began slowly to push into central Anatolia in an effort to recover these core lands. Tactical misjudgement once more contributed to checkmate on this front, however, when in 1176, in an attempt to knock out the organized Seljuk opposition in central Asia Minor, the emperor allowed his forces to be ambushed and defeated at the battle of Myriokephalon. This effort, which had cost the treasury dearly, was thus wasted, and the empire was never again in a position to mount such a campaign in the region. The 'Turkification' – and Islamization – of central Asia Minor was already under way; there was little the empire could now do to prevent its completion.

While the empire faced the Hungarians on the Danube with some success, its failure in Asia Minor spelled the end of the East Roman Empire in its established territorial form. It

Türkmen nomad tents in eastern Asia Minor.

Pamphylia, southern Asia Minor.

became an increasingly European state. During the later eleventh century a number of relatively new political powers entered the historical stage. On the one hand, the maritime power of Venice (followed by Genoa, Pisa and Amalfi) introduced a new element into the economic as well as the political relations between Byzantium and the West. In their efforts to secure Venetian support against both the Normans and other enemies, the emperors made several concessions in respect of customs and trading privileges to these city-states – originally to Venice alone, which was regarded (in spite of its entirely autonomous regime) as still part of the empire – with the result that by the end of the twelfth century imperial naval power had been fatally compromised, and Byzantine merchants had proved unable to compete effectively in terms of long-distance commerce. While this influence has certainly been exaggerated in the past, it is also true that the economic influence of powers such as Venice had considerable effects on imperial politics.[6]

On the other hand, the empire faced a complex situation in its relations with the German emperors and with the nascent power of the Sicilian Norman kingdom. It was partly the Crusades which had transformed the traditional situation: while the Crusaders themselves established a series of fragile principalities around the kingdom of Jerusalem, they also brought with them the political interests of the western powers, who now began increasingly to intervene in what had been an exclusively Byzantine sphere of influence. John II and Manuel tried hard to maintain friendly relations with the German emperors, playing them off against the ambitious Normans of Sicily, in an effort to hold both the latter and the Papacy in check in central and southern Italy and the Adriatic. The emperor Manuel I, who pursued an effective foreign policy that permitted the empire to appear as a major power in the region, was able to attain some success through marriage alliances; yet on his death the system he had built up quickly fell apart, and the fragility of the imperial position – based on inadequate resources – soon became apparent.

Unfortunately Manuel left no heir competent enough to deal with this political inheritance. His son Alexios II, aged 10, was under the influence of his mother (Maria, a Frankish princess); but the hostility towards 'Latin' – that is to say, western – influence at court, which Manuel had promoted, came to a head in 1182 when Andronikos I Komnenos seized the throne and had the young Alexios murdered. The situation slowly worsened: the empire's alliance with Venice had collapsed in 1171 as Manuel attempted to use Genoa and Pisa as a counterweight to Venetian maritime power, and Andronikos unleashed a massacre of Genoese and Pisan merchants and other westerners in 1182, which turned these powerful city-states against the empire. In 1185 the Normans exploited the empire's disorder by attacking and sacking Thessaloniki, the second city of the empire. Andronikos' seizure of power inaugurated some twenty years of internal strife, as the frequent coups d'état demonstrate. Andronikos was himself deposed and killed in 1185 and succeeded by Isaac II Angelos (1185-95), a relation of the Komnenos clan; he was replaced by his brother Alexios III Angelos in the years 1195-1203, who was in turn removed by Alexios III. In 1203, however, the armies of the fourth Crusade appeared before Constantinople. Alexios III was removed, to be succeeded by Alexios IV.

Further problems arose in the Balkans. A rebellion in Bulgaria in 1186 led to the defeat of imperial garrisons and the re-establishment of an independent Bulgarian state. Isaac II was himself heavily defeated in 1190 in an effort to check the revolt; while Serbia, which had occupied the position of a vassal state for some time, began also to distance itself from the empire, partly a result of the empire's wars with Hungary. Isaac was able to stabilize the situation through a successful military campaign and a marriage alliance, but it was apparent that imperial power and authority were in decline on every front. By 1196 Serbia had turned to Rome rather than Constantinople for political support, while the situation in Bulgaria was hopeless. With the arrival of the third Crusade in 1189, Cyprus was also lost to a western power (initially the English under Richard I, then the Knights Templar, and finally – in 1192 – the Lusignans).[7]

The death blow to the Byzantine empire in its late Roman form, which had survived so many threats and challenges, came from the West, and in the form of the Fourth Crusade. Originally intending to attack Egypt, the Crusading forces found themselves heavily in debt to Venice, which had hired them ships and provided some of the finance for the expedition. The Venetians had been looking for an opportunity to intervene in the confused situation at Constantinople in order to consolidate their trading privileges and their hold over the commerce of the eastern Mediterranean. The presence at Venice of a pretender to the imperial throne, Alexios IV Angelos, rendered the task of the Venetians in requesting a diversion to Constantinople fairly easy. In 1203, the crusader army arrived before the walls of the Byzantine capital and within a short time had succeeded in installing Alexios IV as co-emperor, with his blind father, Isaac II, whom his uncle Alexios III had deposed, and who had been brought out of prison after the latter fled the city. Once installed, Alexios IV found it impossible to pay the promised rewards; and as the situation worsened, he found himself increasingly isolated. Early in 1204 he was deposed and murdered by Alexios Doukas (Alexios V); but this only exacerbated the problem. Although the new emperor strengthened the defences and was able to resist an initial crusader attack, the city fell on 12 April. The booty taken was immense – one crusader account asserts that so much booty from a single city had not been seen since the creation of the world. The city which had amassed a store of precious objects, statues, liturgical and ceremonial vestments and objects since its refoundation by Constantine I, and which had never before fallen to violent assault, was mercilessly sacked and pillaged for three days, during which countless ancient artefacts were destroyed, while precious metal objects were melted down or stolen. Some of the most spectacular late Roman objects can still be seen in Venice today.

Alexios V, who had fled, was captured shortly afterwards and executed, and a Latin emperor was elected in the person of Baldwin of Flanders. The empire's lands were divided among the victors; Venice receiving the provinces and maritime districts it had coveted. Greece was divided among several rulers. The Principality of Achaia (the Morea) and the Duchy of the Archipelago were subject to the Latin emperor at Constantinople; a kingdom of Thessaloniki was established, to whose ruler the lords of Athens and Thebes owed fealty; while the county of Cephalonia (which – along with the islands of Ithaca and Zante – had been under Italian rule since 1194) was nominally subject to Venice, although it was in practice autonomous, and after 1214 recognized the prince of Achaia as overlord. The lord of Euboea (Negroponte) was subject to the authority of both Thessaloniki and Venice.

But the empire did not cease to exist. On the contrary, in spite of the parcelling out of much imperial territory, a number of counter-claimants to the imperial throne asserted

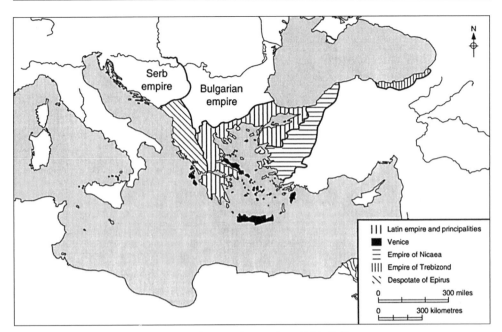

Map 6: The empire's territories c.1204-1240.

their position. In the western Balkans, with its focus in north-western Greece, a branch of the Angelos family established an independent principality, the Despotate of Epiros, which lasted almost to the fifteenth century. In central and eastern Pontus, where the dynasty of the Komnenoi governed a more-or-less autonomous region, the 'empire' of Trebizond appeared. At Nicaea, where the noble Constantine Laskaris continued to exercise effective control over much of Byzantine western Asia Minor, the empire of Nicaea evolved. Constantine's brother Theodore was crowned emperor, and since he was the son-in-law of Alexios III, he had a certain legitimacy. And apart from these 'legitimist' territories, the Bulgarian Tsar Kalojan was in the process of establishing a Bulgar power to rival that of the Tsar Symeon in the early tenth century. Indeed, he captured the Latin emperor in 1205 after decisively crushing his army. By the 1230s the Bulgars were threatening to reduce the Byzantines of Epirus to vassal status.

The Latin empire of Constantinople had an unpromising future. The rulers of Epiros attempted, with help from the German emperor Frederick II, and later with the king of Sicily Manfred, to establish a balance in the Balkans, with the intention of recovering Constantinople. But the emperors of Nicaea were able to make an alliance with Genoa, thus achieving a naval balance of power with Venice. Throughout the 1240s and 1250s they were able to extend their territories in Europe; the recovery of some of the territory held by Frankish rulers followed, although Monemvasia actually fell (for a while) to a Frankish force in 1248. By the end of the thirteenth century, parts of central Greece were once again in Byzantine hands: the Byzantine Despotate of Morea controlled much of central and south-eastern Peloponnese. The principality of Achaia, however, remained an important power to its north. In Asia Minor, a policy of rapprochement with the Seljuks

47

Mosiac, imperial palace at Constantinople.

permitted a stabilization of the frontier for a while. In 1261, taking advantage of the absence of most of the Latin garrison of Constantinople on an expedition, a small Nicaean force was able to gain entry to the City, reclaim it for the empire, and drive out the remaining western troops and Latin civilian population. Constantinople was the capital of the East Roman Empire once more.

In spite of this success, and the consolidation and temporary recovery of some territory in Asia Minor, the last two centuries of Byzantine rule in Asia Minor and the southern Balkan region is a tale of ever-contracting boundaries, the loss of Asia Minor, and the reduction of the empire to a dependency of the growing Ottoman Sultanate. Under Michael VIII (1259-1282), the empire was able to expand into the Peloponnese and to force the submission of the Frankish principalities in the region. International political alliances with Genoa and the kingdom of Aragon and, briefly, with the Papacy, enabled Byzantium once more to influence the international scene and to resist the powers which worked for its destruction and partition. But under Andronikos II (1282-1328), the empire was unable to meet the needs of a much less friendly international environment. Indeed, with the transfer of imperial attention back to Constantinople, the Asian provinces were neglected at the very moment that the Mongols weakened Seljuk dominion over the nomadic Türkmen (Turcoman) tribes, allowing them unrestricted access to the ill-defended Byzantine districts. Most of the south-western and central coastal regions were lost by about 1270, and the interior, including the important Maeander valley, had become Turkish territory by 1300. Independent Turkish principalities or emirates, including the fledgling power of the Ottomans, posed a constant threat to the surviving imperial districts. By 1315, the remaining Aegean regions had been lost, and Bithynia had succumbed by 1337. In addition, the mercenary Catalan Grand Company (hired by Andronikos II in 1303 to help fight the Turks and other enemies) turned against the empire when its demands for pay were not met and, after defeating the Burgundian Duke of Athens in 1311, seized control of the region, which it held until 1388. Other mercenary companies behaved similarly. The empire's resources were simply insufficient to meet any but the smallest hostile attack on its territory, and it was rapidly losing even the possibility of hiring mercenaries.

By the time of Andronikos' death in 1328, the empire held only a few isolated fortress-towns. With the loss of the semi-autonomous region about Philadelphia in 1390 to the Ottomans, the history of Byzantine Anatolia comes to an end. The situation was greatly exacerbated by the civil wars which rent the empire in the period after the death of Andronikos II; wars which were for the greater part inspired by the personal and family rivalries of a small group within the Byzantine aristocracy. Andronikos III rebelled against his grandfather Andronikos II in 1321, and after four years of squabbling, marching and countermarching, succeeded in becoming co-emperor in 1325. Conflict flared up again in 1327, but Andronikos II died in 1328 leaving the empire to his grandson, who ruled until 1341; but it broke out again in 1341, when the regency representing the young John V, son of Andronikos III (dominated by the dowager empress Anne of Savoy and the Grand Duke Alexios Apokaukus) declared John Kantakouzenos an enemy of the empire.

John was Grand Domestic and had been the leading minister under the previous emperor; he now had himself proclaimed emperor and assembled an army. The situation was complicated by religious and social divisions. The rise of hesychasm – a mystical and contemplative movement which found particular support in monastic circles – had polarized opinion within the Church, since much of the regular and higher clergy, including the patriarch, were fiercely opposed to its teachings. The regime at Constantinople thus found that the hesychasts – particularly on Mt Athos, the centre of Byzantine monasticism – allied themselves with John Kantakouzenos, who thus gained the support of Gregory Palamas, one of the greatest theologians of the last centuries of Byzantium, a leading proponent of hesychasm, and a powerful speaker. At the same time, the regency whipped up discontent in the provincial towns against the fundamentally aristocratic party led by Kantakouzenos, so that popular movements sprang up and expelled many of the latter's supporters, with the result that Kantakouzenos fled to the Serbian king Stefan Uroš IV Dušan (1331-55). This alliance suited Serbian expansionist interests, of course, but did not last long, for John then allied himself with the governor of Byzantine Thessaly (a practically autonomous region), John Angelos, . In response, Dušan negotiated an alliance with the regime at Constantinople. Using Turkish allies, Kantakouzenos prosecuted the war until 1345 and, following the collapse of the regency and the murder of Alexios Apokaukos, had himself crowned John VI at Adrianople in 1346. He entered Constantinople the following year, where his coronation was repeated by the patriarch.

John's victory meant also the victory of hesychasm, which was opposed to any compromise with the Western Church. From 1351, when hesychastic doctrine became the official doctrine of the Byzantine Church, its conservative anti-western values came to the fore and proved an important influence on the last century of Byzantine culture and politics, especially in respect of attitudes to western culture and Christianity. Politically and economically the empire was now in a desperate situation. Dusan had exploited Byzantine weakness to swallow up Albania, eastern Macedonia and Thessaly. The empire was left with Thrace around Constantinople, a small district around Thessaloniki, surrounded by Serbian territory; together with its lands in the Peloponnese and the northern Aegean isles. Each of these regions was, in practice, a more-or-less autonomous province, constituting together an empire in name and by tradition alone. But the civil wars had wrecked the economy of these districts, which could barely afford the minimal taxes the emperors demanded, a point well illustrated by the fact that the Genoese commercial centre at Galata, on the other side of the Golden Horn from Constantinople, had an annual revenue seven times as great as that of the imperial city itself.

From the 1350s a new European enemy appeared, for the Ottomans had expanded into Europe during the civil wars, following a request in 1344 from Kantakouzenos for Ottoman help against John V. As a result, they began permanently to establish themselves in Europe, taking the chief towns of Thrace in the 1360s, and Thessaloniki in 1387. By the beginning of the fifteenth century, and with the exception of the Despotate of the Morea and certain of the Aegean isles, there remained no imperial possessions in Greece.

The history of the empire's territories in the period after 1204 is extremely complex as territories were allocated to the conquerors; transmitted directly and laterally to heirs, and by marriage alliance; conquered by a neighbour or a more distant power; recovered; ceded by treaty, and so on. The history of the islands provides a good illustration. After 1204, much of the southern part of the Aegean came under Venetian authority; and although Byzantine power was restored for a while in the late thirteenth century, Naxos remained the centre of the Latin Duchy of the Archipelago, established in 1207 among the Cyclades by Marco Sanudo – a relative of the Venetian Doge – with a body of freebooting merchants and nobles. Initially under the overlordship of the Latin emperor at Constantinople, the duchy later transferred its allegiance to Achaia (in 1261), and to Naples (in 1267), although Venice also laid claim to it. The Sanudo family were replaced in 1383 by the Lombard Crispi family, who retained their independence until after the middle of the sixteenth century, when the duchy was conquered by the Ottomans. The remaining islands were held at different times by the Venetians, Genoese, the Knights Hospitallers and, eventually, the Turks. Rhodes played a particular role in the history of the Hospitallers' opposition to the Ottomans from 1309 until its fall in 1523, when the Knights were permitted to remove to Malta. In the northern Aegean, Limnos remained Byzantine until 1453, before coming for a while under the rule of the Gattilusi of Lesbos (whose independence of the Ottomans finally ended in 1462). In 1460, it was awarded to Demetrios Palaiologos (formerly *despotes* or Lord of the Morea), along with the island of Thasos, which fell to the Ottomans in 1455, until it too was occupied by Ottoman forces in 1479. Other islands had equally checkered histories – Naxos and Chios fell only in 1566, while Tenedos remained under the Venetians until 1715.

The advance of the Ottoman power in Europe brings with it the decline and extinction of Byzantium. By 1371, they had defeated the Serbs on the Maritza, in 1388 Bulgaria became a tributary state, and in 1389 at the battle of Kosovo – in what in fact may well have been a drawn encounter (in spite of the local tradition) – the Ottoman forces were able to

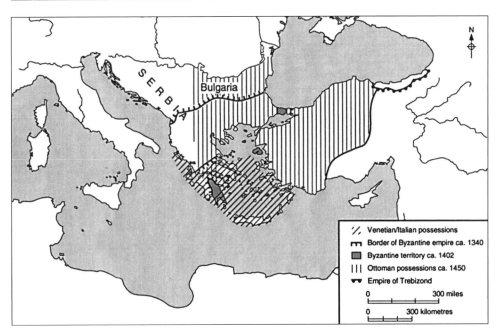

Map 7: The empire and its neighbours c.1350-1453.

compromise the possibilities of further Serb resistance sufficiently for the Serbs to accept tributary status. The Ottoman advance caused considerable anxiety in the West. A crusade was organized under the leadership of the Hungarian king, Sigismund, but in 1396 at the battle of Nicopolis his army was decisively defeated. The Byzantines, caught between the Ottomans and the western powers, attempted to play the different elements off against one another. One possible solution, the union of the two Churches – with the inevitable subordination of Constantinople to Rome which this entailed – was espoused by some churchmen and part of the aristocracy. Monastic circles in particular, and much of the rural population, were bitterly hostile to such a compromise, to the extent even of arguing that subjection to the Turk was preferable. Hostility to the 'Latins' had become firmly entrenched in the minds of the majority of the Orthodox population, both inside and outside the empire's territories. Hesychasm, which represented an alternative to the worldly politics of the pro-westernists, thrived on this ground and further exploited the alienation between the two worlds. Neither party was able to assert itself effectively within the empire, with the result that the western powers remained on the whole apathetic to the plight of 'the Greeks'.

In 1401 the Ottoman Sultan Bayezid began preparations for the siege of Constantinople. But the end was not yet reached. As the siege was under way, Mongol forces under Timur (Timur Lenk – Tamburlane) invaded Asia Minor, where, at the battle of Ankara in 1402, the Ottomans were defeated and forced to accept tributary status. In the Peloponnese, the Byzantines were able to use the opportunity to bring the remaining Latin princes under their authority. But the respite was of short duration. Timur's death shortly afterwards brought with it the fragmentation of his empire and the revival, indeed strengthening, of Ottoman power. The Sultans consolidated their control in Anatolia, and set about expanding their control of the Balkans. The emperor John VIII travelled widely in Europe attempting to muster support against the Islamic threat, even accepting ecclesiastical union with the Western Church at the council of Florence in 1439, but this did little to hinder the inevitable. A last effort on the part of the emperors led to the Western Crusade which ended in disaster at the battle of Varna in Bulgaria in 1444, and in 1453 Mehmet II set about the siege of Constantinople. After several weeks of the siege the Ottoman forces, equipped with heavy artillery, including cannon, were able to effect some serious breaches in the Theodosian walls. In spite of a valiant effort on the part of the imperial troops and their western allies, who were massively outnumbered, the walls were finally breached by the elite Janissary units on 29 May 1453. The last emperor, Constantine XI, died in the attack and his body was never found. Constantinople became the new Ottoman capital; the surviving Aegean isles were quickly absorbed by the Ottoman state; the Despotate of Morea was conquered in 1460; and Trebizond (capital of the empire of the Grand Komnenoi) fell to a Turkish army the year after. The empire which had fought off enemies on every front for a thousand years was no more.

PART II

THE BYZANTINE WORLD

3 The peoples and lands
of Byzantium

Overview of the later Roman world

It is easy to overlook the fact that the history of all societies is determined in many respects by their physical context: geography, climate and the availability or not of certain types of resource, both in terms of foodstuffs as well as in respect of minerals and other raw materials. The late Roman world was dominated by three land-masses (Asia Minor or Anatolia[2], very roughly modern Turkey; the Levant[3] or Middle Eastern regions down to and including Egypt; and the Balkans[4]), and by the Mediterranean and Black Seas, which united these very different regions both to each other and to the outlying regions of Italy and the North African coastal zones with their hinterlands. The climate of these very different areas determined the patterns of agricultural and pastoral exploitation within the empire's borders and the nature of the state's surplus-extracting activities. Asia Minor can be divided into three zones: central plateau, coastal plains, and the mountain ranges which separate them. The plateau is typified by extremes of hot and cold temperatures in summer and winter, in contrast to the milder and friendlier 'Mediterranean' climate of the coastal regions, with the result that the density of agricultural activity and of population is generally very much higher in the latter than the former, where, with some exceptions in sheltered river valleys, it is a pastoral economy which predominates (sheep, cattle and horses). The Balkans is in many ways more rugged and fragmented than Asia Minor, but if we include the broad Thracian plain, the plain of Thessaly and the fertile south Danubian plains it is also productive and potentially quite rich agriculturally. In contrast, the fertile Nile valley and the rich agricultural lands of Palestine and western Syria are very much wealthier, while the long coastal plains of Tunisia produced both olives and cereals. Indeed, Rome imported most of the grain to support its population from Africa, just as Constantinople was heavily dependent upon Egypt to meet its needs. These were satisfied by state contracts with shippers who undertook to carry the requisite supplies and to work for the government at fixed tariffs and under government supervision, in return for specific fiscal and legal privileges.

While it originally included all these lands within its boundaries, and while (after the disappearance of the western empire and the loss of Italy, Spain and North Africa to Ostrogoths, Visigoths and Vandals respectively) much of North Africa and Italy was recovered during the reign of the Emperor Justinian I (527-565), for most of its long existence the lands of the empire were restricted to the Balkans and Asia Minor, with the Aegean islands and Crete and Cyprus. It was the era of the Islamic conquests which introduced such dramatic changes to this picture. After about AD 700 and until the later eighth or early ninth century, remnants of imperial possessions survived under more-or-less autonomous local rule, in northern and southern Italy, the Balearics and Sardinia.

*A landscape in western
Asia Minor, looking east.*

Briefly, during the tenth and eleventh centuries, parts of northern and western Syria and the Lebanon region were recovered. The losses in manpower and fiscal income (that is, taxes) incurred during the seventh century led to a radical transformation of late Roman institutions. The nature of the lands which remained under imperial control, together with their much more limited resources, were henceforth the prime elements which determined the political, economic, and strategic possibilities open to Byzantine rulers.

The provinces which remained in imperial hands were among the least wealthy of former Roman territories. Egypt, the most productive, had contributed the main source of grain for Constantinople, and represented a major source of the state's tax income. From figures given by a range of late Roman sources for the eastern half of the empire (excluding Italy and Africa, which have been reckoned to have contributed only one eighth or so of the total revenue), it has been calculated that Egypt contributed something like one third of the state income (both gold and grain) derived from the near eastern and Balkan provinces (the prefectures of Oriens and Illyricum) together. Further, it has been calculated that the income of the Balkan region south of the Danube, and that of Anatolia, were very approximately equal. Yet in the late Roman period the bulk of the state's income outside of Egypt had been derived from the rich provinces of Syria, Mesopotamia (northern Iraq), Euphratensis, Osrhoene (to the south and north of the upper Euphrates, respectively), Phoenicia (the Lebanon and southern Syria), Palestine and Cilicia (the modern Turkish province of Adana), all lost to the Arabs after the 640s and only partially, in their northern perimeter, recovered in the tenth century. Therefore, with the loss of Egypt and these eastern provinces, and with effective control over all but the coastal periphery of much of the southern Balkans lost during the later sixth and first half of the

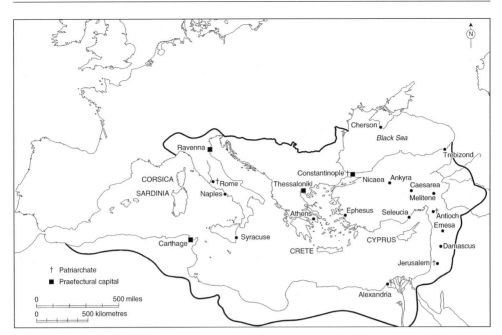

Map 8: The empire at the death of Justinian c.565.

seventh century, the overall income of the state collapsed to a fraction of the sixth-century total: one proposal plausibly suggested is that it was reduced to a quarter. Maps 8 (above) and 3 (p.32) illustrate these changes and fluctuations.

The most densely settled regions of Asia Minor were the narrow coastal plains in the north and south and the much broader plains of the Aegean region, dissected by the western foothills of the central plateau which run from east to west. Urban settlement was concentrated in these areas, although there were groups of cities in some inland regions where a milder situation afforded some protection from the extremes of winter and summer found in the more exposed central plateau and eastern mountains. Land-use throughout the medieval period and into modern times was predominantly pastoral on the plateau, with the cultivation of cereals, vegetables, vines and olives dominating the fertile coastal regions. All cities depended upon their agricultural hinterlands for their economic survival: the costs of transporting foodstuffs in bulk overland – especially cereals – were prohibitive over long distances. Only those with good harbour facilities or other access to the coast could develop as centres of long-distance – as well as local – trade and exchange, and could afford to ship in supplies in times of dearth. Politically and militarily, Anatolia was at peace throughout the Roman period and until the beginning of the seventh century, except for the existence of brigandage in less accessible regions such as Isauria, and the brief civil wars of the later fifth century, which involved both this region and parts of western Anatolia.

The Roman state often transferred populations from one area to another in attempting to deal with demographic and fiscal problems, as well as to eradicate religious opposition, and this was especially true of the Byzantine rulers of the later seventh to ninth centuries. Anatolia thus gained from the import of Slav and other Balkan groups, while south-east

The north-central Asia Minor plateau.

A mountain pass in north-east Turkey., looking north.

A fertile valley in south-east Asia Minor.

Mesembria, on the Black Sea coast north-east of Constantinople.

Landscape in the Mani, southern Peloponnese.

Europe received heretical groups who brought with them dualist ideas and stimulated the growth of heterodox beliefs such as Bogomilism in Bulgaria during the tenth and eleventh centuries. During the eleventh century and after, there was a large-scale migration of Syrians and especially Armenians into south-western Asia Minor; partly a result of imperial expansion eastwards in the tenth century, partly a result of the Seljuk threat in the middle of the eleventh century.

With the arrival of the Seljuk Turks in the 1060s, the defeat of the imperial army at the battle of Mantzikert in 1071, and the political power-struggles which followed, eastern and central Asia Minor fell to the Turks. Imperial efforts to recover some of these lost regions met with partial success during the reigns of Alexios I (1081-1118) – with the assistance of the armies of the First Crusade – and his successors John II and Manuel I up to 1180. But lack of resources and the strength of Turk resistance meant that by the end of the twelfth century the empire was effectively confined to the northern and southern littorals and the western coastal plains of the region. During the period of the Latin empire (1204-1261), the successor empire of Nicaea was able to reassert imperial control to some extent in western Anatolia. The restoration of an imperial Byzantine state at Constantinople in 1261, however, meant that priorities shifted away from this frontier, and Turkish groups under the leadership of a variety of warlords and clans reduced imperial possessions to a few coastal enclaves and fortified centres. By the early fourteenth century Byantine control over Asia Minor had effectively withered away.

The Balkan peninsula is dominated by mountains, and although not particularly high, these cover some two thirds of its area. The main formations are the Dinaric Alps, which run through the western Balkan region in a south-easterly direction and, in the associated Pindos range, dominate western and central Greece. Extensions and spurs of these mountains dominate southern Greece and the Peloponnese. The Balkan chain itself (Turkic *balqan*, 'densely wooded mountain'; Greek *Haimos*) lies north of Greece, extending eastwards from the Morava river for about 550km as far as the Black Sea coast, with the

The Bosphorus.

Rhodope range forming an arc extending southwards from this range through Macedonia towards the plain of Thrace. River and coastal plains are relatively limited in extent. Thus, there are very distinct climatic variations between the coastal, Mediterranean-type conditions and the continental-type conditions of the inland and highland regions. This has in turn generated a very accentuated settlement pattern consisting in a series of fragmented geo-political entities, separated by ridges of highlands, fanning out along river-valleys towards the coastal areas.

The history of the region has been heavily marked by these features. Communications were particularly clearly affected. In addition, the southern Balkan peninsula has no obvious geographical focal point: the main cities in the medieval period were Thessaloniki and Constantinople, yet these were peripheral to the peninsula and its fragmented landscape. The degree and depth of Byzantine political control during the middle ages is clearly reflected in this. In the Rhodope mountains, perhaps the most inaccessible of those mentioned, as well as in the Pindos range, state authority has always remained a somewhat distant factor in the lives of the inhabitants, whether in the Roman, Byzantine, Ottoman or more recent period. Here, as in the more inaccessible districts of Asia Minor, paganism and heresy could survive with little interference or control from a central government or Church establishment.

This geophysical structure also affects land-use. The highland regions are dominated by forest and woodland; the lower foothills by woodland, scrub and rough pasturage. Only the plains of Thessaly and Macedonia offer the possibility of extensive arable exploitation; the river plains and the coastal strips associated with them (such as the region about the Gulfs of Argos and Corinth, much more limited in extent) present a similar but more restricted potential. These are the regions where orchards, as well as vine and olive cultivation, are chiefly located. Inevitably, the pattern of settlement of both larger urban centres as well as of rural communities is largely determined by these features. The relationship between this landscape of mountains, valleys and coastal plains and the sea is fundamental to the political,

61

military and cultural history of the region, in particular in the southern zone. For example, surrounded by the sea (except along its northern boundary), the extended coastline, with its gulfs and deep inlets, serves as a means of communication with surrounding areas and for the dissemination of common cultural elements even to the interior districts of the Balkans. By the same token, of course, easy sea-borne access from the west, the south or from the north-east via the Black Sea made the southern Balkan peninsula – Greece and the Peloponnese especially – vulnerable to invasion and dislocation. The political geography of the Byzantine world played a key role in its overall historical evolution.

Communications

The construction of a network of major arterial roads – granting the rapid movement of men and materials from the inner provinces to the frontiers, and connecting these provinces to one another and to major political centres – was undoubtedly one of the major achievements of the Roman armies during the great period of expansion and conquest from *c.*100 BC–AD 100. While it was certainly this system of roads which made the Roman army so efficient in its response to external threat, and in its use of resources, it also greatly facilitated non-military communications and the movement of goods, people, news and ideas. During the later Roman period, however, and particularly from the later fourth and fifth centuries, the regular maintenance of roads – which was a state burden upon towns and which was administered and regulated at the local level – appears to have suffered a serious decline. In part, this reflected different priorities in the allocation and consumption of resources by those who governed urban centres. It may also reflect a decline in the necessary engineering skills in the empire, and especially in the army. One result of such changes, and the difficulties which they brought for wheeled transport, was an increasing reliance upon beasts of burden for the movement of goods and people. The late Roman government laid down strict regulations on the size, loads and use of different types of wheeled vehicle employed by the public transport system, which was divided into two branches: the slow post (ox-carts and similar heavy vehicles) and the fast post (faster-moving pack-animals, light carts, and horses or ponies). A transport and courier service continued to operate through the Byzantine period, although the two branches seem to have been merged.

Roads were not all constructed for the same purpose, nor to the same standard. Wide roads and narrow tracks or paths, paved and unpaved roads, roads that were suitable for wagons or wheeled vehicles and roads that were not, all receive mention in the sources. For obvious reasons, roads that possessed some strategic value for the state were usually more regularly maintained. The limited and sometimes contradictory evidence suggests that certain key routes only were kept up after the sixth century, for the most part through compulsory duties upon the labouring population and the craftsmen of the districts through which the road passed. Thus in Asia Minor a much less extensive but still effective network of predominantly military routes emerges from the middle of the seventh century, associated with imperial and provincial marching camps situated at strategically important points. The same applies also in the Balkans, although marching

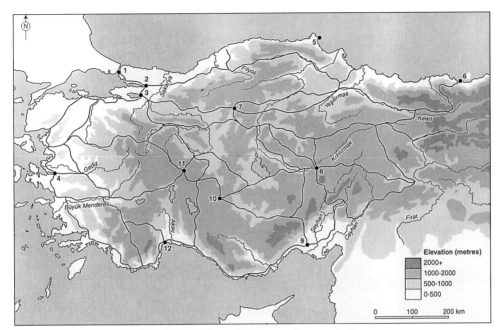

Map 9: Asia Minor – landscape and communications

	Places	Modern river names	Byzantine river names
1	Chalcedon	Sakarya	Sangarios
2	Nikomedeia	Filyos	Billaios
3	Nicaea	Yeşilirmak	Iris
4	Smyrna	Kelkit	Lykos
5	Sinope	Kızılırmak	Halys
6	Trebizond	Gediz	Hermos
7	Ankyra	Büyük Menderes	Maiandros (Maeander)
8	Caesarea	Aksu	Eurymedon
9	Tarsos	Şeyhan	Saros
10	Ikonion	Ceyhan	Pyramos
11	Akroinon	Firat	Euphrates
12	Attaleia		

camps such as those found in the Anatolian region are known only from the later period (twelfth century and after). The maintenance of these stretches was a localized and irregular matter, and the limited evidence suggests that many became little more than paths or tracks suitable only for pack-animals, with paved or hard surfaces only near towns and fortresses.[5] Maps 9 and 10 provide an overview of such major routes.

Transport by water was immeasurably cheaper than by land, at least over medium and longer distances, and was generally also much faster. Long-distance movement of bulk goods such as grain was generally prohibitively expensive – the cost of feeding draught-oxen, maintaining drovers and carters, paying local tolls, combined with the extremely slow rate of movement of ox-carts, multiplied the value of the goods being transported beyond the

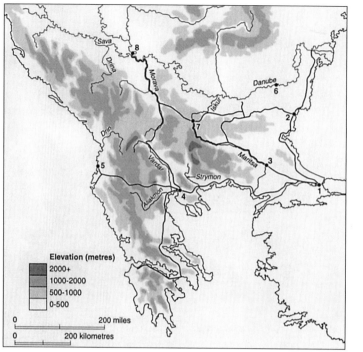

Map 10: The Balkans –
landscape and
communications.

1 – Constantinople
2 – Varna
3 – Adrianople
4 – Thessaloniki
5 – Dyrrhachium
    (Dürres)
6 – Dorostolum
7 – Serdica (Sofia)
8 – Singidunum
    (Belgrade)

price of anyone who would otherwise have bought them. This does not mean that the bulk transport of goods over long distances did not take place. But for the most part it was the state (to supply the armies), with some activity funded by wealthy private individuals, which was engaged in this. In contrast, the cost-effectiveness of shipping, by which large quantities of goods could be carried in a single vessel managed by a small number of men, gave coastal settlements a huge advantage in terms of access to the wider world.

Peoples and languages

The late Roman world was a multi-ethnic, multi-linguistic collage of cultures, united chiefly through the fiscal administrative apparatus of the central government. Roman law and Roman governance, at least at provincial level, served to reinforce the notion of a single state with a single ruler, the emperor. The issue and universal use of a coinage which bore the emperor's portrait bust and other symbols, along with an inscription invoking the emperor's right to rule, further reinforced this political unity; and by the later sixth century – the Latin 'western half' of the empire having dissolved – the Greek language itself served to remind people of both Rome's past and also to promote different ways of thinking about the 'Roman' past and what that actually implied.

Since the conquests of Alexander of Macedon in the second half of the fourth century BC and the consequent fragmentation of his empire into its major constituent parts, Greek – and more particularly Attic Greek – had been the common language of the urban cultures of these regions. It also filtered down, through the presence of the army as well as through service in the army, or through trade, into the ordinary population of the affected provinces. In the process, a whole range of new dialects evolved under the influence of the indigenous languages of the regions concerned, with the result that by the first century BC a purifying movement had appeared, centred in Egypt at Alexandria, which aimed at cleansing Attic Greek of the numerous barbarian accretions which had come to afflict it. Needless to say, this movement was largely unsuccessful: languages are living, flexible and constantly changing, and generally not amenable to such directed pressures. Yet one result was forthcoming, a result which, moreover, has affected the Greek language, Greek literature and Greek politics, especially the politics of education, to the present day. This was the creation of a diglossy, that is to say, of several (but at least two) forms or versions of the language: ordinary spoken Greek, and the so-called 'Atticizing' or 'classicizing' Greek of the cultural and educated elite, whose Greek, it came to be felt, should not be full of barbarisms but should be as pure and as near to the classical Greek of fifth-century BC Athens as possible, precisely in order to establish a degree of social and cultural differentiation within society. In fact, since this was a 'dead' language that was being artificially cultivated, writers and speakers with different educational backgrounds and training tended to produce different versions of this version of Greek, thus confusing the issue even more. The gap between the 'Atticizing' Greek of learned people and the various demotic or spoken forms in currency across the empire was such that we hear, on occasion, of Greek speakers unfamiliar with the educated language having it explained or translated for them.

Anatolia was always a region of considerable cultural diversity. Most of the non-Greek indigenous languages (Isaurian, Galatian, Cappadocian, Lycian, for example) had died out by the later sixth or seventh century, although certain languages may have survived for longer in the more isolated regions. But with the exception of Armenian and some related dialects in the north-east, Greek dominated, in a wide range of dialect forms, some of which survive until today (although no longer in Turkey: Pontic Greek, for example, which moved with its refugee speakers, expelled during the 1923 exchange of populations between Greece and Turkey, can still be heard in those regions of Greece where they were settled).

The situation in the Balkans appears to have been very much more complex after the sixth century. Until then, the languages of the region can be grouped into three major blocs: Greek, with associated dialects in the south; the Latin dialects of the central and northern Balkans, including the Danube plain to north and south of the river, which had for the most part replaced the indigenous languages (Dacian, for example) during the centuries following the Roman conquest of the region during the first and second centuries AD; and the isolated language groups of the western coastal regions, such as Illyrian, the ancestor of the modern Albanian groups. The populations of the second region generated the languages of the Daco-Rumanian and Macedo-Rumanian groups, the ancestors of that known from the thirteenth century as Rumanian, rooted in late Latin and thereafter heavily influenced by the Slav dialects with which the Daco-Thracian populations were in regular contact. Two factors transformed this situation: the arrival of large numbers of Slavs during the later sixth to eighth centuries; and the migration across the region of nomadic or semi-nomadic pastoralists such as the Vlachs and Albanians, firstly in the tenth and eleventh centuries, and later from the thirteenth century onwards. The evidence of place-names suggests some lasting Slavic influence in parts of Greece, but the re-Hellenization which occurred from the later eighth century probably eradicated many traces of their presence. Evidence of Slavic 'tribal' names in the Peloponnese and in northern Greece suggests extensive Slavic-speaking populations in many districts; and from the tenth century to the fifteenth century, Slav occupants of various parts of the Peloponnese appear in the sources as brigands or as independent communities with a fierce warrior tradition. The Slavs of Macedonia and Thessaly retained their original dialects, becoming only patchily and incompletely Hellenophone in certain districts; those who settled in the more southerly regions eventually adopted Greek.

The origins of the Albanians, who first appear in the later Byzantine sources, remain uncertain. They represent the descendants of the Illyrian populations who fell back into the highlands of the central Dinaric chain in pre-Roman times, and their language probably evolved from ancient Illyrian (now generally recognized as an independent member of the Hellenic group of Indo-European languages), heavily influenced by Greek, Slavic and Turkish as well as medieval Italian. For reasons which remain unclear, they began in the fourteenth century to expand seawards from their mountain homeland into the western coastal plain, serving both Byzantine and Serbian overlords as mercenaries and establishing independent chieftainships under various warlords. They appear also in considerable numbers in Thessaly, Boeotia, Attica and the Peloponnese, serving as soldiers and as farmers, and colonizing deserted lands. Albanians arrived in large numbers in the Peloponnese during the reign of the *despotes* (overlord) Manuel Kantakouzenos (1349-1380), who introduced them to serve as soldiers and to resettle depopulated regions.

In the central Balkan region and northern Greece another people known as the Vlachs played an important role. They have generally been identified with the indigenous, pre-Slav populations of Dacian and Thracian origin, many of whom migrated into less accessible, mountainous regions of Greece and the northern Balkan region – as a result of the Germanic and Avar-Slav invasions and immigration of the fifth-seventh centuries – and maintained a transhumant, pastoral economy. Their language belonged to the Macedo-Rumanian group noted already. By the eleventh century they appear in the sources as transhumant pastoralists moving with their flocks between winter pastures in Thessaly and the summer pastures of the Grammos and Pindos ranges; they also served in Byzantine armies. Byzantine sources, which were frequently imprecise with ethnic and other names and identities, regularly confused the Vlachs with the Bulgarians, through whose territory they wandered according to their seasonal routes.

The Bulgars were a people of Turkic language, nomads whose arrival and occupation of the easternmost segment of the south Danube plain in the later seventh century was radically to transform the political contours of the whole Balkan region. While of Turkic origin, they were always outnumbered by the Slav and other populations upon whom they imposed their rule, and by the later ninth and tenth centuries had been almost entirely absorbed, both linguistically and culturally, by the subject populations. Later medieval and modern Bulgarian is a Slavic language.

These regions are the core territories of the Eastern Roman Empire after the middle of the seventh century. Before that time, we must also take into account the Semitic languages of the provinces of the East – chiefly Syriac, but with considerable Arabic elements long before the Islamic conquests; Coptic in Egypt; and the various Hamitic dialects of North

Africa, although the coastal regions, both towns and rural communities, were entirely Latin-speaking as far as the sources can tell us. The urban populations of Syria and Egypt, and considerable elements of the rural populations of these regions, were also Hellenophone, which makes the linguistic map more complex. In Italy, Latin dominated, with the exception of the Greek dialects of Sicily and the south, reinforced during the seventh century as Greek-speakers from western Greece and the Peloponnese fled the warfare and disruption caused by the immigration of the Slavs, to the extent that new dialects evolved and remained a prominent feature of the linguistic map of the region until modern times.

Resources: agricultural production and industry

The Roman Empire was dominated by an agrarian economy. From the mountain valleys of the central Balkans to the fertile Nile, and from the coastal plains and hill country of southern Italy across to the broad plains of northern Syria, agrarian production was the mainstay of life, the essential corollary for the existence of towns and cities, and the basis for the state's taxation. Commerce and industry were, in places, essential elements of local, especially urban, economy; yet overall they played but a minor role in the economic life of the people of the Roman world. At any given time of the empire's existence, it has been estimated that a minimum of 80% of the population was engaged in agricultural and pastoral production; only in its last years, when it was reduced to the city of Constantinople and its immediate hinterland in Thrace, will this proportion have changed.

Bread was the basic food of all the populations of the Mediterranean and Near- or Middle-Eastern zones, and cereals were therefore the dominant crop grown by the majority of rural producers. Egypt (with the rich alluvial soils of the Nile valley) produced by far the greatest quantity per head of the producing population; but the plains of northern Syria, the coastal regions of Asia Minor, Thrace and Thessaly, and the North African provinces also produced substantial quantities of cereals, and North Africa provided the oil and grain for Rome. An important change in the type of wheat grown began during the sixth and seventh centuries, as a harder grain was introduced: hard wheats have a somewhat higher protein content than soft wheats, and produce a flour better suited to bread-making. One of the results was that the proportion of bread to other elements in the diet of people in the Islamic and Byzantine worlds thereafter seems to have declined, a smaller amount of bread made from hard wheat offering the same protein content as a larger amount of soft-wheat based bread. As well as wheat, a substantial element in the grain-production of the empire was barley, with smaller amounts of millet – regarded generally as inappropriate for human consumption. Where the climate allowed – predominantly along the coastal plains of the Aegean and Mediterranean and in some sheltered inland districts – fruit, vines and olives were also cultivated, sometimes extensively and, in the case of olives and vines, sometimes as cash crops to meet the demand from urban markets both near and far. Vegetables and pulses were also cultivated throughout the region, usually on the basis of household garden plots rather than extensively, so that villages and towns were for the most part supplied

Ploughing in western Asia Minor in the 1960s using traditional technology.

Threshing wheat by the traditional method in eastern Asia Minor.

Traditional harrow, eastern Asia Minor.

Traditional ox-cart, eastern Asia Minor.

with all the essentials of life – food, drink, clothing, the materials for housing and the livestock for transport – from their immediate hinterlands. But self-sufficiency was never absolute: villages were also part of a wider world of exchange consisting of several communities within a particular region, by which the inhabitants of one community could obtain goods and services they did not produce themselves, and through which – perhaps through holding an annual fair to celebrate a particular holy day – they might also attract trade and commerce from very much farther afield. But only the largest cities, and then mostly those with access to ports and the sea, had the resources to import goods from further away than their own locality on a regular basis, and these were mostly luxuries for those who could pay for them. Rome and Constantinople imported bulk goods – chiefly grain and oil – on a large scale; but they were notable exceptions, with unusually large urban populations and the seats of major administrative apparatuses for Church and state. Such dependency on distant centres of production was possible only because it was paid for by the state. Inland towns were generally entirely dependent on what was produced locally, strongly inflected in terms of variety and availability by seasonal and regional fluctuations.

Sowing and harvesting and the pattern of seasonal activities depended on location. For those regions dominated by a Mediterranean climate, vegetables were harvested in June, cereals in July; after which the land was normally opened to livestock for pasturage and manuring. Ploughing and tilling generally took place in October and November, and planting/sowing followed immediately thereafter in order to take advantage of the winter rains and the seasonal humidity of the soil. But the cycle might be different in more arid regions: in Syria harvesting takes place in November, with ploughing and planting in July and August, for example. In those areas in which agricultural activity was supported by systems of irrigation, as in the Nile valley, or drier regions with very low annual rainfall, the pattern was different again. Returns on planting similarly varied: the highest average returns in fertile regions appear to have been of the order of 7:1 or 8:1, with variations in either direction. Lower returns in drier or less well-watered districts have been calculated at some 5:1, but all these figures varied slightly across each district and according to the type of crop and seasonal climatic fluctuations.

Long-distance trade in the period up to the later sixth and early seventh century displayed particular patterns which reflected the prosperity of the regions where certain goods were produced. Thus oil and grain were exported (along with the pottery in which they were transported) from North Africa throughout the Mediterranean world; oil and wine similarly travelled from the Syrian coast to the western Aegean and south Balkan coastlands, whence it was re-exported inland or further west to Italy and southern Gaul. The distribution of ceramic types can tell us a great deal about these movements, since not only were many types of import carried in pottery containers of one sort or another – amphorae, often very large vessels, were used for transporting and storing liquids such as wine and oil, as well as solids such as grains, the shape varying according to need. They were moved around chiefly by sea, and were often accompanied by other ceramic products, including fine tablewares, which were exported alongside the bulk goods. Finds of such wares, in conjunction with knowledge of their centres of production, offer a fairly detailed picture of such trade in this period. Some of these goods, indeed, travelled even further afield. In the later sixth century

Above, right and below: A fifth- to sixth-century village in the limestone massif of Syria.

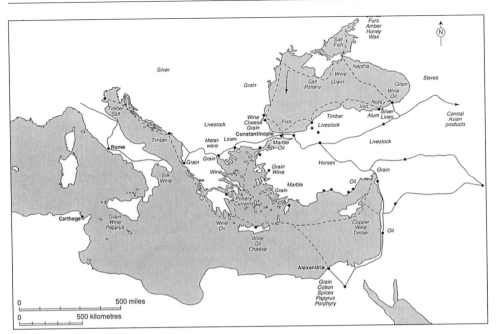

Map 11: Trade and land use

ships were still sailing from Egypt into the Atlantic and around to south-west England, trading corn for tin. This Mediterranean trade did not reflect private, market-led demand alone: it appears that much of the commerce in fine wares, for example, travelled in the ships of the great grain convoys from North Africa to Italy and from Egypt to Constantinople, the captains of the ships being permitted to carry a certain quantity of goods on their own account for private sale in return for a percentage of the price obtained (as did the officers and crews of the east Indiamen which sailed from the Indies to England in the eighteenth and nineteenth centuries, or the West Indies mail packets at the same period).

A marked difference existed between those centres of population and production with access to the sea and inland towns and villages. The economy of the late Roman world was intensely local and regionalized, and this was reflected also in the attitudes and outlook of most of the population. None of this means that the Roman world was poor in resources, however (although some regions were certainly poorer in natural and man-made resources than others). But the expense of transport, especially by land, meant that patterns of settlement and the demographic structure of the empire conformed to the limits of the resources that were locally available. But even here, it was chiefly the major urban centres which were involved.

Livestock – sheep, goats, cattle, horses and pigs – were a feature of most rural communities, but certain areas concentrated in stock-raising more than in other spheres of production. The raising of mules and horses was an essential for the state, both for the public postal and transport system as well as for the army. Substantial stud farms were maintained in parts of Asia Minor (Phrygia, Lydia and Cappadocia), but are also known from North Africa, Italy and Syria. The Anatolian plateau was dominated by stock-

Eastern Asia Minor pastureland.

farming, often on large ranch-like estates, and while agriculture played an essential role in the maintenance of the population, the richest landlords of the region seem generally to have based their wealth on this type of production. But stock-farming played an important role throughout the East Roman world, and sheep and goats, along with pigs, formed an important element in the productive capacity of many rural communities, sharing with cereal production the attentions of the peasant farmer. Livestock were the source of many essential items, not just meat, skins or milk, but also felt, glues and horn, for example, as well as bone and gut for both decorative and practical purposes.

Raw materials other than these products – wood, stone and ores in particular – were usually derived from more restricted contexts. The woodlands of the Mediterranean and Black Sea coasts produced timber for shipbuilding, and there is evidence that the government developed an organized policy for the exploitation of woodlands. Stone for building could be quarried throughout the empire, where the materials were available and appropriate, but certain types of stone, marble in particular, was quarried by specialists from particular sites. The much-sought-after high-quality marble of Prokonnesos, for example, was shipped all over the Mediterranean. Stonemasons similarly were in high demand and itinerant specialist groups are known to have been hired for particular building projects in Syria in the fifth and sixth centuries. Changes in demand and cultural priorities seems to have brought this widespread industry almost to an end during the sixth and seventh centuries, but the wealthy could still afford to import expensive marble throughout the medieval period, and a more localized vestigial trade in stone continued.

Of the metallic ores mined or collected in the Roman world, iron was probably the most important, needed for weapons and tools. Centres of iron mining included north-eastern Anatolia and the central southern Black Sea coastal regions, and central Syria, although ores were also mined in the Taurus mountains and the south Balkans. Tin, generally alloyed with copper to make bronze or with zinc to make brass, was mined in the Taurus, but was also imported to the east Mediterranean from the south-western parts of Britain. Bronze was commonly used – both for low-value coins as well as for a huge range of household utensils and tools, and ornamental objects. The sources of copper remain uncertain, but the Caucasus and southern Pontic regions, north Syria, and the central Balkans and Spain seem to have supplied some of the empire's needs up to the sixth century. Crucial to the empire's economy was gold, of course, obtained from the Caucasus, from Armenia, which had rich deposits, and to a lesser extent from the Balkans, although the location of Roman and Byzantine gold workings remains largely unclear. Silver was extracted in the Taurus, central Pontic Alps and Armenia, as well as in the central Balkans. In the case of both these precious metals the state tried as hard as possible to control both their import and export. The export of both, indeed, was strictly prohibited for much of the empire's history, although the state's success in enforcing such regulations was extremely variable. Control over stocks of precious metals was achieved partly through recycling, of course, although this could not ensure a constant supply. Crude oil was also employed, chiefly in the preparation of the 'liquid fire' projected through tubes at enemy warships, and obtained from a small number of sites in the Caucasus, Georgia and the south Russian steppe to the east of the Crimea. Alum, found chiefly in the eastern Pontic mountains and Bithynia, was also exploited, chiefly for use in fulling and dying, but also in medicinal applications, although the alum industry was a relatively late development.

This, then, is the physical world of later Rome and medieval Byzantium. It was this context which set limits to or facilitated the political programmes of different emperors and which determined the ability of the East Roman state to respond to its enemies, deal with its neighbours, organize its administration and recruit, move and support its armies. It would be wrong to suggest that this physical context was the only factor: of course, cultural constraints, traditional ways of doing things, ideas about what could and could not be done, all contributed to the complex network of causes and effects, the results of which constitute what we call 'history'. But it would be equally misguided to ignore the fundamental role of geographical factors in that history. The nature of roads and communications, the speed with which news, resources and people could travel, the effectiveness of armies, the availability of certain types of resource, and the ways in which these are affected by climate and seasonal variation are all factors of fundamental importance. They directly affected how the government functioned, the amount of agricultural production that it could appropriate for itself, the health and well-being of the peasantry, how much they produced and consumed, the regional availability of livestock, and so on. In short, without a grasp of these issues, making sense of the historical evolution of the Byzantine world becomes impossible.

4 The Byzantine state

Resources and logistics

The power and authority – and therefore the effectiveness – of the government at Constantinople was largely determined by the degree to which it was able to exercise control over the resources necessary to its continued existence and to the maintenance of its army and its administrative machinery. Integral to the ways in which it achieved this were also certain social-economic and ideological interests. It is the relationship between these elements and the extraction and redistribution of resources which determines both the internal limits and the extent of state power. The ways in which states exercise power and authority vary along a scale which alternates between two poles: at one extreme, power is concentrated at and exercised from the centre, through the ruler and an administration which remains under close and effective central supervision even in the provinces; at the other, state power is diffused, through an economically and sometimes politically independent elite (nobility or magnate class), with a consequent parcelling-out of surplus distribution and the attendant danger that the state or rulers lose effective power over the resources necessary to their own continued existence. Such changes and fluctuations are found in the history of the Byzantine state, and provide important insights into why the empire evolved in the ways it did.

The first priority for the government at Constantinople was the maintenance of its territorial integrity – without territory there was no state. To achieve this end it required two things: an army, with which to defend itself against external foes and to maintain order internally, and a fiscal system through which the resources to achieve this – as well as to support the other apparatuses of government – could be extracted from the producing population. Late Roman and Byzantine society was an agrarian society of peasants and rural artisans, and they were the only realistic source of surplus wealth production. It was dominated throughout its history by a system of extracting resources characterized by the appropriation of wealth through a variety of forms of tax and rent. This does not mean that they were the only *existing* forms of surplus appropriation: slavery continued to exist, but (even as early as the fourth century in the East) seems to have played only a very limited role in production and, more importantly, in the production of the wealth of the dominant class, being restricted for the most part to the domestic or industrial sphere. Indeed, during the late Roman period agricultural slaves came to approximate more and more to various degrees of tied but free tenant, and the result was that the economic reality of slavery disappeared. Rent and tax, not the intensive, plantation-based exploitation of chattel-slaves, was the main form of surplus appropriation from the later third century and afterwards.

Surplus appropriation could take many different forms. Private landlords normally collected rent in cash or kind, according to the nature of the contract or lease and according to the economic conditions of the time or area, or both. The existence or not of a market for each locality, and thus of the possibility for producers to exchange their surplus goods for cash, determined the form. The state exacted surplus in both cash and kind from the regular taxes on land, as well as through a variety of labour-services: maintenance of the postal stations and horses, or the production of iron-ore, woven cloths, and so on, which would be calculated according to centrally-determined tables of equivalence. By the same token, local communities were on occasion required to help with the building of roads and bridges or fortifications, and to billet and feed soldiers and their officers, imperial officials and messengers, and so on. By the ninth century, the state demanded the production of weapons and various items of military equipment from provincial craftsmen, imposed as additional corvées. Extraordinary levies in food or grain were common. Military service always brought with it exemption from these extra demands, but did not merit exemption from the chief state taxes on land. All these forms of surplus appropriation were obtained through 'customary' obligations and the force of law, as in most cases, backed up ultimately by imperial military might, or by simple threat and bullying, by state officials, churchmen or private landlords. Only at the very end of the Byzantine period, when the state was reduced to a few districts in the southern Balkans and the Aegean islands, did commerce become a significant element in the state economy. But by then, as we have seen, the Byzantine empire was itself an insignificant political force in the east Mediterranean.

Moving wealth around the empire was easiest in the form of coin, and the state always preferred to use coin where possible. But the existence of isolated regions without market possibilities meant that some resources always had to be raised in kind or services. At the same time, it meant that the state could use the presence of soldiers in particular (who were usually paid in coin) as a sort of mobile market, and it was frequently the case that, by demanding that local populations sold goods to the army at artificially low prices, the state benefited at the cost of the producers where there was no access to a normal market. As we have seen, transport of bulk goods overland was very costly, and was practicable only for the state, which invested in a system of fast and slow transportation to serve its own requirements, in particular supplying the army with equipment and food, and moving news and information.

The role of the state transport system, the Roman *cursus publicus* or, in Greek, *dromos*, remained crucial throughout the empire's history. During the period from the fourth to the middle of the sixth centuries it was organized in two divisions, regular (*cursus clabularis* or *platys dromos*) and fast (*cursus velox* or *oxys dromos*), responsible respectively for the transportation of goods in bulk, whether by ox-cart or by mule and pack-horse, and for the rapid movement of messengers and imperial officials of all kinds around the empire. Some changes to these arrangements were made by reforms carried through by the Praetorian Prefect of the East, John of Cappadocia, in the first years of the reign of Justinian I. Thereafter it seems to have been reduced to a single division for both slow and fast services. But even though it may have been trimmed and reduced from its original extent, a system of post-stations, with small teams of riding- and pack-animals, continued to be maintained. In the later fifth and early sixth century, the post had been maintained by state-funded purchases of provisions (paid for with gold and obtained from landowners and, presumably, other producers); the animals were supplied by the state ranches on which they were bred and raised; and they were staffed by hereditarily inscribed personnel exempted from extraordinary state taxes and corvées. The use of the animals attached to the post-stations was strictly controlled by the issue of state warrants issued either by the praetorian prefects of the appropriate prefecture – who were responsible for the administration of the system – or the office of the *magister officiorum* (the 'master of offices', who was in charge of the state's messengers and couriers). By the 760s, and following upon the changes which occurred in the administration of the state during the later seventh century, it was an independent department under its logothete, a high-ranking officer for whom numerous seals survive.

The operations of the *dromos* were closely associated with those of the *logothetes ton agelon* (logothete of the herds), the officer in charge of the imperial stud ranches, in particular the *metata* (stud ranches) of Asia and Phrygia, and successor of the older *praepositus gregum* ('overseer of the herds'). He supplied a proportion of the horses and pack-animals for the army, and for the imperial household and stable service. By the eleventh century, the system was maintained in the same way as military units on active service, by the attribution to them of a portion of the land-tax assessment in kind from the locality they served. Those producers who thus contributed were in turn inscribed as a special category in the fiscal registers, freed from other state burdens, just as were soldiers' properties.

Government and administration

To a large extent civil government was effectively the same as fiscal administration. The main function of the administration was the assessment, collection and redistribution of fiscal resources, in whatever form, towards the maintenance of the state. Justice was associated with the different levels of the administration, so that justice was effected at the same levels as fiscal administration. The amount of tax required by the government varied year by year according to the international political situation and according to internal requirements. By the time of Constantine I state finances had come to be controlled and administered through three departments: the praetorian prefectures, the 'sacred largesses' (*sacrae largitiones*) and the 'private fisc' (*res privata*). The most important was the praetorian prefecture, through which the land-tax assessment was calculated, collected and redistributed. Each prefecture comprised a specific territory, although they were reorganized and redistributed on several occasions. At the beginning of Constantine's reign there were three major prefectures: Oriens (stretching from Moesia and Thrace in the Balkans around to Upper Libya in Africa); Illyricum, Italy and Africa; and the Gauls, including Britain and Tingitana in North Africa. By the 440s these had been rearranged into four prefectures: the Gauls, Italy, with North Africa and parts of Illyricum, and the East (Oriens). The Gallic, Italian and much of the North African prefectures were lost during the middle and later fifth century, leaving Illyricum and Oriens only; but with Justinian's reconquests, new prefectures for Italy and for Africa were established. Each prefecture was subdivided into dioceses (the Roman form of the term was *dioecesae*, 'directorates'), under a deputy (*vicarius*) of the praetorian prefect; and each diocese was divided into provinces under provincial governors. The lowest unit of administration was then the city (*civitas* or *polis*) each with its district (*territorium*) upon which the assessment and collection of taxes ultimately devolved. Taxes were raised in a variety of forms, but the most important regular tax was the land-tax. This could be raised in money, and traditionally had been so; but during the financial crisis which the state suffered in the later third century, and as a result of the restructuring of finances and military arrangements under Diocletian and Constantine, much of it was actually raised in kind – grains, other foodstuffs and so forth – and deposited in a vast network of state warehouses, where it could be drawn on by both soldiers and civil administrators; who received a large portion of their salaries in the form of rations (*annonae*). As the financial situation of the government improved during the fourth and into the fifth century, so these rations could be commuted once again for cash – assuming the producers were able to obtain it – but the government always kept available the option of raising revenues in kind, especially when military requirements demanded it. The prefectures, through their diocesan and more particularly their provincial levels of administration, were also responsible for the maintenance of the public post, the state weapons and arms factories, and provincial public works. The latter – maintenance of roads, bridges, granaries, the provision of crafts and skills for particular tasks – were provided through special levies or impositions upon the population, or specific groups within the population, depending on the task in hand.

The other finance departments, the sacred largesses and the private fisc, had evolved out of earlier Roman palatine departments, and had more limited functions. The sacred largesses were responsible for bullion from mines, minting coin, state-run clothing workshops, and the issue of military donatives – regular and irregular gifts of coin to the troops for particular occasions such as an imperial birthday, accession celebration and so forth. It had local branches in each diocese, and representatives in the cities and provinces to administer the revenues drawn from civic lands (which it administered after the middle of the fifth century) and from other income, such as the cash for the commutation of military service or the provision of horses for the army. The *res privata*, under its *comes*, was essentially responsible for the income derived as rents from imperial lands, whatever their origin (from confiscation, for example, or by bequest or escheat). It was as complex as that of the *comes sacrarum largitionum*, with different sections responsible for its various tasks. During the sixth century its responsibilities were divided between income destined for state purposes and that employed to maintain the imperial household, and a new department – the *patrimonium* – was established.

During the course of the sixth century both the sacred largesses and the private fisc were further altered: the various estates administered by the latter were organized into five sections, each independent (including the original *res privata*) responsible for different types of estate and expenditure; while the diocesan level of the activities of the sacred largesses was gradually subsumed by the provincial level of the praetorian prefectures. The situation of the seventh century speeded up this process. Under Heraclius, a major centralization of minting took place, involving the retention of mints at Ravenna, Carthage and Alexandria, apart from Constantinople, and the closure of the remaining six provincial mints. During his reign, and over the following twenty years or so, the *sacrae largitiones* disappears as a separate department. Over the same period, the praetorian prefecture of the East (that of Illyricum effectively disappears with the loss of imperial control over most of the Balkans) is broken up, so that each of its sub-sections becomes an independent bureau, mostly under its own *logothetes*, or accountant. But these are now quite senior officials subordinated in the first instance to the supervision of the *sakellarios*, and then the emperor himself.

The role of the *sakellarios*, as superintendant of the imperial household finances, is illustrative of the sorts of changes which occurred. His close association with the emperor and the imperial household shows that a process of centralization was taking place in which the emperors played a much more active managerial role; a reflection of the crisis in the empire's financial and political situation in the years from 640 on. By the middle of the eighth century, the new structures are more apparent in the sources. A logothete for the general finance office (*genikon logothesion*) was responsible for the land-tax and associated revenues; similarly a department for military finance (*stratiotikon logothesion*) dealt with recruitment, muster-rolls and military pay; while another department, the *idikon*, or special *logothesion*, dealt with armaments, imperial workshops and a host of related miscellaneous requirements. The various departments which were once part of the *res privata* became similarly entirely independent and placed under their own officials. The public post, previously under the *magister officiorum* (the master of offices) became independent under its own logothete. Other departments which had originally been part of the imperial household, such as the sacred bedchamber, evolved into special treasuries and storehouses for special state requirements, while the bedchamber itself, known as the *koitôn*, evolved its own personal imperial treasury for household expenditures.

The difficulties with which the government had to contend during the second half of the seventh century are exemplified by the temporary transformation in the role of the officials called *kommerkiarioi*, the earlier *comites commerciorum*. Originally subordinates of the *sacrae largitiones*, by the middle of the sixth century they were under the praetorian prefecture, and until the early years of the seventh century their chief role lay in supervising the production and sale of silk, which was a state monopoly. But they seem later to have been made responsible for supplying troops with equipment and provisions, and the levying and storing of fiscal income in kind. The *kommerkiarioi* and the warehouses which are associated with them in the evidence thus represented a pre-existing institution (dealing with state-run luxury production and commerce) to which – as a result of the fiscal and administrative crisis in the middle years of the seventh century – fell the essential task of supplying the army; thus presumably filling a gap created by the new situation with which the administration of the prefecture could not cope. This arrangement operated until certain reforms and changes were introduced around 730 by Leo III (717-741).

From about 730/731 there seems to have taken place a gradual reduction in the importance of individual *kommerkiarioi*: instead of high-ranking general *kommerkiarioi* associated with warehouses (*apothêkai*) there appear instead *kommerkiarioi* associated with no specific region and with no warehouse. In their stead we now find institutions called imperial *kommerkia* which appear to have fulfilled a related but more limited function, at least until the 830s; while the *kommerkiarioi* themselves now occur in association with

Tenth-century Byzantine sculpture.

specific military provinces (*themata*) or, more usually, specific ports or entrepôts, underlining their reversion to the role of customs officials controlling trade and exchange activities with regions outside the empire. From the later eighth century, there is sound evidence for the levying of a duty on trade, referred to as the *kommerkion*, and there is no doubt that *kommerkiarioi* were associated with its collection. As these developments occurred, a transformed fiscal organization evolved, evidenced by the appearance of provincial or thematic (military provincial) fiscal officials – *dioiketai* – responsible for collecting the taxes, which were assessed and verified by *epoptai* and *exisotai*, all under the general authority of the *genikon* logothesion. Thematic fiscal affairs and the co-ordination of military and fiscal arrangements was the sphere of the *protonotarios* – an official who appears during the 820s – who was responsible to the central financial department of the *sakellion*.

These structures remained in force until the later eleventh century, with minor modifications. From this time on, the tax collection and assessment came increasingly to be in the hands of a single official for each province – the *praktor* – originally a low-ranking fiscal agent; but by the twelfth century, a tax-farmer, who worked in conjunction with another assessment official – the *apographeus* – responsible for drawing up detailed accounts of the taxable lands in a *praktikon* (a statement of taxes owing on each fiscal unit or group of units and of tenants' obligations to their landlord).

Tenth-century sarcophagus.

Alexios I was responsible for a series of major reforms in the central and provincial fiscal administration of the empire. New supervisors of the central bureaux were created: the *logothetes* of the *sekreta* (departments) who acted as a general overseer; the grand *logariastês*, to supervise the administration of taxation; and the grand *logariastes* of the imperial domains and related institutions (including charitable houses). At the same time, he ordered a fundamental reassessment of all basic taxes, and began to issue a reformed coinage, with a greater number of fractional denominations to meet the increased demand for precious-metal coin in commercial and day-to-day transactions.

A major change in the ways in which resources were administered occurred during the twelfth century with the expansion of the institution known as *pronoia*, literally 'care' or 'forethought'. The term referred to the concession by the state of the right to receive the revenues from certain public (i.e. fiscal or taxed) districts; or of certain imperial estates, and their tenants, along with part or all of the rents and taxes raised from them. Such grants were made to individuals by the emperors for a variety of reasons. They took the form of personal grants from the ruler, who represented the state in the institutional sense; and while there was also a more general meaning of the term *pronoia*, the most important involves *pronoia* grants in return for military service. This was a new departure, and – involving as it did, for the first time, the temporary alienation of state revenues to private individuals – marks a further move along the line from absolute to devolved state power referred to in the opening sections of this chapter. It is important to emphasize that *pronoia* grants were at first limited to members of the extended family of the imperial clan, the Komnenoi; and that although the emperor Manuel I appears to have employed them a little more liberally, they first appear on a wider scale after the events of 1204 and the introduction into many areas of the Byzantine world of western, feudal arrangements. These no doubt had an influence on the Byzantine way of doing things, and may have speeded up the development of *pronoia* on a more generalized basis. But such grants were given not only on a large scale to individuals, but also to groups, and sometimes on a very small scale; while the government, at least in theory, always retained the right to revoke such a grant. They rarely became hereditary in the proper sense.

The structure of fiscal administration remained largely the same from this time until the end of the empire's history, although a number of minor modifications were effected, some at the central level, some of provincial importance. But increasingly, as the power of the magnate elite increased at the expense of the central government, especially during the Palaeologan period from 1261 until 1453, the state's share of the resources of the empire declined, while the burden on the depressed tax-paying peasant producers grew. The bureaucracy of the empire also became increasingly corrupt, and the vested interests of those who could afford to buy fiscal officials or otherwise influence fiscal policy ensured that the situation was not rectified. Already during the later eleventh and twelfth centuries, the number of complaints about the vast number of different officials who visited the provinces and exploited and bullied the peasantry as well as many landlords is considerable, and the situation appears to have worsened as time progressed. Under particularly able financial administrators, such as Andronikos II, the government was able to re-establish its authority and rebuild its resources; but such gains were eroded by bureaucratic incompetence and oppression, magnate vested interests, and civil war. The ultimate result was the complete inability of the government to support an effective army and to defend itself against its enemies.

Taxation: demand, assessment and collection

A fundamental principle of late Roman and Byzantine taxation was to ensure the maximization of exploitation and hence of revenues. In the later Roman period this had been achieved by a system whereby land registered for taxation but not cultivated was attributed for assessment to neighbouring landlords, a process known as *adiectio sterilium*. Tax was assessed according to a formula tying land – determined by area, quality and type of crop – to labour power, a formula referred to as the *capitatio-iugatio* system. Land that was not exploited, either by agriculture or for pasturage, was not taxed directly. The tax burden was reassessed at intervals, originally in cycles of five, then of fifteen years, although in practice it took place far more irregularly. From the seventh or eighth centuries a number of changes were introduced. Each tax unit was expected to produce a fixed revenue, distributed across the tax-payers, who were as a body responsible for deficits, which they shared. The tax-unit – the community, in effect – was jointly responsible for the payments due from lands that belonged to their tax unit but were not farmed, for whatever reason. Remissions of tax could be requested or bestowed to compensate for such burdens, but if the community took over and farmed the land for which they had been responsible, they had also to pay the deficits incurred by the remission. During the same period, the cities lost their role as crucial intermediaries in the levying of taxation, which was now devolved for the most part upon imperial officials of the provinces and upon the village community.

The most important change which took place after the seventh century seems to have been the introduction of a distributive tax assessment, whereby the annual assessment was based on the capacity of the producers to pay, rather than on a flat rate determined by the demands of the state budget. This involved, of course, accurate records and statements of property, and one important result was that the Byzantine empire evolved one of the most advanced land-registration and fiscal-assessment systems of the medieval world, as well as one of the most sophisticated bureaucracies for administering it. It also appears to have been associated with the ending of the connection between the land-tax and the poll-tax: instead of a combined *capitatio-iugatio* assessment, the land tax, or *kanon*, was now assessed as a separate item, with the replacement for the poll-tax, known as the *kapnikon*, or 'hearth' tax, raised on each household. These changes may not have happened overnight, and there is no imperial legislation to give us a clue as to when and how they occurred; but they had been completed by the middle of the ninth century, and probably long before.

The regular taxation of land was supplemented by a wide range of extraordinary taxes and corvées, noted already, including obligations to provide hospitality for soldiers and officials, to maintain roads, bridges, fortifications, and to deliver and/or produce a wide range of requirements such as charcoal or wood. These continued unbroken into the middle and later Byzantine periods, although their Latin names were mostly replaced with Greek or Hellenized equivalents. But certain types of landed property were always exempt from many of these extra taxes, in particular the land owned or held by soldiers and those registered in the service of the public post; in both cases because of traditional favoured conditions of service, and because they depended to a degree on their property for the carrying out of their duties (see below on soldiers).

Although the basic land tax and the accompanying hearth-tax now became the fundamental elements of the tax system, it was complicated by the addition of a vast range of extra and incidental impositions. Quite apart from the extraordinary taxes in kind or services mentioned already, government tax officials began to add more and more extras to their demands, in the form of fees for their services and demands for hospitality (which could then be commuted for money), so that the system became immensely ramified. During the second half of the eleventh century, depreciation of the precious-metal coinage, combined with bureaucratic corruption, led to the near-collapse of the system.

Fundamental changes were not made until the early twelfth century when the emperor Alexios I was forced by inflationary pressures and the complexity and *ad hoc* nature of the old system to introduce important changes. The older charges were rationalized, standard rates were established, and the bureaucracy was trimmed. But increasingly, as the wealthy and powerful managed to extract exemptions for themselves and their lands from many fiscal burdens, so the weight of the state's demands fell upon an increasingly hard-pressed peasantry, so that the social divisions within the empire – which had grown with the evolution of the new, middle Byzantine elite as it gradually turned itself into an aristocracy of office and birth – became more and more apparent. During the later ninth century the system of communal responsibility for untilled lands was transformed into a system whereby land could be temporarily exempted from taxation, removed from the fiscal district to which it originally belonged and administered separately, or granted special reductions in taxation. Such interventionist measures seem to have been intended to maintain as close a degree of control as possible over fiscal resources in land. Yet over the same period, and in order to retain control over its fiscal base and to compete with the elite and the powerful, the government itself began to transform fiscal land into state lands, so that rents to the government in its capacity as a landlord now became indistinguishable in many respects from taxation. The evolution of *pronoia* represented an alternative means of redistributing resources by the government, but also encouraged this overlap.

Until the end of the twelfth century the government was able to retain a fairly effective control over fiscal resources. But the growth of the aristocracy, which had first challenged the state in the tenth century, had continued. It was from members of that elite that the emperors from the later eleventh century were drawn, and whose hold on power was determined largely by their ability to maintain a series of family alliances – through marriage, governorships and so on – with their peers. After 1204 in particular, the devolution of imperial authority became the chief means by which emperors governed and administered, and through which imperial resources were mobilized. Central taxation – the land tax and its associated impositions – remained the basis of government finance; but as the empire shrank territorially, so commerce came to play a more important role, yet one which was already limited by the strength and dominant position in the carrying trade of Italian merchants and maritime power. The fact that the *kommerkion* on trade was, by the end of the empire, more important a source of income than the land-tax, illustrates the insoluble problem faced by the emperors of the last century of Byzantium.

By the later thirteenth century the land tax was raised on the basis of a flat rate, assessed at regular intervals, but modified in accordance with local conditions and other factors, while the tax on labour power had reappeared as an imposition on individual peasant tenants and their households. Supplementary taxes and impositions continued to be raised, some of them devolved onto landlords, for example, and many of them designated for specific types of government expenditure or to cover the expenses of particular state requirements, such as the hiring of mercenary forces or the paying of tribute top foreign powers. In one case, in the Peloponnese during the first half of the fifteenth century, taxes introduced by the Ottomans – who had controlled the region for some 16 years after 1404 – were retained by the Byzantine administration which took over, so that Islamic taxation terms appear in a Byzantine context: *ushr* (tithe) and *haradj* (land-tax), for example.

Armies and fleets: structure and resources

The late Roman armies in the sixth century can be divided into two branches: stationary frontier units known as *limitanei*, consisting largely of the older legions and auxiliary units; and the mobile field forces, called *comitatenses*, composed chiefly of units established during the later third and fourth centuries. There were also units based near the imperial capital or in the imperial palace referred to as *palatini*. There was a great deal of cross-posting, while many field units were established in their garrison towns more-or-less permanently, so that such formal divisions were in fact somewhat artificial. The mobile

Above and below: Monemvasia, eastern Peloponnese, a Byzantine fortress from the seventh century.

forces were grouped into divisions under regional commanders or *magistri militum* ('masters of the soldiers'), each covering a major defensive hinterland with the stationary units based under their overall authority. In *c*.AD 600 there were nine such major divisions, including two based around Constantinople. Naval units for maritime and riverine operations were stationed at key Balkan and Syrian ports, the former part of a special arrangement established by Justinian known as the *quaestura exercitus*, whereby naval and land forces along the Danube were supplied and provisioned from the Aegean region by sea.

Soldiers were recruited partly from volunteers, partly from conscripts drafted on the basis of the *capitatio-iugatio* tax-assessment, although voluntary recruitment was the norm for the field armies by the sixth century. The mobile field armies were complemented by more localized forces, including the *limitanei*, along and behind the frontiers, commands which also included provinces in which local trouble – brigandage, for example – might be expected, also subject to the regional field-army commander. In the 560s there were some 25 such commands covering the frontiers and their hinterlands.

This dual-level arrangement evolved out of changes which took place in the third century, and coped with the defensive needs of the empire – with some problems at times – until the great war with the Sassanid Persian kingdom from 602-626, but failed to resist the pressures which resulted from the early Islamic conquests and the disastrous loss of tax revenue and resources from the eastern provinces between 634 and 642. The government responded by withdrawing the various field armies back into the core territories between 637 and 640, mostly in central and western Asia Minor. There, they were billeted across Asia Minor, and a process was begun by which the groups of provinces occupied by each field army came collectively to be known by the name of that army. The field forces themselves were gradually transformed into provincialized militia-like forces, each with a central core of professional soldiers supported by both central and provincial revenues. The groups of provinces evolved into military regions or *themata*, each commanded by a general, or *strategos*, who had eventually – by the later ninth century – also a supervisory authority over the civil and fiscal officials in his district. Later *themata* received purely geographical names. The civil administration subsisted in an increasingly altered form until a series of measures to recognize the sort of changes which had occurred was undertaken, and the military and civil/fiscal arrangements were harmonized. The difference between mobile field units and stationary frontier forces vanished.

The state faced serious problems in maintaining its armies after the 640s. Already short of cash before the Arab-Islamic conquests, the way in which the troops were garrisoned across the provinces of Anatolia shows that taxes were raised chiefly in kind in order to maintain the troops, rather than paying them in cash (as had usually been the case in peacetime). It was this process of localization that reduced much of the field army in each region to little more than a militia, with localized loyalties competing with the armies of other *themata* for imperial favour. Another result of the crisis was the reintroduction, probably in the later seventh century, of hereditary conscription for certain categories of recruit. While these processes were developing, soldiers with landed property were encouraged to provide some of their weapons and equipment from their own resources, and some of the traditional protection from fiscal charges applied to such property also. The result was the evolution by the tenth century of a distinct category of 'military lands', which had a specially-protected status and were regarded by the government as the basis for the recruitment of the provincial armies. Thus the armies of the later eighth century and after consisted of several different types of recruit: regular professionals making up the core of the thematic forces, the militia-like majority of the *themata*, full-time 'professional' regiments – the imperial guards units or *tagmata* – at Constantinople, and foreign mercenaries (Chazars, Kurds, Turks and others). The imperial naval forces were likewise completely restructured over the same period, with the establishment of several provincial fleets for coastal defence, since Arab warships had begun to pose a serious naval challenge to the empire from the 650s.

The armies were supported by various means. From the fourth until the seventh centuries all units were issued with rations, although from the later fifth century in the

East these could be commuted into cash, so that regimental commissaries bought provisions and other needs at local markets or direct from the producers, before issuing them to the soldiers. Mobile units drew supplies from the revenues of the provinces affected by their presence, in return for issuing receipts against the following year's tax demands. These arrangements were made by the administration of the praetorian prefecture, in order that military supplies could be taken into account when making the regular tax assessment. For forces passing through a region, the administration was informed in advance, so that supplies could be provided along the route of march.

Equipment, including clothing, mounts and weapons, was provided by levies in kind and from state workshops. There were several arms factories in towns throughout the empire. At the end of the sixth century weapons and clothing could be purchased by the troops with a special cash allowance. Military horses were provided by levy and purchased at fixed prices, some from imperial stud-farms. Supplies such as iron-ore, wood and charcoal were similarly provided by levy.

The crisis of the second half of the seventh century meant changes to these arrangements. Much of the burden of supporting the armies was transferred directly onto local populations. Cash payments were reduced to a minimum, and a system of supporting troops in kind – by levying supplies directly from the population in the areas where troops were based – had to be established. The troops were distributed over wide areas to facilitate this, resulting in an increasing dependency on soldiers' households for provisions and even weapons. By the later eighth century, many provincial soldiers were called up for only part of the year. Weapons, military clothing and mounts and pack-animals continued to be raised by levies. Yet in spite of these shifts, the provisioning and supplying of the armies – particularly those on campaign – remained very similar to that operated before the 650s; and by the ninth century it was a shrunken and transformed but still essentially late Roman structure which operated.

The structures which evolved during the seventh and eighth centuries are collectively referred to as the 'theme system'. The re-establishment of internal economic and political stability and dissension among its enemies enabled the empire to re-establish a certain equilibrium by the year 800. In spite of some significant defeats, a more offensive policy in both east and north, combining diplomacy and missionary activity with military threats, against the Bulgars, for example, eventually helped to confer an advantage; so that, despite the fierce opposition of local Muslim emirs during the first half of the tenth century, the empire was able to attain a series of brilliant reconquests of large tracts of territory in north Syria and Iraq, the destruction of the second Bulgarian empire, and the beginnings of the reconquest of Sicily and southern Italy. By the time the soldier-emperor Basil II died in 1025, the empire was once more a major political and military power in the eastern Mediterranean basin, with only the Fatimid Caliphate in Egypt and Syria to challenge its power. The offensive warfare of the period from the mid-ninth century, however, had important effects upon imperial military organization. As the thematic militias became less able to meet the needs of aggressive warfare, regular field armies – with a more complex tactical structure, specialized fighting skills and weapons, and more offensive spirit – began to evolve, partly under the direction of the developing elite of provincial landed military officers. Full-time professional units played a growing role as the state began to

St Theodore 'the recruit', a popular soldier-saint.
Eleventh-century mosaic, monastery of Hosios Loukas,
Greece.

commute thematic military service for cash payments, which were then used to hire mercenaries. The result was a colourful and international army – remarked on by outside observers – consisting of both indigenous mercenary units as well as Russians, Normans, Turks and Franks, both infantry and cavalry. Perhaps best-known among these are the famous Varangian guard, first recruited during the reign of Basil II, consisting of Russian and Scandinavian adventurers and mercenaries. Among their most notable leaders was Harald Hardrada, later king of Norway (1046-1066), until he met his death at the hands of the English king Harold Godwinsson at the battle of Stamford Bridge in 1066. Harald fought with the Varangians from 1034 until about 1041.

By the same token, the declining relevance of the thematic armies under their *strategoi* meant that new tactical and strategic command structures evolved. New military districts under independent commanders evolved, beginning with the conversion of former *kleisourai* – small frontier commands – to *themata* along with the incorporation of conquered regions as *themata*. But these were usually quite small, based around a key strongpoint. This system then evolved further as ever larger and militarily more effective detachments of the imperial *tagmata* and similarly-recruited professional units were established along the frontiers. From the 970s, these divisions were grouped into larger commands, each under a *doux* or *katepano*, independent of the local thematic administration. They formed a screen of buffer provinces protecting the old *themata*, tactically independent of one another in terms of their available manpower. Similar arrangements were established in the Balkan and western provinces. These field armies, whether on the frontiers or within the provinces, consisted increasingly of mercenary, professional troops or of forces sent by the dependent rulers of the various smaller states bordering the empire.

But the offensive and successful warfare of this period had some negative results. Greater state demands for resources to pay for the warfare met greater aristocratic resistance to tax-paying; during the first half of the eleventh century the development of new social tensions within society as a whole were reflected in political factionalism at court. The over-estimation of the empire's military strength and the neglect of defensive arrangements by the central government, as it attempted to neutralize the power of the provincial (military) elite, weakened its capacity to respond flexibly to external threat or attack. The thematic forces faded into insignificance; the mercenary armies began themselves to exploit the political divisions within society and take sides, leading to civil war and the collapse of the defensive structure of the empire. The result was, in effect, the loss of central Anatolia to Turkic pastoral nomads and their herds.

Major military and fiscal reforms under the emperors of the Komnenos dynasty after 1081 re-established stability and, to a degree, the international position of the empire. While foreign mercenary units continued to play a prominent role, the recruitment of indigenous Byzantine units specializing in a variety of arms restored the ability of the imperial armies to fight external enemies on their own terms. This was partly based on a reformed fiscal administration, on the one hand, and the raising and maintenance of troops on the basis of grants of revenue to certain individuals in return for the provision of trained soldiers, both infantry and cavalry. Increasing western influence, in the form of the introduction of weapons such as the crossbow and the adoption of western heavy cavalry tactics, differentiate this period from the preceding century. In respect of strategic management, while the term *thema* was still used, it meant merely 'province', and the system of ducates inherited from the later tenth and eleventh centuries constituted the basic pattern of military commands. By the end of the reign of Manuel I (1143-1180), the restored *themata* of Asia Minor stretched from Trebizond on the south-eastern stretch of the Black Sea coast westwards through Paphlagonia and around the western edges of the central plateau down to Cilicia. The commanders of the forces based in each of these regions were *doukes*, and they usually also combined military with civil authority, their commands being usually more-or-less coterminous with the province in which they were based; while the fortresses and towns were administered by imperial officers called *prokathemenoi* aided or supported by a *kastrophylax* (fortress warden) responsible for the defences.

The construction and garrisoning of fortresses and the maintenance of a costly standing army was an expensive strategy, however, and proved ultimately too much for the imperial exchequer and for the resources at the emperor's disposal. As the structural weaknesses within the Komnene system of administration and rule were revealed following Manuel I's

Nicaea (modern-day Iznik), western Asia Minor.

death in 1180, the intervention of the Normans of Sicily in the Balkans, and the Fourth Crusade, finally put an end to any hope of a Byzantine recovery in Asia Minor. Yet Komnene defensive structures survived to form the basis upon which the rulers of the empire of Nicaea – established in western Asia Minor after the seizure and sack of Constantinople by the Crusaders in 1204 – owed much of their success, at least temporarily, in throwing back and holding the Turkish advance in the region. The system of *themata* with military units based in them under *doukes* required continuous expenditure, and it was this that the Palaeologan emperors were able to afford for only a short while. The degree of reliance upon foreign mercenary units depended at first upon the situation, since the emperors of the Paleologus dynasty did not abandon attempts to raise and maintain indigenous forces. The Nicaean emperors had employed considerable numbers of Latin mercenaries – chiefly cavalry – and this practice certainly continued, although a difference soon appeared between the salaried Latin mercenary troops on the one hand, and the individual Latin knights granted *pronoia* revenues, on the other. Locally-recruited units, both mounted and foot, garrisoned the frontier and other fortresses, paid a small salary and supported by a variety of fiscal privileges. In the later thirteenth century, the main distinction between the field armies and the provincial garrison troops was that the former were recruited on a mercenary basis or supported by *pronoiai*, whereas the latter were supported primarily through fiscal exemptions. But at the same time there is increasing evidence for the decline of the Latin mercenary element in the imperial armies, and its replacement by Turks, who played a more prominent role thereafter, many of them referred to as *Tourkopouloi* (a term used to refer to the offspring of christianized Turks).

As resources became straitened, so more and more soldiers of the field armies were supported through *pronoiai*, thus slowly eliminating the distinction between field troops and garrison units. From the later thirteenth century the sources mention various special categories of soldier, employed as soldiers for the revived fleet established under Michael VIII, and distinguished by their conditions of recruitment and service: the *Gasmouloi*, originally persons of mixed Greek and Latin race, were paid as mercenaries; the *Tzakones* or *Lakones* – drawn from the southern Peloponnese – served as light-armed troops on a similar basis. Another group, referred to as *Thelematarioi*, or 'volunteers', served on the basis of grants of land given by the emperors, in the region of Constantinople; while the *Prosalentai* appear similarly to have been given lands in certain coastal regions and islands to support their service as oarsmen in the imperial ships. The status of both the *Thelematarioi* and the *Prosalentai* seems to have been hereditary. The reduction of the fleet after 1285 (following peace with Venice) seems to have led to the merging of the first two groups and their becoming more like the latter in the ways they were supported. As the Anatolian lands were progressively lost during the fourteenth century, the local garrisons of the European provinces appear still to have depended upon land allocations and fiscal privileges; while the imperial field armies soon came to be made up from similar sources, complemented by mercenary units hired for specific campaigns from various foreign sources as well as among the indigenous Byzantine population. Taxes were raised also from *pronoia* holders to support mercenary units.

By the early fourteenth century, the commanders of provincial armies and administration were entitled *kephale* (head), and the regions they controlled were referred to as *katepanikia*; usually comprising a fortress and its hinterland. The older *doukes* and *prokathemenoi* with their *themata* disappeared as the empire shrank and its territorial structure adjusted and evolved accordingly. As already noted, the fiscal administration remained independent and under direct central control.

The armies of the fourteenth and fifteenth centuries were a motley body: allied soldiers from neighbouring territories, such as Serbs, Bulgars, Alans (the latter from the northern Caucasus) and Cumans (Turks); peasant militias in the provinces serving on the basis of tax exemptions; foreigners who were given land in return for military service (the arrangement by which the Cumans were recruited in the early fourteenth century, for example); foreign mercenary companies, such as the Catalans; and holders of *pronoia* grants of varying size. From the 1320s and especially the 1330s Turkish soldiers from the various allied emirs of Asia Minor were employed in Byzantine campaigns in Europe. By the 1330s, most of Asia Minor (except for a few coastal cities) had been lost anyway, so that the only practicable strategy for the region was henceforth one of containment and diplomacy. Such troops normally served for a single campaign before returning to their homes. By the late fourteenth century Turkish 'allies' dominated, while the erstwhile Serb and Bulgar allied forces had virtually ceased to operate on the Byzantine side, a change emphasized by the beginnings of the Turkish (Ottoman) occupation of the Balkans, beginning with Gallipoli in the 1350s.

The frequent civil wars in the last century of the empire's history served only to drain its resources and make it almost entirely dependent upon foreign armies for its survival and for the authority of the emperors at Constantinople. By the 1360s the empire was

Fifth-century mosaic, Great Palace, Constantinople.

reduced to the districts around Constantinople and Thessaloniki, the southern Peloponnese, some Aegean islands and coastal towns. Soldiers of the empire were counted in hundreds rather than thousands, although the names of some of the older formations still appear in the narrative sources, and it has been assumed that they survived – in a reduced state – until the fall of the capital in 1453. But most Byzantine 'armies' were dominated by Italian or Turkish forces, serving either as 'allies' or mercenaries. The army which fought to defend the capital against the forces of Mehmet II in 1453 was probably typical: some native soldiers, Italians from several cities (Genoa, Venice and others), Cretans, islanders from Chios. There were perhaps some 7,000-8,000 altogether, of whom possibly as many as 5,000 were Byzantines. All such estimates are based on the often contradictory information given in the sources, many of them eye-witness accounts; but this reasonable estimate gives some idea of the situation of the empire in its last days, bearing in mind the fact that many of the foreigners as well as the Byzantines were effectively serving as volunteers (the Venetians, for example, were present to defend their own quarter and interests).

The empire's naval forces were relatively limited in the later Roman period. Small flotillas were based along the Danube, there was a fleet based at Ravenna, and a flotilla at Constantinople. Transport ships were generally requisitioned from private sources, perhaps also from the grain fleets which normally supplied Constantinople. With the establishment of the *quaestura* a further fleet of transports was also established. But the districts which comprised this administrative entity did not survive the Slav and Avar invasions of the Balkan provinces, although the Aegean regions continued to be the source of men, ships and resources. In the later seventh century the maritime corps known as the 'ship troops' (*Karabisianoi*) appears, probably the surviving element of the *quaestura*. It was based at first on Rhodes, even though it drew its soldiers from the mainland as well. In view of the enormous threat posed by Arab seapower from the 660s to the coastal regions of the empire – especially the Aegean basin – this unit evolved into the central element in the provincial naval power of the middle Byzantine state. A fleet attached to the region of Hellas also evolved, certainly by the 690s. At the same time, the imperial fleet based at Constantinople was probably expanded, and was involved in many actions with Muslim war-fleets from the 650s on, being instrumental in the defeat of the sieges of the period 674-678 and 717-718.

As the empire recognized the need for effective fleets, it expanded its naval resources. By about 830, there were three main naval *themata* – of the Aegean, of Samos and the Kibyrrhaiotai – in addition to the imperial fleet, and the small fleets of Hellas and the Peloponnese. These developments served to check and occasionally throw back hostile ship-borne attacks; but the situation in the West was rather different. The loss of Carthage in the 690s and of the North African coast deprived the empire of its naval bases there. Sicily may have continued to support imperial naval activity, and there is a little evidence for imperial naval activity in the Balearic Islands. But from the late 840s, the Balearics also provided shelter for pirates and raiders, and by the early ninth century the empire seems to have lost interest in the western Mediterranean. The failure adequately to support the fleet when Sicily and then Crete were invaded in the 820s proved costly, since the latter in particular rapidly became the source of constant maritime raids on the empire's coastal lands.

As with the land forces, the (compulsory) commutation of naval service for cash in the coastal regions during the later ninth to eleventh centuries necessarily meant a reduction in provincial naval resources. Emperors from the time of Basil II clearly found it cheaper to call upon allies and dependants (such as Venice) to supply warships, than to pay for an expensive standing fleet at Constantinople. The result was that the imperial fleet was considerably reduced in numbers during the eleventh century, while the increasing dependence of the empire on non-Byzantine powers, whose interests were potentially hostile to those of Byzantium, was an important contributory factor in the political-military difficulties the empire experienced throughout the later eleventh and twelfth centuries.

The imperial navy underwent a brief recovery under Alexios I. In his first few years he was entirely dependent upon Venice for maritime aid in his struggle with the Normans, but he reorganized the command structure of the fleet, establishing a new supreme commander – the *megas doux* – and amalgamating the remnants of the provincial fleets and the imperial flotilla at Constantinople. Some effort was spent on re-establishing a respectable imperial naval presence in the Aegean and Adriatic. Special naval impositions on the Aegean islands for the provision of a certain number of warships and sailors, or

Fifteenth-century city walls, Trebizond (modern-day Trabzon), on the Black Sea coast.

provisions and supplies in money or in kind, were made to support the imperial fleet. But the emperor Manuel allowed these obligations to be commuted. Yet he could still raise and support substantial fleets of warships and transports for major operations. Mercenary sailors and ships, as well as allies, continued to play a central role, but Manuel's successors allowed the fleet to decay once more. By the end of the twelfth century the empire was helpless against the overwhelming naval force that could be assembled by Venice or the other major maritime Republics of Italy. Only briefly, with a short-lived reform under Michael VIII, was any attempt made to establish once again an independent imperial naval power, but this foundered in the lack of resources from which the empire suffered, compounded in the first half of the fourteenth century by the disastrous civil wars which took place.

5 Life in town and countryside

The Roman town and its hinterland

The classical city, the *polis* or *civitas*, occupied a central role both in the social and economic structure of Mediterranean society during the Roman period (and to a lesser extent in those Northern European regions to which it was imported), as well as in the administrative machinery of the empire. Cities might be centres of market-exchange, of regional agricultural activity, occasionally of small-scale commodity production or, where ports were concerned, major foci of long-distance commerce. Some fulfilled all these roles; others remained merely administrative centres created by the state for its own fiscal administrative purposes. Crucially, all cities were also originally given the status of self-governing districts with their own lands, and were responsible to the government for the return of taxes. Where such cities did not exist, the Roman state created them, sometimes establishing entirely new foundations, sometimes amalgamating or changing the nature of pre-existing settlements and providing them with a corporate identity, institutional structure and legal personality of a *civitas*. These cities were usually quite dependent on their immediate hinterlands for their (usually highly localized) market and industrial functions, where these existed at all, as well as for the foodstuffs from which the urban populace lived. They acted as local centres, but on the whole were parasitic on their *territoria*. And as the social and economic structure of the empire evolved away from the relationships and conditions which gave rise to and maintained these urban structures, so the cities became the first key institution of the classical world to feel the effects of these changes.

The form which these changes took are complex, but mirror the effects of a growing conflict between state, cities and private landowners to extract surpluses from the producing population, and the failure of the cities to weather the contradictions between their municipal independence on the one hand, and on the other the demands of the state and the vested interests of the wealthier civic landowners. Although, well into the first half of the seventh century, there is evidence in the East that many *curiales* – the city councillors, members of the *curia* or town council – continued to honour their obligations to both state and city, it is clear by the later fourth century that many did or could not. These *curiales* – who were the chief landowners and leading citizens – had been responsible both for the upkeep of their cities by voluntary subscription, and for the local assessment, collection and forwarding of the revenues demanded by the state. But as many were able to obtain senatorial status (in other words, they became members of the *curia* of either Rome or Constantinople), which freed them from such duties, so the burden fell more and more upon the less wealthy and privileged, who were in consequence less able to extract all the revenues demanded, especially as tax evasion among the wealthy, through bribery as well as physical resistance, was endemic. The process was both very complex and regionally nuanced, according to traditional pattern of landholding and urbanism, but these were the most obvious features. As a result, and over the period from the later fourth to the later fifth century, the government intervened more and more directly to ensure the extraction of its revenues. This it did both by appointing supervisors imposed upon the city administrators, as well as through the confiscation of city lands (the rents from which were now the guarantee that the state's fiscal income was at least to some extent assured), and eventually through the appointment of tax-farmers for each municipal district. The *curiales* seem still to have done the actual work of collecting, but the burden of fiscal accountability seems to have been removed during the reign of Anastasius (491-518). While this certainly relieved the pressure, and possibly helped promote the brief renaissance in urban fortunes which appears to have taken place in some eastern cities in the sixth century, it did nothing to re-establish their traditional independence and fiscal responsibilities.

By the early years of the seventh century, all the evidence suggests that cities as corporate bodies were simply less well-off than they had been before about the middle of the sixth century. But this does not mean that urban life declined in any absolute sense, still less that there was less wealth available to the local elite and landowning class; or that cities no longer fulfilled their role as centres of exchange and production. They continued to function as centres of exchange and small-scale industry, as well as for the social activity for the landowners and the wealthy of their districts. It seems, in effect, that there was as much wealth circulating in urban environments as before, but towns as institutional bodies now had only very limited access to it. They had had most of their lands and the income from those lands taken from them. The local wealthy tended also, during the later sixth century in particular, to invest their wealth in religious building or related objects, and it is important to bear in mind an evolving pattern of investment as well as the possibilities of a decline in investment. In addition, the Church was from the fourth century a competitor with the city for the consumption of resources. And however much their citizens might donate, individually or collectively, this can hardly have compensated for this loss. Indeed, such contributions became the main source of independent income for many cities. The archaeological data – especially from surveys of late Roman cities such as Ephesus, Smyrna and Ankara, for example, but also from many other sites in the Levant and Balkans – suggests a shrinkage of occupied areas of many cities, and even an increasing localization of exchange activity; but again, this does not have to mean a change in their role as local centres of such exchange.

The state played an important role in the ways in which towns evolved during this period. During the third, fourth and fifth centuries the government had quite deliberately followed a policy of 'rationalizing' patterns of distribution of cities. Many cities in over-densely occupied regions were deprived of the status and privileges of city; others which were of importance to the state in its fiscal-administrative structure were 'incorporated' and received city status for the first time. This had nothing to do with economic interests, but reflected rather the desire of the emperors to establish a network of centres adequate to the demands of the fiscal system. Considerable numbers of the 'cities' which were suppressed in this process had been little more than villages representing the autonomous or semi-autonomous communities of the pre-Roman states incorporated into the empire. By

1. The emperor Justinian with guards and members of the clergy, sixth-century mosaic, San Vitale, Ravenna.

2. Deatil of Justinian, sixth-century mosaic, Ravenna.

3. Christ pantokrator ('the ruler of all'), church at Cefalu, Sicily, twelfth century.

4. Christ pantokrator, Pammakaristos church (Fethiye Camii), fourteenth century.

5. Adam and Eve, late twelfth-century mosaic, church at Monreale, Sicily.

6. The creation of Man, late twelfth-century mosaic, church at Monreale, Sicily.

7. *Jacob's ladder, fourteenth-century fresco,*
Church of the Chora (Kariye Camii).

8. *The Archangel Michael, eleventh-century*
mosaic, Nea Moni, Chios.

9. St Ignatios, tenth-century mosaic, St Sophia, Constantinople.

10. A depiction of a Byzantine ship and the use of Greek fire, twelfth-century manuscript of the history of John Scylitzes (Biblioteca Nacional, Madrid).

11. A mill, fifth-century mosaic, Imperial Palace, Constantinople.

12. *Gold* nomisma
*of Constantine VI
(780-797).
Obverse: The emperor
and his mother, Irene.
Reverse: Leo III,
Constantine V and
Leo IV.*

13. *Gold* nomisma
*of Theophilos
(829-842).
Obverse: The
emperor.
Reverse: Michael II
and Constantine,
Thophilos's son.*

14. *Gold* nomisma
*of Leo VI (886-912).
Obverse: Christ
enthroned.
Reverse: The emperor
and his son
Constantine VII.*

15. *Silver* milarêsion
*of Leo VI (886-912).
Obverse: Cross.
Reverse: 'Leo and
Constantine, in
Christ pious emperors
of the Romans'.*

16. Gold histamenon nomisma *of Constantine VIII (1025-1028). Obverse: Christ. Reverse: The emperor*

17. Gold histamenon nomisma *of Isaac I Komnenos (1057-1059). Obverse: Enthroned figure of Christ. Reverse: The emperor, standing with a sheathed sword.*

18. Gold hyperpyron *of Isaac II (1185-1195). Obverse: The Virgin Mary enthroned with Jesus. Reverse: The emperor with the Archangel Michael.*

19. Gold hyperpyron *of Michael VIII (1258-1282). Obverse: The Virgin Mary within the walls of Constantinople. Reverse: The emperor kneeling before Christ.*

20. Tenth-century chalice, Constantinople (St Mark's treasury, Venice).

21. Nicaea, modern Iznik, from the air.

22. Monasteries, Meteora, north-central Greece.

23. Eleventh-century church at Famagusta, Cyprus.

24. Church of the Holy Cross, Aghtamar, Armenia, tenth century.

25. Nea Moni, Chios, eleventh century.

26. Church of Hosios Loukas, Greece, eleventh-twelfth century.

27. The Pontic Alps near Trebizond, Turkey, looking south.

28. Monasteries, Meteora, north-central Greece.

29. Mount Ararat, eastern Anatolia.

30. Sardis, western Asia Minor. In the background is the citadel.

31. Medieval walls of Ani, Armenia.

32. Miletos, western Asia Minor.

Mosaic portrait of the donor, Theodore Metochites, Church of the Chora (Kariye Camii).

endowing certain settlements with city status and, more especially, with local fiscal-administrative functions and responsibility, the state assured such cities of their continued existence and at the same time enhanced their local importance, whatever their original economic and social situation may have been. But the result was that, when the elites in such communities were no longer able or willing to fulfil this role, and when the state began to supervise city fiscal affairs directly – employing the *curiales* merely as assessors and collectors of tax rather than guarantors – the continued existence of such cities would become a matter of indifference to the central government. The ideological and symbolic importance of cities and urban culture in the Roman world, expressed through imperial involvement in urban building and renewal in several cases, meant that they continued to play an important role culturally. In addition, cities particularly associated with a local saint's cult or fulfilling some other cult function within the Christian world view enhanced their chances of flourishing where they did not already possess a primary economic character.

Transformation: from polis *to* kastron

The effects of the warfare of the seventh century – first the Persian invasions, then the devastation of the Arab invasions and raids – proved too much for many of these fragile provincial cities and their localized economies. The great majority of cities shrank to a

Pammakaristos church (Fethiye Camii), Constantinople.

fortified and defensible core which could support only a very small population, housing the local rural populace and, where present, a military garrison and an ecclesiastical administration. Unlike late Roman cities, Byzantine towns were merely walled settlements. Civic buildings were for the most part non-existent; the state and the Church built, for their own use (churches, granaries, walls, arms-depots), but the cities had no resources of their own, no lands, no revenue, no corporate civic juridical personality. Wealthy local landowners could and probably did invest in building, although there is virtually no evidence until the eleventh century. But the majority of these invested whatever social and cultural capital they had in Constantinople and in the imperial system which, after the loss of the eastern provinces, became focused almost exclusively on the capital. This 'Constantinople factor' was important for the contours of middle Byzantine society. The establishment in the fourth century of a new imperial capital on the site of the ancient city of Byzantion had far-reaching consequences for the pattern of exchange and redistribution of goods in the Aegean and east Mediterranean basin; at the same time, the development of an imperial court and a senate, with all its social, economic and administrative consequences, had a similar effect upon patterns of investment of social wealth. By the early seventh century, the focus for the investment of personal wealth and the accretion of prestige and status was increasingly focused on Constantinople, since this was the most direct way of ensuring a niche within the imperial system. There were exceptions to this, such as other major urban centres: Alexandria, for example. But the changing pattern of imperial administration and patronage was a central factor bearing on the ways in which late Roman elites invested their wealth, and hence on the amount of social investment in provincial cities. The loss of the eastern provinces and their major towns further accentuated this picture.

Due to these changes, the government and its military establishment promoted the transformation of many towns into fortresses, with the needs of local administration and the army firmly in the foreground. The 'city' effectively disappeared, and in its place there evolved the middle Byzantine *kastron* or fortress-town – distinguished by its limited extent and strongly defensive character – so that in many texts of the period from the eighth century on, the traditional Greek word for city, *polis*, is replaced by *kastron*, even when urban life began to flourish once more, in the later tenth and eleventh centuries.

The archaeological and literary evidence speaks volumes: the major city of Ancyra shrank to a small citadel during the 650s and 660s, the fortress occupying an area of a few hundred metres only; the city of Amorion, which was defended successfully in 716, for example, by 800 men against an attacking army more than ten times larger, was reduced in effect to the area of the citadel, or *kastron*, with an area of a few hundred metres. The occupied medieval areas of most cities seem to have been similar in nature. In fact, it seems often to have been the case that separate areas within the late Roman walls of many cities also continued to be inhabited, functioning effectively as distinct communities whose inhabitants regarded themselves (in terms of their domicile quite legitimately) as 'citizens' of the city within whose walls their settlement was located, and that the *kastron*, which retained the name of the ancient *polis*, provided a refuge in case of attack (although in many such cases it may not necessarily have been permanently occupied, still less permanently garrisoned). Many of the *poleis* of the seventh to ninth centuries survived as 'cities' because their inhabitants, living effectively in distinct communities within the area delineated by the walls, saw themselves as belonging to the *polis* itself, rather than to a village.

These changes are accompanied by an increasing 'ruralization' of Byzantine society, for as the fiscal role of cities changed, and as they then suffered from the invasions and economic dislocation of the second half of the seventh century in particular, the state appears to have transferred its attention to the village community as the focus of its fiscal administration. The central importance of the village in the state's fiscal considerations in the later seventh century and after is very clear. The language itself reflects this, for the medieval and modern Greek word for a village – *chorion* – meant until the middle of the sixth century or so a fiscal unit, the property of a landlord occupied by his tenants, in contrast to the standard Hellenistic and Roman word for a village, *kome*. From the later sixth and increasingly during the seventh century and after, *chorion* became the standard word for a village, which was also (and understood to include also the lands belonging to it) a fiscal unit. The properties within each fiscal district – in turn centred on the village and the lands held by its inhabitants – were assessed by centrally-appointed officials operating from a local administrative base (sometimes a town, sometimes a fortress or provincial military headquarters). The fiscal community was approached through its representatives – usually the wealthier villagers, who might also be landlords in their own right – who had to collect the assessment and deliver it to the state's officials. The arrangements for carrying this out varied over time. But the city disappears entirely as an intermediary, and we can reasonably describe the Byzantine empire from the eighth century on as a patchwork of village economies.

As a result of the stabilization of the political and military situation in Asia Minor after the early ninth century many urban centres recovered their fortunes; chiefly those which had an obvious economic and market function for their locality. Thebes in Greece provides a good example of an urban centre that made a good recovery in the later period, for by the middle of the eleventh century it had become the centre of a flourishing local silk industry and local merchants and landowners had houses there, which attracted artisans, peasant farmers with goods to sell, and the landless looking for employment – thus further promoting urban life. In addition, this urban regeneration is also connected with the growth of a middle Byzantine aristocracy or social elite of office and birth, which possessed the resources to invest in agricultural and industrial production, in the context of competition for imperial favour and economic pre-eminence.

Thus during the later tenth and especially in the eleventh and twelfth centuries towns become economically much more important. This reflects in part the improved conditions within the empire for trade, commerce and town-country exchange-relations to flourish. It also reflects the demands of Constantinople on the cities and towns of its hinterland for the provision of both foodstuffs and other goods. Concomitantly, towns begin to play a central role in political developments, so that whereas in the later seventh through into the mid-eleventh century most military revolts had been based in the countryside and around the headquarters of the local general, during the eleventh century and thereafter such political opposition to the central government is almost always centred in towns, whose populace also appear in the sources as a body of self-aware citizens with specific interests. Communal identity did not go much beyond this, although Byzantine Italy presents some exceptions, especially in connection with local efforts to attain a degree of local self-determination. For example, there was a revolt at Bari in 1009/1010, which was clearly associated with local aristocratic and urban desires for a greater degree of autonomy, for Byzantine towns also fell under the sway of local magnates who held both landed wealth as well as (and this is particularly important in the Byzantine context) imperial titles and offices. In itself, this development is no different from that found elsewhere; in Italy, for example, where it was the local elites which were the basis for the evolution of urban communal identities.

In Byzantium, it is partly also a reflection of the military organization of the empire from the middle of the tenth century and after, when many towns became the seats of local military officers and their soldiers; in turn, a reflection of the improved ability of the state after the crisis of the seventh and eighth centuries to supply and provision its soldiers through cash payments only, relying upon the existence of local market-exchange relationships to do the rest. Finally, it reflects the increasing domination of the countryside by these magnates, who gradually absorb considerable numbers of formerly free peasant holdings into their estates. The consequence was a reversal of the process of ruralization of economic and social life which typifies the seventh and eighth centuries. However much they now came to flourish as centres of local economic activity, both productive and commercial, they remained *kastra*, fortresses, and represented a very different sort of urban culture from that late Roman urban society which they had replaced.

This shift is illustrated in several contemporary or near-contemporary accounts. In the eleventh-century *Life* of a certain St. Nikon, we read how the saint settled near Sparta at the end of the tenth century, where he was invited by the local *archontes*, the landowners and leading secular and ecclesiastical officials of the district, to move into the town and rid them of a plague. In return, they helped him establish a monastery on the site of the ancient *agora*, and two of the *archontes* donated classical columns: eloquent testimony to the fate of the ancient town! The story makes it quite clear that the town was run by these men, and in this respect was hardly different, except perhaps in the degree of social differentiation, from a rural village community. In many cases (although lack of evidence makes any generalization dangerous), it is clear that there was nothing to choose institutionally between an undefended village settlement and a *kastron*: the inhabitants of many *kastra*, for example, were assessed for their taxes on a communal basis, just like any village, and there was very little to differentiate town from village from the institutional perspective. Size was certainly not an important feature. A major difference between the typical late Roman 'city' and the medieval town was that public buildings were no longer funded from 'public' sources. The role of the city corporations was taken over by the Church and by monasteries, by private individuals, or by other associations.

At the juridical institutional level there were no differences between town and village, except where a bishop was resident: this qualified a settlement for the title *polis*, and seems to have been the only formal definition of the term *polis* which survived beyond the ninth century. Naturally, there were many functional differences between towns and villages: towns had a greater role as markets, as residences for representatives of the military or other state administrators, as foci for traders and artisans, for an ecclesiastical establishment with economic requirements and effects, a more regular market or fair, and a range of other services and functions not available in a rural village context. The structure of town society had always been different from that of the rural village, even when the town in question was a small *kastron*: such communities tended to develop communal, non kin-based organizations, such as confraternities, specialist 'societies' focused on a particular saint's cult, for example, or the supporters' groups associated with chariot- or horse-racing. The *archontes* who dwelt in such urban centres may also have had informal arrangements for conducting their business, shadowy successors to the late Roman town councils, although very little is known about them. Only after the Fourth Crusade in 1204 do specifically urban institutions of government appear in the sources for a handful of major cities; and it is this lack of differentiating features which constitutes one of the most important contrasts between Byzantine towns and those of the late Roman world or the medieval West.

Rural society

The rural population of the empire was, as we have already noted, concerned almost exclusively with agricultural production of one sort or another. Some areas specialized in particular crops and products – vines and olives, and their derivatives, for example – and, once the political and military situation had stabilized, these regions became centres of thriving cash-crop economies. But the social structure of the countryside also underwent some changes between the Late Roman period and the tenth and eleventh centuries, of course. In the sixth century (and earlier) land was farmed for the most part by dependent peasants of one category or another, such as *coloni adscripticii* (registered as attached to the land they farmed) and *coloni liberi* (free peasant tenants), who collectively constituted the majority, working their farms which formed part of the estates of the landowning elite. The adscripted peasants could be released from their obligations only by their landlord; the free tenantry paid taxes directly to the state, and continued to be entered in the tax registers under their own names, rather than under a landlord's name. Alongside these two groups were free smallholders, in practice hardly different in their economic situation from the *coloni*, whose village communities they might share. They were of slightly higher status legally, of course, since they owned their properties, and could alienate them at will. But since they were subject to both pressure from the fisc for tax, on the one hand, and from the more powerful landlords around them, their position was very insecure.

The extent to which this pattern of landownership and land-exploitation survived into and beyond the seventh century is difficult to say. The Church and the state were major landlords in their own right, and there is no doubt that they continued to be major landlords within the territories remaining to the empire after the losses of the seventh century. Bishops represented the Church in this respect, and belonged in effect to the class of provincial magnates in respect of their economic power. It was often the bishop who was responsible for directing municipal action in respect of works of fortification and supplying a city in times of danger, for example, even extending their role to the administration of the public (state or municipal) granaries and the provisioning of locally-based troops.

The continued existence of the senate in Constantinople, the power and authority it wielded on occasion during the seventh century, and its reinforcement through newcomers from the imperial bureaucracy and administrative apparatus, meant that large landed properties also survived. The actual composition of the senate, and the degree of continuity from the sixth century in terms of families and specific estates, remains impossible to assess. But the older senatorial families lost out in many ways to the rising service aristocracy of the Constantinopolitan establishment, recruited at least in part on the basis of talent as well as connections or family. Nevertheless, it is likely that a proportion of the old elite was assimilated to the new service establishment of the second half of the seventh century. Whatever the origins of the military and civil officials of the period, personal wealth could only be assured beyond one generation through the acquisition of land. Landed property remained an essential element in securing one's future and also in cementing one's position within the establishment. And there is enough evidence to show that large private estates existed – side by side with those of the state and the Church – in the later seventh and eighth centuries, although the degree of physical continuity remains unknown. The sources refer also to the large estates of the Church, and to villages of independent peasants, who own and farm their holdings, paying taxes directly to the state. The extent of such communities was especially important for the government, since it was greatly to its advantage to have as large a proportion of the producing population directly under its fiscal authority as tax-payers, and thus maximize its share of the surplus appropriated.

Seventh-century church, Cappadocia.

Importantly, the proportion of free tenants and freeholders seems to have increased during this period, a process begun already in the sixth century, as imperial legislation suggests, in particular the number of those who leased land on an emphyteutic basis, paying a fixed rent (in kind or cash), the leases for which were transferable and were often held in perpetuity and hereditarily. Over the same period, it appears that a gradual assimilation of all three categories of tenant smallholder (*coloni liberi*, free tenants and emphyteutic lessees) into a single body of tenants occurred during the seventh and eighth centuries; tenants who paid a rent to their landlord and tax to the state, bound to their holdings or not according to the nature of their tenancy (which meant that emphyteutic lessees could cede or sell their lease – in effect, their land – and were often regarded, at least in respect of non-Church lands, as the *possessor* and not simply the tenant). Villages of predominantly free peasants seem henceforth to represent a more important element in the rural social landscape, and it appears that the village community became an economic and social element of much greater relative importance than had hitherto been the case, particularly in the state's administration of revenue extraction and collection. The evidence may also imply that the number of such villages increased as a result of several factors: in particular the abandonment by landlords of their estates in threatened areas, and the consequent assertion by the agrarian producers of their independence; the state-organized immigration of large numbers of Slav settlers with their own community structures and organization; and the increasing independence of peasant smallholders with perpetual or long-term, heritable leases, paying low and fixed rents to landlords who may often have been permanently resident away from their properties.

The expansion of independent smallholding appears to have been both a result of the changes in the relationship between agricultural producers and landlords, and to a degree

Summer transhumant village, north-east Turkey.

also the result of the reorganization of the system of fiscal assessment by the state, in turn brought about by the dislocation of the warfare of the second half of the seventh century. At the same time, it has been suggested that the conditions promoted by war and constant insecurity cast a large number of the agricultural population of threatened areas adrift, as refugees – either from the tax-collector, the rent-collector and bailiff, or the Arabs. It stimulated an increase in demographic mobility. The relocation by the state of refugee populations in several different areas of the empire further complicated the picture.

There was, of course, a good deal of social differentiation within peasant communities, facilitated in particular by the sub-division of holdings among heirs, leading to properties which might eventually become too small to be economically viable. Poor harvests, seasonal or climatic fluctuations, natural disasters and similar perennially present elements, quite apart from the demands of the fisc and of the local provincial or military administration, always left peasant farmers very vulnerable to changes in fortune and sudden household economic failure. The abandonment of holdings and the attribution of the taxes due from these to the owners of neighbouring lands was clearly a normal occurrence for the compilers of the legal hand-books of the eighth and ninth centuries, and their evidence portrays a rural society with many internal gradations.

Peasants of *colonus* status (the Greek term is *paroikos*), bound to their land by private contract, continued to farm the estates of powerful landlords – whether private, Church or state – spread over several provinces or districts. They shared villages with free tenants, and lessees of various kinds. In areas relatively free from hostile threat, the well-established bond between landlord and tenants remained, whatever the legislative intervention of the state may have done to relax or weaken the connection. Thus not all areas within the empire will necessarily have been affected in the same way. While the overall effect of the economic and social dislocation of the second half of the seventh century and the opening years of the eighth century seems to have promoted an increase in peasant mobility and in the numbers of peasant freeholders directly subject to the fisc, already the disadvantages which accompanied a peasant subsistence economy – together with the rise of the new magnate elite of the provinces – were leading to a new phase of polarization between estate owners and peasant communities, on the one hand, and within such communities, on the other. The evidence of eighth- and ninth-century sources in respect of the tax-burdens of the rural population, especially of those which affected the poorer members of each community, makes this clear. The long-term result was a general decline in the numbers of these independent communities, and the reduction of the vast mass of the peasantry to the status of tenants of one condition or another by the later eleventh century. Peasant freeholders survived well beyond this period, but in declining numbers. The emperors of the twelfth century maintained and appear to have enforced, as far as was possible, the legislation of the tenth century aimed at protecting the peasantry from the encroachments of wealthy landlords, for example; and it is clear that substantial imperial revenues were derived from such producers, whether they remained entirely independent, or whether they had been incorporated into the government's own system of estates.

Towns, trade and the wider world

There existed a fundamental tension in the Byzantine world between the fiscal interests of the state and the non-state sector of private merchants, bankers, shipping and so on. The state represented a particular set of ways and means of regulating the extraction, distribution and consumption of resources, embodying a strongly autarkic relationship between consumption and agricultural production. The export of finished goods, the flow of internal commerce between provincial centres, as well as between the provinces and Constantinople, and the movement of raw materials and livestock, were determined to a large extent by three closely connected factors: the demands of the state apparatus (army and treasury) for raw and finished materials and provisions; the state's need for cash revenues to support mercenary forces and the imperial court; and the demands of the imperial capital itself, which dominated regional trade in the western Black Sea and north-west Asia Minor, north Aegean and south Balkans. The pattern of supply and demand was already heavily slanted towards Constantinople, as we have seen, and this pattern became even more accentuated after the loss of central Anatolia to the Turks in the 1070s and 1080s. Trade in the Byzantine world was mostly inward-looking, from the provinces and from the empire's neighbours to Constantinople and between the provinces. Such trade represented after the later ninth century a flourishing aspect of the internal economy of Byzantine society, and large numbers of traders and entrepreneurs were associated with it. But the exploitative state apparatus still dominated, although, as in the later Roman world, while state-dominated trade may have had an inhibiting effect in some respects, it may also have encouraged trade and commerce along the routes most exploited by the state itself, precisely because private entrepreneurial activity can take advantage of state shipping and transportation. And given the number of trading ports around the Black Sea, from which Italians were excluded before the Fourth Crusade, it has been suggested that long-distance trade by Byzantine merchants before 1204 must have been substantial.

But this essentially late Roman pattern left little room at the level of production and distribution of wealth for outwardly-directed commercial activity or enterprise. Even when the state farmed fiscal contracts, the opportunities for private entrepreneurial activity were limited, not just by state intervention, but by social convention. What one did with newly-acquired wealth was not invest in independent commercial enterprise, but rather in the state: titles, imperial sinecures or actual offices, and court positions were first on the list of priorities. And although land and the rent accruing from landed property (in addition to the ideologically positive realization of self-sufficiency) were important considerations, it is clear that imperial titles and pensions were just as fundamental to the economic position of the power elite. Investment in commerce was ideologically marginalized, even though the developing group of *archontes* – the local middling and small-scale landed elites of the provincial towns and cities – had in many regions of the empire an active involvement in small-scale commodity production and manufacturing and the associated movement of goods which resulted. The best-documented examples come from the south Balkan silk industry, but there is no reason to doubt that other regions witnessed similar activity. There is every reason to think that there existed a flourishing and successful merchant class in the Byzantine empire during much of the ninth, tenth and eleventh centuries, but little is known about it. In the later Roman period and afterwards traders and merchants, as well as various categories of craftsmen and artisan, were organized in bodies called 'colleges', *collegia* (or *systemata* in Greek), very crudely comparable with later medieval guilds, although with fewer legal and social obligations attached. In Byzantine times such organizations were further differentiated according to whether their members pursued manual or more 'entrepreneurial' activities: the former were regarded as lowlier and humbler in status, the latter could aspire to a certain social standing, depending on the income they derived from their trade, and their contacts. Roman (and therefore Byzantine) law allowed for business associations as well as the charging of interest on loans, and there is no reason to doubt that – conditions being favourable – commerce and trade did not flourish where markets existed. This depended very much, however, on both the historical situation at the time, and on regional variations in terms of transport and communications, settlement patterns, and so forth. Yet merchants do not actively seem to have sought out new trade routes and markets outside the limits of the immediate political influence of the empire, except possibly in the brief period from the 1030s to 1080s, when commerce attained a slightly higher status than had been usual under emperors who needed to build up a metropolitan political base. Even in the Black Sea, it was state policy which protected Byzantine commerce, not merchants themselves.

For most wealthy Byzantines, their resources were derived predominantly from agricultural production. The social elite, both great magnates and local gentry or *archontes*, derived status from the possession of land and, in particular, membership of the imperial system. The wealth which the members of this elite could expect to derive from trade and commerce, both during the earlier period of its evolution and in the tenth and eleventh centuries, was of far less significance in comparison with that derived through rents and state positions. Thus, while merchants were an active element in urban economies by the eleventh century, playing an important role in the distribution of locally-produced commodities, they appear to occupy a relatively subordinate position in the process of wealth redistribution as a whole. In particular they played no role in the perceptions of the society in general in the maintenance of the empire and in the social order as it was understood. The social elite had no interest in their activities, except as suppliers of luxury items on the one hand, and as a means of selling off the surpluses from their own estates in local towns or fairs, or the capital, on the other. At the same time, the government exercised a somewhat inhibiting control over entrepreneurial enterprise, insofar as it carefully supervised the relationship between traders selling goods to the capital, and those who bought those goods and sold them on or worked them into other commodities. Thus all those dealing in a particular textile, or a particular type of livestock, who approached Constantinople had to do so as a body, and were admitted to trade with the City only through a similarly-constituted body of Constantinopolitan merchants or artisans. These regulations are most clearly expressed in the late ninth- or early tenth-century *Book of the Eparch*, a regulatory guide issued by the office of the governor of Constantinople. Their purpose was primarily to ensure the regular and orderly supply of the city with all its basic and secondary requirements, and to avoid overburdening its resources with extraneous immigrants, but they seem also to have had a significant dampening effect on independent commercial enterprise. In view of the fact that such control was exercised also over the import and export of other goods, such as grain, between the empire and its neighbours, it is easy to see that trade can have offered only minimal inducements, except where a particular loophole in these arrangements could be exploited, or where a hitherto unregulated commodity was involved. Even foreign traders were subject to these controls, at least until their power and economic influence became too powerful, in the later twelfth century. Groups of foreign merchants were thus normally resident in a specific quarter, and had to be accompanied by imperial officials when they did business.

This contrasts very clearly with the situation in the Italian merchant cities with which the Byzantines did business in the later eleventh and twelfth centuries, especially Venice, Genoa and Pisa. To begin with, while the major trading cities possessed an agricultural hinterland from which most members of the urban elite derived an income, leading elements of the elites of these cities were at the same time businessmen whose wealth and political power was often dependent as much on commerce as on rents. As they evolved during the eleventh and into the twelfth century, the city-states themselves – increasingly dominated by merchant aristocrats and their clients – came to have a vested interest in the maintenance and promotion of as lucrative and advantageous a commerce as possible. Therefore, the economic and political interests of the leading and middling elements were identical with the interests of the city, its political identity and its independence of outside interference. State/communal and private enterprise were inseparable. The economic and political well-being of the city as a state was thus to a large extent coterminous with that of the social elite and its dependants. The Byzantine state, in contrast, played no role at all in promoting indigenous enterprise, as far as we can see from the sources, whether for political or economic reasons, and viewed commerce as simply another minor source of state income: commercial activity was regarded as – and was in respect of how the state worked – peripheral to the social values and political system in which it was rooted.

This difference is not a reflection of the failure of an archaic and statist political-economic system to respond to new conditions, both in respect of international commercial relations as well as internal economic growth. As we have noted, there did exist a relatively active, albeit more or less entirely inwardly-directed commerce, and a merchant 'class' to conduct it. Interest in trade and commerce clearly existed and involved both members of the provincial urban and rural as well as the metropolitan elites. But the interests of commerce were subordinate to the relationship between the political and ideological structure of the imperial state on the one hand and the interests of the dominant social-economic elite on the other. Commerce was seen as neither economically nor politically relevant; an apathy conditioned by the way in which state and society had evolved over the centuries. For those at the top of the social scale, it was perceived as both economically unimportant and socially and culturally demeaning; while for those who were involved in trade it brought no social advancement and, for the most part, no great social wealth.

Given these preconditions, and the rise of the Italian maritime cities – especially Venice and Genoa – the longer-term results for the Byzantine economy and state were unfortunate. The internal conflicts and military failures, followed by political collapse of the 1070s and early 1080s, the establishment of a series of hostile Turkish states in Anatolia and the need for the Byzantines to call upon allies with military and especially naval resources which they could themselves no longer mobilize, pointed the way. The naval weakness of the imperial government throughout the twelfth century, particularly in respect of the threat from the Normans in Sicily, directly promoted reliance upon Venetian assistance, purchased through commercial concessions. Together with the role played by Venice, Pisa and Genoa (among several cities) during the period following the First Crusade (and the competition between Venice and Genoa in particular), this paved the way for Italian commercial infiltration of the Byzantine economic and exchange sphere during the twelfth century; culminating in the concessions achieved under the emperors following Manuel I. Indeed, it was because Italian commerce was on a small scale, and regarded as unimportant to the economic priorities of both state and aristocracy, that it was enabled to prosper. Demographic expansion in Italy stimulated the demand for Byzantine grain and other agrarian produce, which meant that Venetian and other traders slowly built up an established network of routes, ports and market bases, originally based on carrying Byzantine bulk (as well as luxury goods) and Italian or western imports to Constantinople, and later expanding to a longer-distance commerce to meet the needs of an expanding Italian market.

Commerce and merchant or banking activity were no less marginal to the Byzantine elite in the twelfth century than they had been before the eleventh century. The Italian

Eleventh-century sculpture, Antalya.

trading cities were able to expand their activities and increase their wealth much more rapidly by virtue of the opportunities thus opened to them. So that, while Byzantine society appeared to be solidly based within the traditional framework, a new and much more complex Mediterranean-wide market was evolving, linking East and West, upon which cities such as Venice and Genoa depended very heavily for their political existence and the relatively new-found power and wealth of their ruling elites. This is made clear by the sharply negative effects upon the Venetian economy of the expulsion of Venetians under Manuel I in 1171, the consequent naval expedition against Byzantium, and its failure. The internal strife in Genoa at the same period reveals similar concerns, as different factions struggled for pre-eminence in the making of policy with regard to the relative importance of commercial and political interests in West and East, and the relations between the Byzantine and German emperors.

The coinage reforms of Alexios I – a priority necessitated by the collapse of the traditional monetary system in the 1060s-1080s – made day-to-day money transactions easier. But greater commercial exchange and commodity production, stimulated by the economic expansion of the eleventh century, combined with the greater flexibility of the reformed coinage, also facilitated an increasing involvement of outsiders in internal Byzantine commerce and investment. This was seen chiefly as an irritant and as a political problem by Byzantine commentators, although some bemoaned also the fate of Byzantine merchants. But the observation was itself made possible because of the successful exploitation by Italians of an expanding market which had not impinged upon Byzantine consciousness a century earlier, although the presence of Italians in Constantinople certainly appears to have stimulated local services, such as the production and supply of naval equipment of all sorts. The real expansion of Venetian and Genoese activity within the empire began towards the end of the twelfth century, when improved relations between the Byzantine government and the Venetians, Genoese and Pisans reflect Byzantine concerns about the political designs of the emperor Frederick Barbarossa and the need to win friends and allies with naval potential as well as political power in Frederick's geo-political back-yard. The concessions granted by Byzantine rulers reflect the notion that trade still occupied a marginal place in the economy of the state. They also reflect both the fact that Byzantine rulers could still effectively exploit the hostile relations between Venice and Genoa as well as the overwhelmingly non-commercial, political emphasis placed by the imperial government on these matters.

The events of 1204 finally destroyed the old order; and when after 1261 a reconstituted central imperial state was revived, it inhabited a very different world indeed, not simply in terms of the well-established political presence of western powers in the east Mediterranean and Aegean regions, but also in terms of its ability to maintain itself. The reduced income derived from the appropriation of surplus through tax on a much smaller, and constantly shrinking, territorial base; the fragmentation of territory and political authority; and the lack of a serious naval power with which to defend its interests, were fundamental. Income derived from taxes on commerce played a proportionately larger role in real terms as well as in the eyes of the central government. Yet the traditional elite, with few exceptions, was still based on the income from land; while the state itself was unable to compete with Italian and other commercial capital and shipping. In the mid-fourteenth century the emperor John VI attempted to exploit the political situation in the Black Sea at the expense of the Genoese and to bolster the position of Byzantine merchants by reducing dues payable at the port of Constantinople, so that they could compete equally with those imposed upon the majority of Italian traders, and thus promote an increase in imperial revenue. But Genoese military and naval power soon restored the situation. Nevertheless, the emperor's plan reveals the importance of revenues of this sort to the much-reduced empire; but by this time it was too late effectively to change the pattern which had evolved, although a number of Byzantine aristocrats had begun to take an active interest in commerce. With a few exceptions, 'Byzantines' or 'Greeks' played a generally subordinate role to Italians, sometimes as business partners, often as small-time entrepreneurs, as middlemen, and as wholesalers; frequently as small-scale moneylenders/bankers; rarely as large-scale bankers (although there were some), or major investors, still more rarely in major commercial contracts. Indeed, the market demands of Italian-born commerce began also to influence the patterns of production within the empire, with the result that the state itself no longer had any effective role in managing or directing the production of wealth.

In the context of economic growth which affected the whole European and Middle Eastern world from the tenth and eleventh centuries, the pre-eminence of Italian shipping in trade and commerce within the formerly relatively closed Byzantine sphere had unforeseen effects. First, it contributed towards the economic growth of those Italian merchant cities most involved, and resulted in turn in an increase in their dependency on that trade for their own internal stability. Second, it deprived the various

Gold hyperpyron *of Alexios I. Left: Obverse showing the enthroned figure of Christ. Right: Reverse with the standing figure of the emperor.*

Byzantine successor states and their elites of any possibility of successfully responding and adjusting to the economic and political conditions which prevailed after 1204 and especially after 1261, since, by the time they showed an interest in commerce and shipping on a large scale, Italian merchants, bankers and shippers had already a long-established dominance, together with a network of markets and a system of business and managerial practices with which Greek enterprise – whether or not supported by a state – could not hope to compete.

Yet commerce became increasingly essential to the growth of local economies within the Byzantine world, at the same time impinging to an ever greater extent on the traditional means of state-directed redistribution of wealth. Its untrammelled operation contradicted the essence of imperial state control and threatened also the traditional mode of operation of aristocratic landholding and consumption. Byzantine entrepreneurial activity thus posed a threat not only to the state's efforts to maintain a position of dominance with regard to the appropriation and distribution of social wealth; it was also a direct challenge to the pre-eminent position of the landed aristocracy within the state. The operation of the traditional fiscal establishment, together with the ideological and cultural devaluation of commerce, prevented indigenous commerce from taking advantage of expanding markets. Inadequate investment in a context already dominated by Italian shipping in respect of external trade, meant that Byzantine merchants were never in a position to mount an effective challenge.

These points can be illustrated in the rise in influence during the middle years of the eleventh century of a Constantinopolitan commercial elite, allied to an artisanate actively involved in the generation of social wealth not dependent upon landed property. It was not to last long, however. The reimposition of the constraints of state control and the reassertion of aristocratic dominance under Alexios I reflected not only a conservative reaction, but also an imperative which burdened any central authority in the Byzantine state of the time which wished to re-establish both political and economic stability and its own credibility: the 'statist' approach was, in real terms, and however modified by the conditions of the time, the only model available through which the Byzantine empire could be governed. Just as in the seventh century, when dramatic administrative-organizational changes were pursued on the logic of an attempt to restore a lost situation, so in the twelfth century the Komnene reorganization represents a conscious effort to re-establish a lost order. While the 'lost' order was itself in part an imagined tradition, the conditions within which the new measures were introduced were so utterly different from those which had generated the older structures, that quite unpredictable results and consequences followed, upon the basis of which emperors inevitably evolved very different responses.

From the tenth and eleventh centuries, the central government and its fiscal apparatus were faced with a more diverse, and therefore more complex, tax-base. They were also presented with a challenge over the appropriation of surplus wealth, the distribution of such surpluses, and the way in which they might be invested. The state wanted as much as it could lay its hands on to support its own apparatus and existence. Private landlords and others were thus in competition with the state, even if this was not always explicitly so. And it was the form taken by the competition between state centre, local gentry, and magnate elite in the particular context of the institutional organization and ideology of Byzantine economy and society which determined the possibilities open to the emperors in reorganizing the fiscal apparatus and methods of rule of the Byzantine state in the later eleventh and early twelfth centuries. In this case, the evolving local elites of the provincial towns adopted for the most part the values of the established state-centred, land-based (but Constantinople-dwelling) and rent-extracting aristocracy.

Neither foreign merchants nor commerce caused the political breakdown of central imperial power, however much they undercut the efforts of the state to retain central control over its resources and, more importantly, the process by which those resources were distributed, especially during the second half of the twelfth century. On the contrary, it was the structural relationship between the centralized bureaucratic state and its fiscal machinery, on the one hand, and the dominant social elite, on the other, which were determinant. This relationship underlay the political and fiscal collapse of the state in the years immediately prior to the Fourth Crusade; after which the movement of goods in the Aegean and east Mediterranean basin was firmly in the hands of Italian commerce and investors, however important the role of Byzantine and Greek middlemen and petty traders may have been within this network. As the empire shrank, so commerce and trade, rather than land, came to be the main source of state income. But by the end of the empire the government shared only minimally in this resource.

6 Byzantine political society

As we have seen in Chapter 5 above, the rural society of the empire was the primary source of productive wealth, upon whose agricultural and pastoral activities both the state and private landowners depended for their own incomes, derived in the form of tax and rent. But the peasantry had no say in the running of the empire, in its political or administrative life, or, saving their own subsistence requirements, in the ways in which the wealth which they produced was distributed and consumed. Only when peasants joined the army and became involved in group 'political' action, such as mutinies, or when the humbler elements in the populations of towns banded together to make political or other demands for example, or when individuals were able to join the retinue of some wealthy magnate or courtier and improve their own social status and rank, could persons from such a background aspire to any influence over such matters. There were exceptions, but they are notable because they were such. Byzantine society was clearly stratified and its culture was deeply hierarchical; a hierarchy that was represented through various writings as both God-given and naturally just, in which each group had its own particular role. This was sometimes conceived of using the metaphor of the body, in which the peasantry, the productive population, were seen as the legs and trunk, supporting and nurturing the arms (the military) and the head, represented by the emperors themselves. There is no allowance in this model, of course, for an aristocracy or social elite, since this was assumed to be identical in its interests, at least in theory, with those of the emperor, and thus with the well-being and governance of the state. But the social elite was, in reality, always a complex series of overlapping and inter-connected groupings and vested interests, sometimes, depending upon the period, involving kinship and family connections as essential elements in its identity, at other times identified through court office and rank; usually a combination of aspects of both.

The late Roman senate

The term 'senatorial aristocracy' usefully describes the nature of the late Roman elite up to the middle of the seventh century. But it is a term that needs to be used with care, since it embodies a wide range of persons of very different economic status, and not necessarily of similar social origins. The senatorial order, which represented the established landed and office-holding elite of the empire was enormously expanded during the fourth and fifth centuries. The emperor Constantine I began to employ senators in the administrative machinery of the state in great numbers, in contrast to Diocletian, who for political reasons had introduced a number of restrictions on the posts senators could fill. In the middle of the fourth century there were perhaps three hundred senators belonging to the senate of Constantinople; by the end of the century there were as many as two thousand, a result of the creation by the emperors of ever more senators, and the tying of increasing numbers of posts to senatorial rank. One result of this was, inevitably, the devaluation of senatorial status, and the consequent establishment of new grades of higher status to compensate for this movement. All senators held the grade of *clarissimus*, which was hereditary; but a re-grading in the later fourth century introduced two new levels – *illustris* and, below this, *spectabilis*. Only the first title was hereditary, the two senior ranks being tied to tenure of an imperial office or post in either military or civil service, although the title of *spectabilis* rapidly lost its status value and was limited to fairly humble posts by the end of the fifth century. The system became increasingly complex as grades internal to the ranks of *illustris* were introduced, according to whether the holder held an active post or not, and whether he was based at court or in the provinces. Since functional posts could also be awarded on an honorary and inactive basis, the degrees of the hierarchy were quite convoluted.

'Senatorial aristocracy' thus refers both to those who held the title *clarissimus* hereditarily – several thousand by the sixth century – as well as to all those who were awarded the higher titles of *spectabilis* and *illustris*, neither of which was hereditary, although the children of those who held these titles were automatically graded as *clarissimi*. Many of these would have been fairly modest landowners, some may even have been in quite straitened economic circumstances, while a substantial number were certainly extremely wealthy and owned very substantial estates. During the sixth century, a further refinement of the grading system occurred, by which new titles – *magnificus* and *gloriosus* – replaced *illustris* at the higher levels, so that most key military and civil posts were of these ranks. The term 'senatorial aristocracy' must also include these persons, therefore, who held high office in Constantinople and the provinces; men who actually exercised state authority at various levels, and whose salaries enabled them – if they were not already from a wealthy background – to establish themselves as major landowners and secure their membership of this economically powerful elite. Once a senatorial family had established itself through imperial service, of course, it had the resources to further the interests of its own junior members and to build up a clientele, so that successive generations were assured of their membership of both a social elite and the ruling establishment. This was never an aristocracy of birth, however, since the emperors were always able to make new senators and fill posts with men whom they preferred, for whatever reason, so that the make-up of this 'class' (if it can be so called) was extremely varied and included families and individuals of widely differing economic status and potential.

The late Roman senatorial elite, internally diverse and highly regionalized though it was, was also the bearer of late Roman literary culture and the guardian of the urban-centred cultural traditions of the earlier Roman and Hellenistic worlds. The transformations in the role of cities, the reduction in the territory of the empire in the seventh century, and the narrowing of cultural and ideological horizons which the Persian and especially the Arab wars ushered in, affected this in many ways. Late Roman culture vanishes almost completely, together with a great deal of the cultural capital it carried with it. Many of the developments which led to this transformation were in train long before the seventh-century crisis; but that crisis brought things to a head and promoted the development of new structures and responses. The nature of literary culture, and the bearers of that culture, change considerably, as the relationships of power to land and to office within the ruling elite change. The old senatorial establishment, with much of the literary cultural baggage associated with it, fades away during the seventh century to be replaced by a service elite of heterogeneous ethnic, social and cultural origins. It is quite likely that the new elite incorporated many elements of the older establishment, but elite culture underwent radical change. Wealthy provincials found access to positions of authority blocked off at the local level, both by local economic conditions as well as by the predominance of centrally-appointed provincial military and civil officialdom. They therefore turned to Constantinople, the seat of empire and source of wealth, status and power, and there they invested their social capital in order to become part of that system. Only the Church provided an alternative and equivalent career structure, but that also was centred in Constantinople. The emperor and the court became – more than ever before – the source of social advancement. And while there were many minor routes to power which were not directly pulled into that nexus, the imperial court nevertheless constituted the dominant mode of entry.

The new order

The new elite thus owed its origins to the period of turmoil and reorganization of state structures which occurred in the seventh century. The needs of the state in respect of finding persons competent to deal with both civil and military matters in the provinces in this period of crisis was a central consideration. The advantages an individual had over both local landlords and peasantry if he occupied a position of military or civil authority in the provinces were considerable – a monopoly of armed force, for example, the power to seize or confiscate food or other produce for the army, and so on. Persons appointed to such posts thus had every opportunity to further their own interests if they desired. These tendencies were reinforced by the fact that many of the military commanders of the Anatolian armies appear to have been Armenians who took service with the empire. This serves as a useful reminder that the government was looking for people with the appropriate skills and resources for the tasks in hand, for such men – usually from the middling or upper nobility of Armenia – often brought their own personal armed retinues with them, thus further strengthening both their value to Constantinople as well as their local power. But what is particularly important is that the composition of both the senate in Constantinople and of the state's leading officials changes. Although there had always been a place for 'newcomers', under imperial patronage, in the state establishment during the later Roman period, the greater proportion of non-Greek names, for example, of officials known from all types of source, is very striking from the 660s and after. At the same time, the old system of senatorial dignities and titles (the *clarissimi*, the *spectabiles* and the *illustres*) seems to drop out of use, only the leading category of the *illustres* group, referred to as *gloriosi* (*endoxos* or *endoxotatos* in Greek) retaining any significance. There seems to have taken place a considerable change in the cultural and social origins of key personnel in the imperial establishment at all levels. At the same time titles which no longer corresponded to either social or political realities become irrelevant, disappearing entirely or being fossilized at a lower level of the system of ranks and status. There occurred, in fact, a restructuring of the whole system of titles and precedence during the seventh century, in which the importance of titles and posts dependent directly upon imperial service in the palace and at court increases, to the disadvantage of older titles associated in one way or another with the senatorial order. Power was concentrated and focused more than ever before on the figure of the emperor and in the imperial palace, while the older, much more pluralistic system of rank, privilege, wealth and power disappears. And all these developments in turn suggest that, while many senatorial landowners probably did hold on to their properties during this period of massive economic disruption and sometimes severe political repression (confiscations of senatorial property and waves of executions are supposed to have occurred in the reigns of Phokas [602-610] and Justinian II [705-711, his second reign]) the old elite must have suffered very considerably as the economic effects of constant warfare came to be felt.

One effect of these changes was to make 'senatorial' titles and epithets part of the common system of titles based on service in the palace and at court. Their survival as 'senatorial' grades was still recognized in the ninth and tenth centuries. The conclusion must be that, if senatorial grades had been reduced to one aspect of an otherwise entirely imperial and palatine hierarchy of ranks, and the older titles marking out membership of the senatorial order in the late Roman sense had fallen out of use, then the senatorial order as such no longer existed. 'Senators' were now imperially-appointed – there was no longer a hereditary clarissimate – which in turn may suggest that the socio-economic and cultural elements which had constituted the older senatorial order in all its diversity no longer existed or, at the least, was no longer able to dominate the state and government. The senate in Constantinople – which continued to wield influence because it included high-ranking state officials – thus no longer embodied the economic or political interests of a broad stratum of landowners, an aristocracy of privilege whose urban-based municipal culture was also the elite culture of the late Roman world.

This does not mean that in the period from the middle of the seventh to the middle of the ninth century there were no wealthy, large-scale landowners; nor that their vested interests were unrepresented in the activities and politics of the ruling elite at Constantinople. But the evidence does suggest that this element in society no longer dominated the state in the way it had previously, and that service at court and imperial sponsorship was now far more important to social and economic advancement. The collective political-cultural strength of the late Roman senatorial elite had lain in its monopoly of high civil office in particular, the civil magistracies, governorships, judicial posts and so forth, in both the provinces and in Constantinople. But many of these disappeared or were reduced in status and importance as a result of the changes in the role of cities and in fiscal and military administration that occurred over the period from *c.*640-650 on, which involved a considerable reduction in the status of many posts, a concentration of supervisory authority in the hands of the emperor and a few close advisors, and a focus on service at court for promotion and advancement.

Thus the incorporation of senatorial titles into a single imperial hierarchy appears to develop in parallel with the disappearance of the senatorial establishment and the system of grades which were its outward mark of identification. A more court-centred, imperial 'meritocracy' evolved, in which members of the old establishment competed on more-or-less equivalent terms, depending upon competence and patronage and connections. In the situation of sporadic near-crisis which characterized the empire's administration from *c.*640 until the 720s, there seems to have been little room for the culture of the old establishment;

a factor reflected also in the reduction in the production of many genres of non-religious literature and other shifts in the cultural pattern of the period. As the importance of the court increased, so that of the senatorial order must have waned, as those who belonged to it came to depend more and more upon the court for their status; in turn a reflection of the decline of provincial centres of wealth and society. This is clearly reflected in the fate of the middling and lesser senatorial titles, which either vanish or sink to the bottom of the hierarchy. Birth and lineage also became less important: the hagiographical writings of the later seventh to ninth centuries, for example, have no commonly-employed vocabulary to describe persons of wealth and power, concentrating usually on descriptions of their wealth and status at the time, rather than their lineage (although this does also continue to be mentioned on occasion).

The result of all these changes was not simply that the dominance of the older aristocracy was broken, or that the state administration was increasingly filled by newcomers. It was that the new 'pseudo-meritocratic' service elite depended, at least in its formative period, entirely upon the emperor; and although the sources are few and often difficult to interpret, one feature above all stands out: the seventh century witnessed a massive reconcentration of power and economic control in the hands of the state. The shrinkage of the empire territorially, the centralization of fiscal administration, the effective disappearance of cities as intermediaries – socially and economically – between the provinces and Constantinople, the apparent increase in the numbers of peasant communities independent of private landlords, as well as the other features outlined already, were all part of this shift in emphasis. And it gave the imperial system a new lease of life which was to last until the eleventh century.

Middle Byzantine elites: factions and clans

But by the eleventh century, the service meritocracy of the later seventh century had become, by virtue of its close affiliation with the state and with imperial patronage, the provincial aristocracy of the middle and later empire. The inherent contradictions between the economic interests of an increasingly independent landowning magnate class dominating at least certain key sectors of the machinery of the state, on the one hand, and the fiscal interests of the state itself and of the particular power elite or ruling class faction which directed it at any given moment, on the other hand – fought out over the surplus which could be wrung out of the producing population – became clear. Should that surplus go to the landed power-elite and magnates as rent, or to the state (and thus, of course, indirectly, to the power elite of the moment) as taxes and other impositions? Part of the resolution, from the eleventh century, given the dependence of the state upon this elite for all its chief civil and military functionaries (although distinct class fractions existed, which used the state against their particular opponents) was for the state to concede revenue extraction to those upon whom it depended. The other part of the resolution was the seizure of the state by the representatives of a particular faction of the ruling elite, and the establishment of a more openly dynastic and aristocratic system of administration, dependent upon a precarious network of clan alliances and patronage supported by the leading magnate families.

Evidence for the rise of a new aristocracy comes in the second half of the eighth century with the appearance of family names associated with particular individuals. It is a feature of many historical societies that consciousness of status, background and family identity is usually indicated by this means, and it is clear from the later evidence that many of the most important middle Byzantine magnate families owed their fortunes to service in the military or civil branches of state service during the eighth and ninth centuries. By the middle of the tenth century the sources repeatedly draw attention to the activities, both political and cultural, of such families, and a number of clan or family names – some twenty or twenty five – recur time and again in connection with the expansionist warfare of the period. But the term 'aristocracy' (*aristokratia*) was usually avoided: terms such as 'well-born' or 'of noble lineage" are more common, underlining the values associated with an honourable family tradition. It is notable that the majority of these magnate clans were of Anatolian provincial origin, associated primarily with the army, with the focus of their lands in the eastern regions. Many of them were of Armenian origins.

While by no means united ideologically, at least until the later eleventh and twelfth century, constituent elements of this group – made up of a number of dominant families with their clients and retinues throughout the provinces as well as in the central administration – came into conflict with those elements which dominated the state apparatus at Constantinople at given moments, especially during the first three-quarters of the eleventh century, and in particular over the appropriation and the distribution of resources. This was exemplified by the clash between the bureaucratic faction, which dominated policy during the brief reign of the emperor Michael VI (1056-1057), and the leaders of the Anatolian armies, all members or associates of well-established 'military' clans; a clash which resulted in the rebellion led by Isaac Komnenos and Katakalon Kekaumenos and the deposition of Michael. But the relations within and between the different elements which made up these groups was fluid and subject to constant change, so that it is impossible to speak of clearly identifiable or long-term political solidarities. There nevertheless developed an awkward problem for any government, since there was a contradiction between the interests of the latter, whose leading personnel had come by the early tenth century to be almost entirely recruited from this dominant social elite, and the interests of those members of this elite who found themselves in the position of both representatives of their clans and families, on the one hand, and as landlords in their own right, on the other. By the middle of the eleventh century contemporary commentators were speaking in terms of identifiable 'military' (provincial) and 'civil' (Constantinopolitan) factions; the former identified with the great magnates of Asia Minor, an elite of birth, the latter with the central bureaucracy and, to a degree at least, an elite based on merit.

This does not mean that the latter did not also possess or invest in landed property in the provinces; nor that the demarcation between the two groups was not always very fluid and subject to a wide range of conjunctural pressures, factional alliances and individual personalities – indeed, interests were represented and embodied precisely in individual family histories and individual careers. Competition for power and influence took place within the context of a patrimonial political structure, dominated by the formal hierarchies and system of honours and status of the imperial state, and between rival clans and families. While, undoubtedly, landed wealth played a crucial role in the consolidation of magnate autonomy, families and individuals invested also very heavily in the imperial system itself: posts and sinecures, state 'pensions', often amounting to considerable yearly incomes in gold and precious cloths, as well as thesaurized coin, jewellery, plate and so on. All members of the dominant social class, as well as their clients, invested and accrued wealth in this way. While many families thus consolidated their position economically over a number of generations through the acquisition of lands, equally large numbers seem to have possessed relatively little landed wealth, and were in consequence much more directly dependent upon the state or, more specifically, the particular ruler and palatine faction of the moment. In fact, such persons may be described as clients of the state itself, and formed thus an important group of interests at the capital and in the palace. And it must be stressed that even the more independent magnates – both individuals and clans – depended on this bureaucratic, imperial system for titles, honours and, to a certain extent (depending upon distance from the capital, relationships with local society and similar factors) social status and respect. Only towards the end of the twelfth century had some of these families attained sufficient wealth and resources to become more independent of the court and its system of titles and precedence.

The growth in the power of the elite was stimulated by two developments. In the first place, the sources show the increasing subordination of the peasantry to both private landlords and to holders of *pronoiai*. This natural process was hastened by the occurrence of a series of natural disasters affecting harvests in the first half of the tenth century, and exposed peasant smallholders in particular to pressure to convert their lands into tenancies in return for support through difficult periods. While the government enacted a number of laws to restrict the alienation of such lands to 'the powerful' (a loose term denoting most of those with the resources to buy up land, and thus not necessarily signifying the very wealthy alone), success was very limited, and in the end , and in spite of draconian measures enacted by the emperor Basil II, the state began to lose control of the fiscal resources which such independent producers represented. The predominantly free peasantry, while they became increasingly liable to the depredations and encroachments of the big landowners and magnates (especially in the tenth century) as well as those who were also the tenants of large landlords, were all still subject to the fisc, that is to say, they were taxed directly (although some estate owners, particularly monastic or ecclesiastical, were exempted as a special privilege by certain emperors).

In the second place, from the later eleventh century, the elite were benefitting from the concession by the state of the right to receive the revenues from certain public (i.e. fiscal, or taxed) districts; or of certain imperial estates, and their tenants, along with part or all of the rents and taxes raised from them. Such grants – known as grants of *pronoia* – were made for a variety of reasons to individuals by the emperors. They took the form of personal grants from the ruler, who represented the state in the institutional sense; and while there was also a more general meaning of the term *pronoia*, the most usual involved *pronoia* grants in return for military service. With the expansion of magnate landholding, a process of alienation of the state's fiscal and juridical rights set in, although the extent to which the institution of *pronoia* contributed to this before the thirteenth century is open to doubt: such grants only seem to have become generalized from the middle of the twelfth century as a means of supporting soldiers, and many of them were very small – not major estates designed to support a knight and his retinue, but quite small revenues intended to maintain a soldier for a limited period.

Nevertheless, through obtaining fiscal exemptions of varying sorts, landlords – both secular and monastic – were able to keep a larger proportion of the revenues extracted from their peasant producers for themselves, as rent, while the government's hold on the remaining fiscal land of the empire was constantly challenged by the provincial elite. This had important consequences, for – in conjunction with developments in the way the government recruited and financed its armies during the later tenth and early eleventh century – it meant that the overall burden placed upon the peasant producers grew considerably. In the period before the changes of the later tenth century, it is likely that this burden was fairly evenly distributed across the rural population of the provinces, and that, although the transit of imperial forces did involve unusually heavy demands on the communities closest to the routes used by military detachments, such demands were neither frequent nor regular.

But the reliance upon mostly mercenary armies, who needed supplies, fodder, housing and other necessities throughout the winter and possibly all year round, and who could not draw upon their families and their own resources as had the traditional thematic forces, must have considerably increased the weight of the state's demands in this respect. In contrast to the general situation in the ninth and earlier years of the tenth century, the bulk of the provincial soldiery could no longer be said to support itself for most of the year. Monastic charters and exemptions are particularly instructive, showing, for example, that the number of groups of foreign mercenaries alone who were dependent upon rights of billeting and provisioning at the expense of local communities and landlords increases very sharply from the 1040s. This was a process which was already under way from about 950, and increased in pace and intensity thereafter. There was probably considerable regional variation, evidence for which is lacking, so that some districts, especially those from which the imperial forces conducted operations over several seasons, will have been more drastically affected. The amount of state resources extracted by these means was probably considerable; a development illustrated by the fact that the value of the *antikaniskion* (the monetized equivalent of the *kaniskion*, a render of produce to imperial officials as a gift or fee for carrying out their duties) could actually be greater than the rate of land-tax imposed. Tenants of landlords with access to imperial patronage, both secular and monastic, attempted to free themselves from many of these impositions through obtaining grants of exemption of one sort or another, although it is clear that in many cases the needs and demands of the local military meant that privileges were often entirely ignored. The amount of resources lost to the state through grants of exemption from additional taxes cannot have been negligible, while the burden of landlords' demands on peasant tenants is hinted at by an eleventh-century writer, who notes that cancelling fiscal privileges freed the rural communities from the burdens which they owed in rents and services.

The divergence between the interests of the landed and office-holding elite and the central authority (or the 'state' as a political entity) – which is evident during the later tenth and eleventh centuries – was papered over from the time of Alexios I and until the end of the twelfth century. This was by virtue of the transformation of the empire under the Komnenos dynasty into what was, in effect, a gigantic family estate, ruled through a network of magnates, relatives and patronage that expanded rapidly during the twelfth century and that, in uniting the vested interests of the dominant social-economic elite with those of a ruling family, reunited also the interests of the former with those of a centralized empire. The factional politics which resulted from these developments, in particular over who would control Constantinople and sit on the throne, become apparent in the squabbles and civil wars which followed the defeat of Romanos IV by the Seljuks in 1071; a situation resolved only by the seizure of power by Alexios I in 1081. By the end of the twelfth century, if not already a century earlier, the vast majority of peasant producers in the empire had become tenants, in one form or another, of a landlord. By the same period, the elite had crystallized into a multi-factional aristocracy of birth, with a few very powerful families at the top, and a number of subordinate and collateral clans and families dependent upon them, often with strongly regional affiliations and identities. Under the Komnenoi, the imperial family and its immediate associates monopolized military and higher civil offices, while the older families who had been its former rivals dominated the bureaucratic machinery of the state. In the provinces, local elites tended to dominate, having benefited from the economic stability of the tenth and eleventh centuries and the revival of urban economies. And it was these social relations which facilitated the internecine strife and factionalism which marks the fourteenth and fifteenth centuries in particular.

Aristocrats and archontes

While these important magnate clans and their clients dominate the political history of the tenth and eleventh centuries and afterwards, other developments in the social composition of the Byzantine world deserve some attention. The economic and political stability achieved by the later ninth century almost everywhere in the empire made possible a recovery of urban life on a widespread basis. Small fortresses grew into flourishing market centres, attracting small-scale industries and trade, and promoting the development of local elites who were able both to invest in these new developments and draw profits from them. This provincial gentry – a middling elite of landowners who were more concerned with local affairs than with those of the imperial capital (although they also had interests there, too) – becomes prominent in the eleventh century and afterwards; both in respect of local politics and in terms of the relationship between the capital and the provinces from which the government drew its income. While they were dependent in part on more powerful patrons among the higher aristocracy, their regional location meant a greater investment than hitherto in local economies, especially in commerce and small-scale manufacturing, such as silk, pottery, glass, olive oil and wine production. Byzantium rapidly became an attractive and lucrative market for outsiders, in particular the Venetians and Genoese, as noted in an earlier chapter. At the same time, and in spite of the enormous concentration of wealth and power in the capital, the provinces, in particular the south Balkan regions and those districts which had access to the Aegean Sea, evolved a much stronger identity in respect of local as well as international trade and commerce. Partly, this reflected the fact that economic life at Constantinople was rigorously overseen by the Prefect of the City, chiefly with the intention of regulating the movement of people and the consumption of resources

The Byzantine and Ottoman walls of Ankara.

in such a large centre of population; so that the provincial cities of the empire were much more attractive to entrepreneurs and artisans of all categories.

While the fiscal system was focused on the village community, the towns – in contrast to the late Roman pattern – remained more-or-less independent of the imperial administration, except that they served as administrative centres and residences for the various local and visiting imperial officials whose business lay in the provinces. The local elite, who more and more preferred to live in their local town rather than on their estates, had a free hand in the running of the towns, in the governance and administration of which they, together with the local bishop and senior clergy, constituted the chief elements. The bishop, in fact, was generally a key member of this elite, and often had family connections with the middling and higher aristocracy of the town and its hinterland. This group supplied also many of the local state officials in both the civil and military administration, so that the interests of the families who were thus represented could be furthered with little real opposition. Indeed, the term used to describe them – *archontes*, a term which may be loosely translated as 'lords' – meant also an official or holder of an imperial post of some sort, and points to their origins. Like the more powerful magnates – who could also be classed as *archontes* – these local town elites represented that group of middling landowners who had supplied, and continued to supply, the local officers of the imperial administration. They likewise derived their income from land and from town property, for the recovery of urban markets and economies meant that town properties were more valuable than hitherto, so that substantial incomes could be drawn from urban rents. Thus the more stable economic situation of the empire together with the emergence of local landlords as an important element which would have the interests of their own town at heart, as much as a career at Constantinople (the centre of local society and economic activity), created a new element in the pattern of relations between capital and provinces. It meant that local interests could now be represented more vocally than hitherto, and also created a basis for opposition to the activities of fiscal officials sent from the imperial capital. The development of ties of patronage and dependence between these archontic families and their tenants and clients reinforced these local solidarities, generating an additional barrier between central government and local tax payers. As a result, the possibility of armed opposition to government officials also arose, and one or two examples of local revolts which were clearly inspired by popular or communal hostility to imperial fiscal policy are recorded in the sources. A good example is the rebellion, during the reign of Constantine X (1059-1067), of the townspeople of Larissa, a small *kastron* in Thessaly in Greece. Led by their *archontes*, they wished to protest against the imposition of extra taxes by Constantinopolitan officials. Although one of these local lords – a certain Nikoulitzas Delphinas – tried to warn the emperor, he was ignored and eventually ended up at the head of the rebels. The revolt ended peacefully, by negotiation (although the emperor broke the promises he made to its leaders), but signalled an important change in the relationship between Constantinople and the provinces.

Provincial *archontes* also developed a sense of local pride which encouraged both the investment of their wealth in towns and gave them a political identity; and through the relations of clientship and patronage which existed between the middling and upper levels of the elite, they were able to exercise substantial interest on behalf of their town. But towns never evolved corporate institutional identities in the Byzantine world, in contrast with Italy and western medieval Europe. In contrast, they remained the foci of these local elites, and it was they and the magnates with whom they were associated who exploited the towns for their own economic and political ends rather than vice versa; a fact which becomes especially clear during the civil wars of the first half of the fourteenth century. Unlike the greatest magnates of the empire, the local *archontes* resided in their provinces and towns, whereas the former generally chose to dwell, for political as well as cultural reasons, in their Constantinople mansions. This gave the local elites an advantage in respect of local commerce and industry, insofar as they were located where production took place, and were consequently in a position to be directly involved. There is some evidence that, while the imperial elite retained its somewhat snobbish attitude towards trade (discussed in Chapter 5 above), local landowners were much more willing to invest their own wealth in a variety of enterprises and be personally involved in these activities, even though this brought no improvement in social standing in respect of the imperial system. This distinction between local 'middling' elites and the great 'imperial' magnates of the various aristocratic clans who dominated the political and the wider economic scene survived until the end of the empire.

There seems also to have evolved a difference in the focus of economic activity between Asia Minor, or those regions which the empire controlled after the loss of the central plateau in the later eleventh century, and the Balkans, especially Greece and Thrace. The former seems to have remained predominantly agricultural, with towns serving chiefly as market centres for livestock, whereas in the latter, while all towns still depended, of course, on agriculture for their existence, artisanal production and cash-crop agriculture for market demands appears to have been a more prominent feature of life after the eleventh century. One of the obvious reasons for this difference is the fact that the empire had still to invest substantial resources from the Anatolian districts in defence and then in the maintenance of armies as well as the building of fortifications. The nature of the Anatolian market for agrarian

Relief, Church of the Taxiarchs, Areopolis.

and other produce was somewhat differently accented, and in eleventh- and twelfth-century Asia Minor, just as in the seventh and eighth centuries, much of the surplus that might otherwise have ended up in the market place was consumed by the state in the form of military supplies and related expenses. This was not – or was certainly less – the case in the Balkans, and goes some of the way to explaining the difference; while there is also some evidence that the government offered some fiscal inducements to some towns and communities which had formerly lain outside imperial control, in order to maintain their loyalty to the empire. But the difference might also lie in the pattern of communications and the fact that state fiscal structures were much more deeply embedded in the network of production, distribution and consumption of resources in Asia Minor than in the southern Balkan region.

In this respect, it seems likely that the role of Italian traders and the demand for Byzantine agricultural produce in the West played a particularly important role in the Balkan region. For it was here that Italian traders were most active; partly a reflection of the fact that southern Greece and the Peloponnese lay between Italy and Constantinople. Neither should we forget Constantinople, which continued to dominate and thus to distort the pattern of supply and demand in the regions around it, both in the north-western parts of Asia Minor and in Anatolia. In either case, external demand stimulated internal production for the market, with its various repercussions. The fact that, as we have noted already, Byzantine merchants were slowly squeezed out of the carrying business (albeit much later) does not alter this.

After the loss of central and eastern Anatolia, the structure of the aristocracy was altered in one very important respect, namely in the balance which had hitherto existed between the great Anatolian magnates who dominated the empire's military apparatus, and the bureaucratically-rooted element of the imperial elite. The great majority of powerful magnate families in the ninth to eleventh centuries came from the central, northern and eastern Anatolian regions, whose economy was dominated by pastoral exploitation and ranching. Imperial control in the southern Balkans had been minimal until the ninth century, so that powerful families from these regions were both fewer and, with one or two probable exceptions, newer. But with the loss of much of the former region the importance of the magnates with predominantly Balkan properties increased proportionately. Whereas the great Anatolian estates had been, for the most part, inland, those of the Balkan and Aegean region were mostly concentrated along the coast, and were thus in a position to profit from both local and long-distance markets. The state seems to have retained control of much of the interior of the Balkans by allocating substantial areas to imperial estates and appanages granted to members of the imperial family; and the fact that at least until the end of the twelfth century it retained and attempted to enforce the tenth-century legislation protecting the rights of peasant freeholders shows that this element of rural society remained an important fiscal resource for the government.

Further shifts in this balance occurred after 1204 and the Latin occupation of the central lands of the empire. Apart from their survival as rulers of the empire of Trebizond in the eastern Pontus, for example, the great clan of the Komnenoi virtually disappears from mainstrean imperial politics at Constantinople; a similar fate affected several other families which had played an important role in twelfth-century affairs. In the longer term, as the empire fragmented after the Fourth Crusade, the rulers of the successor states increasingly appointed members of their own families as governors of substantial regions, allocations which often became effectively hereditary. Even where they did not – and this process was by no means either universal or complete – it nevertheless involved the consumption of fiscal resources on a regional basis, rather than their being forwarded to the capital. The consequence was a substantial reduction in the income received by the central government, and a real increase in the constraints under which it had to function; while at the same time, revenues derived and consumed regionally rivalled those of the centre. In effect, in its last one hundred and fifty years, the empire was held together by family relationships between these more or less autonomous aristocratic groups, reinforced by the still-powerful belief in a single, unified imperial state which was a central pillar of the imperial ideology, as much as by any coherent administrative structure.

Bureaucrats and administrators

To a degree, the upper levels of the bureaucracy were always coterminous with the social elite of the empire: those who attained the more important imperial offices and titles, however humble their background and regardless of their race, were automatically co-opted into the elite, since they disposed of the wealth, contacts and status to exercise power and authority over those less fortunate than themselves; those who inherited wealth and social status invariably became part of that establishment, or that of the Church, at least after the middle of the seventh century. Before this time late Roman society was a little more pluralistic in the opportunities it offered for careers and status, given the existence of several important provincial cities such as Alexandria or Antioch. Yet there was an important middling stratum of officials who were both numerate and literate, at least insofar as they could maintain records, make assessments of fiscal and related demands, and carry out all the other functions necessary to the running of a fairly complex administrative system. They often rose by virtue of their talent and ability to high office and thereby became members of the 'elite' already discussed, so that there is, throughout the history of the empire, even in its last centuries when the aristocratization of the state establishment was well advanced, a constant flow of talent upwards into the higher state positions and thence, depending on circumstances, into the aristocracy.

The incentives to join the administrative establishment were considerable, not least the promise of a secure income and attendant status, but involving also (depending on the post achieved) a lucrative income from less formal sources: bribes, perquisites of the system, 'customary' payments for services rendered, and so on. Even quite humble officials could, depending on the context, be important, and were able to exploit the opportunities their posting might offer them. Most obvious in this respect were those associated with the assessment and collection of taxes, but others could equally benefit.

It should not be thought, however, that this system was, in its own terms, 'corrupt'. Most of the customary fees and perquisites taken by administrative officials were recognized by the government, and it is only when they become obviously excessive or unfair that we read of appeals and protestations. Whether anything was then done depended once again upon the political and historical context. Such protests in the tenth century often met with a favourable response, whereas in the later twelfth century the excessive greed and admitted corruption of provincial fiscal officials was widely recognized but rarely challenged. On the whole, and given the social values of Byzantine culture, the Byzantine administrative apparatus was no more corrupt than that of any other comparable pre-modern society supporting a fairly complex state system.

For bureaucrats and administrators at all levels the hierarchy of imperial ranks and offices embodied in the system of titles described in documents ranging from the later fourth to the thirteenth centuries was of crucial significance, for it summed up the means of their advancement as well as the outward forms that advancement would take. The imperial hierarchy was an ordered system embodying the notions of harmony and order – *harmonia* and *taxis* – symbolizing the divine order of the heavenly sphere, which the Christian Roman Empire was meant to emulate on earth, under the guidance of the divinely-appointed emperor. The emperor thus represented a concentration of power and authority, the imperial palace was the focus of that authority, and the officers of the palace were its agents. All agents of the state, down to the simple soldiers of the provincial armies, were part of this hierarchical order, and it brought together also the Church and the secular administration, since they were integrated at various levels in the same order of precedence. The principles were neatly summed up in the introductory passages of the so-called *Book of Ceremonies*; a mid-tenth-century compilation originally commissioned by the emperor Constantine VII (913-959), although completed only after his death:

> Many things are apt to disappear in the process of time... among them a
> great and precious thing, the exposition and description of imperial

ceremony. To neglect this ceremony, and to sentence it, so to speak, to death, is to be left with a view of the empire devoid of ornament and deprived of beauty. If the body of a man were not gracefully formed, and if its members were casually arranged and inharmoniously disposed, one would say that the result was chaos and disorder. The same is true of the imperial polity, for if it be not guided and ruled by order, it will in no way differ from vulgar deportment in a private person.

Constantine had, perhaps, an unusually historical perspective on such matters, and the average court official, and in particular those responsible for maintaining this system of ranks and precedence, had more practical concerns of ensuring that the titles and grades were properly observed during imperial ceremonies and at imperial banquets, which by the tenth century (if not much earlier) were described in notes and memoranda in order to ensure the correct procedures were followed. It is these notes which were assembled in the so-called *Kletorologion of Philotheos*, the 'hierarchy of the imperial table', produced in 899 by an imperial *atriklines* or chief butler, and which provide invaluable information on the system of precedence as well as the complete calendar of major imperial festivals and banquets for which this official was responsible. Although these lists also give a somewhat artificial account of the system, since they 'freeze' it at a particular moment in time when in reality the system was constantly evolving as new titles appeared, older titles were reduced in status, or the relationship between them was altered, they nevertheless demonstrate the importance of these ideas for the imperial court.

Bureaucrats and administrators were therefore entirely embedded in this system, which determined both their social status and income as well as the possibilities for their career and advancement. The whole structure depended upon the central position of the emperor, and the closer an official was to the emperor, the better his opportunities for promotion or advancement. Of course, patronage and 'interest' were also crucial elements, along with an ability to oil the wheels of the machinery with appropriate amounts of cash suitably dispersed, so that the system was never really meritocratic; and as time passed, the development of an aristocracy further biased the system away from individual talent towards one of interest and of connections.

Access to the state administration could be achieved through various means. In the period up to the seventh century, study of the law was always an excellent foundation, since this qualified one for court posts as well as provincial positions of authority and responsibility, although a general acquaintance with traditional classical scholarship was sufficient. During the later seventh and eighth centuries this changed, and we read in the introduction to the *Ecloga* of Leo III and Constantine V, issued in 741, that many provincial officials were entirely ignorant of the law and of the administration of justice. Although some illiterate officials are known from the sources, literacy and a decent education were, except in unusual circumstances, always an advantage, since this was a literate and record-keeping state administration which depended upon the transmission of vital information in written form, not just between officials, but from one generation to the next. By the tenth and eleventh centuries a knowledge of the law was once again regarded as an important part of the education of any would-be senior official. In the middle Byzantine period various sources describe how parents who had been able to provide their children with the appropriate basic education would then send them to the capital, where they would be placed under the protection of a relative who would supervise their further education, use his influence to obtain openings for them, help them to advance their careers, and so on. In return, of course, the children's immediate family would at some point be called upon to reciprocate in whatever ways were deemed appropriate. Such was the case of Euarestos, for example, a young man whose family sent him to Constantinople under the tutelage of his patrician relatives during the reign of Theophilos; or of a certain Theophylact, similarly despatched to the capital to take up a post secured for him through family patronage in the office of the imperial private secretary. Another case, of a certain Eudokimos, is similar. Coming from a wealthy Cappadocian family, he was educated at Constantinople, and on completing his studies received the dignity of *kandidatos* and an appointment to a command, first in Cappadocia and later in Charsianon. There are many other similar examples from the later eighth and ninth centuries and afterwards.

Such a system of connections and interest was not confined to families, of course: many wealthy persons maintained clients and a ramified system of patronage which operated in much the same way, with the principles of reciprocity and mutuality underlining their effectiveness. In theory, all posts were open to all persons, and even in the thirteenth century and after, when the aristocratization of the higher levels of the government was more-or-less complete, individuals of humble origins could still find their way to quite high positions. In practice, of course, and as already noted, the system was heavily inflected by the existence of a powerful social elite and the networks of patronage which were a part of any such society. And the ability of a family to pay for the schooling and tuition which would furnish their offspring with the requisite classical and Christian learning was clearly crucial. Yet in the fourteenth century, for example, Alexios Apokaukos, a simple scribe in the bureau of the *domestikos* of the provinces, was able to rise to the rank of Grand Duke – admiral of the fleet – and Eparch, or Prefect, of Constantinople.

By the same token, although the administrative hierarchy was graded according to military and non-military posts, as well as, by the tenth century, ranks normally held by eunuchs and non-eunuchs, this was not an exclusive system. There are many examples of officers holding posts which were technically not open to them. At the same time, clergymen and monks sometimes occupied state positions, often very powerful ones, since ultimately it was the emperor who decided who held which posts. In the late seventh century, the emperor Justinian II appointed his associate Theodotos, a monk, to the post of general finance minister, while a few years later a deacon of the Great Church in Constantinople, a certain John, was given command of a fleet. Such examples underline the centrality of physical proximity to the rulers and their circle, and serve to remind us that the apparently fixed hierarchy, in the various lists of grades and titles which have been preserved, tell only part of the story.

Officials were inducted into their posts by a formal ceremony at which they received the signs of their office – a ceremonial military girdle and a robe or other garment specific to their department and rank – and during which they swore an oath of loyalty to the emperor and declared their orthodoxy. By the ninth century the great majority of junior posts were conferred by the award of a token of office, so that the emperor did not need to be present. Senior posts, in contrast, which were of greater significance to the emperor and which were often directly chosen by him, were appointed by word of mouth at a ceremony formally conducted by the ruler and during which the official or officer, if the post was military, did formal obeisance to the emperor. Such ceremonies applied to the clergy of the Constantinopolitan churches also, since they, too, were members of this hierarchy of state positions. Promotion depended upon a regular rhythm of movement within each department; in the fifth and sixth centuries everyone moved up a grade each year, although originally the period had been longer. The extent to which this practice remained the same thereafter is impossible to say, although it is clear that during the eighth and ninth centuries the emperors did move the commanders of thematic regions fairly frequently, sometimes across to an alternative post, sometimes upwards. Where the move was from one post to another comparable one, however, the incumbent would sometimes receive a higher-ranking title, so that salary and social standing would rise accordingly. If all went well, an individual of reasonable talents could expect to rise to a fairly senior position by the end of his career and, if he came to the attention of the emperor or another powerful senior official, perhaps even become a senior minister or official himself. Salaries rose incrementally with promotion, and upon retirement, since there was no system of pensions as such, officials received an enhanced sum, together with certain judicial rights and sometimes also fiscal exemptions. Some administrative officials, especially in the period from the tenth century, sold their posts in advance of their retirement as a means of putting a sum aside.

The lower-ranking posts, while part of the scale of grades, had no titles attached to them. But the middling and higher-ranking functions were always accompanied by a title, which conferred a particular rank upon the holder; and with that title went also a salary. All titles, whether they involved active posts or not, had a salary attached to them, and we have already noted how complex the system of titles became during the late Roman period. Posts and titles could thus always be purchased, although this practice was formally permitted only from Leo VI, who was responsible for relaxing many of the stricter regulations governing bureaucratic behaviour and career structures. In particular, such purchases served as investments for the future – in view of the yearly income which accompanied them – and provided thus some security. The bureaucrat Michael Psellos bought a post as an investment for his son-in-law to-be in the mid-eleventh century, but then had to pursue the young man through the courts in order to recover his expenses when the engagement fell through. Those at court generally received their pay directly from the emperor – even quite lowly persons – during a long ceremony held during the Easter period; those in the provinces received their salary by courier or – again depending on the period and the local situation – from the revenues of the regions where they were based. Salaries consisted not just of pay (nearly always, except in special circumstances, issued in gold coin) but included also other items, such as silken garments, the production and dyeing of which were an important part of the imperial household industries.

The highest military and civil posts in the empire were, because of their functional importance, especially in the military sphere, rarely subject to the same abuses as the ordinary administrative-bureaucratic positions in the various departments of the central government. They were also much more directly in the emperor's eye, and were therefore not often subject to the normative pattern of bureaucratic advancement – it was the ruler who chose to hire and fire such senior officers, and this was done with an eye on their effectiveness and competence as much as for any other reason.

During the last two centuries of the empire's existence the members of the aristocratic elite of the empire assumed that all senior positions were theirs by right, and normally filled them. The administration came to be entirely dominated by members of a few family lineages such as the Tarchaneiotes, Philanthropenos, Branas, Tornikios and Synadenos families and others (together with members of the 'imperial' clans, such as the Palaiologos, Komnenos, Doukas and Laskaris families). But emperors still selected men according to their talents and suitability for the job as much as for their social origins and family, and many in the middling and lower levels of the fiscal administration, for example, were still drawn from the humbler levels of society. The so-called 'Pseudo-Kodinos', a mid-fourteenth-century treatise on imperial offices and dignities, shows that the hierarchy was still very much in place, although it had been substantially modified over time. The principles around which the bureaucracy and court service were traditionally based, certainly until the time of the Komnenos dynasty, had revolved around the notion of separation, at least in theory, of government administration from imperial household. In practice, the two had always merged at certain levels, so that officials of the imperial household had often been awarded state positions, in military, civil and ecclesiastical spheres. Under the Komnenos emperors the state had increasingly been treated as a family patrimony, with state officials describing themselves as *doulos* (servant) of the emperor. By the time of the composition of the 'Pseudo-Kodinos', a position in the imperial household and a kinship association with the imperial family, however attenuated, were the keys to government service. As time went on, government and imperial household effectively merged, with the result that the patrimonial system favoured by the rulers of the Komnenos dynasty eclipsed the vestiges of the late Roman bureaucracy which had dominated until the end of the eleventh century.

In spite of such changes, the East Roman Empire, a state whose roots lie in the late Roman world of the fourth and fifth centuries, retained a remarkably effective administrative apparatus for over a millennium. It would be no exaggeration to claim that this was, perhaps more than any other single factor, the reason for its survival for so many centuries against such heavy odds.

7 Church, state and belief

The evolution of the 'Established Church' (4th-7th centuries)

The political ideology of the East Roman world incorporated ancient traditions, Hellenistic, Roman, oriental and early Christian. The official theological system reflected the evolution of a formal, sophisticated set of beliefs in which different elements had contextually-different effects, and in which the syncretistic cultural backdrop to its development meant that a variety of pre-Christian traditions could play an important role. Christianity represented not simply the formal or official 'political theology' of the Roman world, it represented also a regional and individual system of moral values. It also came to constitute – certainly by the seventh century for the majority – the metaphorical space within which the world could be apprehended and through which it could be affected. While overtly pagan beliefs and cults had died out by this time, many of the day-to-day beliefs and practices which had formed part of the cultural universe of rural populations in particular for centuries, if not millenia, remained, and were given a Christian context and a Christian interpretational and explanatory gloss, when they were raised at all. This was the context in which both the Church and monastic structures had to operate, and it provides the essential context for an understanding of the ways in which Byzantines responded or reacted to the situations with which they were confronted; whether at the level of imperial politics or at that of individual beliefs and responses to personal issues.

The patriarchate of Constantinople was one of the five major administrative units into which the Christian Church had organized itself territorially within the Roman world, the others being Rome, Jerusalem, Antioch and Alexandria. Constantinople was the last to be raised to ecumenical status (that is to say, the superior status held by the other patriarchates), which it first claimed formally at the council held there in 381, but which was always contested by Rome (and which was not in fact formally adopted as part of the patriarch's title until the later ninth century). Each see had an apostolic tradition, and the history of their relations with one another are heavily inflected by claims and counter-claims about precedence and rights. The position of the patriarchate of Constantinople was enhanced by the fact that the city was also an imperial capital – and after 476, *the* imperial capital – but the Roman see never admitted Constantinopolitan equivalence. While the development of the see of Constantinople took place in an environment which transformed it slowly but surely into an 'imperial' Church, Rome was – with a few exceptions – independent of direct political influence from the emperors. One of the results was that Rome appeared at times as an independent authority, and conflicts within the Byzantine Church could be referred to Rome, with the result that the tensions between Rome and Constantinople were further heightened, on the one hand, and within the Byzantine world, between different factions within the Church, as well as between the secular power and one or another of these factions.

The Church represented one of the most powerful ideological and economic institutions of the late Roman and Byzantine world. By the early seventh century, Christianity of one variety or another was without doubt the majority belief system of the Roman world, although isolated pockets of pre-Christian traditions and cults survived in some areas. In philosophical terms it represented a theology which claimed universal validity and a system of belief based on faith in a messianic saviour, and during its first four hundred years of existence had evolved a sophisticated and highly-developed theological armoury. In practical terms it incorporated a plurality of ways of interpreting the world, influenced by the inherited patterns of belief from the cultural traditions in which it developed and upon which it had been imposed. Through its formal teaching and theology it was presented by the clergy and the literate and learned minority as the single correct form of belief – orthodoxy – even though its first centuries were marked by a series of intellectual and political clashes over the definitions at issue.

A fundamental feature of the East Roman Church was the close political-ideological relationship it held with the secular power, embodied by the emperor. The development in the fourth century of an imperial Christian ideological system rooted in both Romano-Hellenistic political concepts and Christian theology established an unbreakable association, which was thereafter to set limits to – yet also to legitimize – the actions of emperor and patriarch. In its most abstract form it was understood as a relationship of mutual dependence, but the onus was on the secular ruler both to defend correct belief as well as to protect the interests of the Church – in the form of the honour and respect accorded the priestly office – which catered for the spiritual needs of the Christian flock. As these ideas were expressed in the sixth century, the conviction that dominated was that the health of the state was assured only when the traditions of orthodox belief (as derived from the Apostles and the Fathers of the Church) are faithfully practised and handed down. This utopian expression of harmony and order – which the earthly kingdom was meant to strive to achieve, in imitation of Heaven – was reflected in imperial religious and secular politics and in the ways in which the emperors understood their practical role in respect of the Church, especially with regard to the convening of ecclesiastical councils and the incorporation of the principles embodied in these ideas in imperial legislation.

From the time of Constantine I, emperors were involved in both church politics and theological matters, and imperial legislation and long-established tradition ensured that, by the time of Justinian in the sixth century, secular ruler, state and Church were inextricably joined in a complex whole. Justinian I issued a novel, an edict, in 535 which summed up these developments, and in which were described the two great blessings with which mankind has been endowed – priest and emperor – both deriving from the same divine source. As God represented the ultimate source of law, so the emperor chosen by God was the ultimate source of earthly law; a formulation which – by defining the priestly authority strictly in terms of ministering to 'matters divine' – left some considerable scope for dissension thereafter.

During the later sixth and seventh centuries, imperial court ceremonial took on an increasingly 'liturgical' aspect which underlined the corporate identity of the secular and

Christ crowning the imperial couple, tenth-century ivory.

spiritual spheres; a development given further emphasis by the development of a Church-led coronation ceremony (that of the emperor Phokas in 602: thereafter all coronations took place in churches), which contrasted very obviously with the traditional highly militaristic and largely pre-Christian tradition through which emperors up until this time had been acclaimed and ratified. What began as the Church within the Roman Empire became by the seventh century – and even more obviously so after the Arab conquests – the East Roman imperial Church; fully integrated into the apparatus of the state and its political ideology, yet retaining at the same time a somewhat ambiguous position in respect of the emperors' rights to intervene in matters affecting dogma, however indirectly.

The tensions inherent in this relationship were most obvious when emperors involved themselves directly in matters of theology or ecclesiastical jurisdiction. Many emperors were themselves extremely able theologians, but they always represented a particular interest, and this was not always perceived by leading churchmen as the same as the interests of the Church. The nature of the conflict depended upon the perceptions of the parties involved and their understanding of the repercussions. There are numerous such conflicts between ruler and Church from the very beginning: the disagreement between the emperor Justinian and Pope Vigilius; the struggle between the government of Constans II and its official monothelete policies and the Churchmen and monks who joined the opposition led by Maximus Confessor, in the middle of the seventh century; the conflict between Germanos I

Tenth-century mosaic of Leo VI, St Sophia, Constantinople.

and the emperor Leo III (generally assumed to be over iconoclasm, but probably a disagreement over aspects of ecclesiastical jurisdiction); the conflict between the emperor Constantine VI and the patriarch Tarasios, over the emperor's remarriage; a similar conflict between Leo VI and the patriarch Nicholas I; the strife between the emperors and the churchmen who supported the opposing factions of Ignatios and Photios; tensions between the emperor Isaac I and the patriarch Keroularios; and the struggle between the supporters and opponents of hesychasm or of the unification of the Eastern with the Western Church during the fourteenth and fifteenth centuries. Depending on the character of those involved, the power constellations and other factors, the victor was sometimes the emperor, but just as often the Church, in the person of the patriarch. In the early stages the emperors were often able to use their secular power to their advantage – as with Justinian's bullying of Vigilius or Constans II's arrest and exile of Pope Martin. But as Italy became more indifferent to – or alienated from – the empire, so this became less possible; the failure of Justinian II's attempts to coerce the Pope is a good example. The patriarch at Constantinople was more exposed, but the strength of character of the two key figures then became an important element in whatever result was arrived at.

The loss of the eastern provinces to the Arabs in the seventh century solved one of the most difficult theological-political issues faced by the emperors of the period: how to overcome the hostility and suspicion which had evolved between the Chalcedonian, or dyophisite, Christians and the Monophysites of Syria and Egypt (see Chapter 1 above). Monotheletism had failed, but the loss of the provinces effectively removed the problem, at least as something which directly confronted the emperors on a day-to-day basis. Until then it had remained unclear as to which way the 'official' Church would eventually go, since several emperors or their consorts were either public or secret supporters of the monophysite position; most famously, perhaps, Justinian's empress, Theodora, who provided considerable cash subsidies to the 'shadow' monophysite Church in Syria. After the middle of the seventh century, however, Christological issues no longer rocked the Church: only the iconoclastic policies of the eighth and ninth centuries – which also had a Christological element – stimulated further major internal rifts, and it is by no means clear that these commanded the interest or commitment of more than a handful on either side, at least until the iconophiles rewrote the history of the period during the ninth and tenth centuries.

Heresy and heterodoxy were two of the constant issues which the Church and the emperors had to confront. The geographical and cultural variety of the Byzantine world meant that in many regions traditional, pre- or non-Christian practices could linger on unobserved for centuries, albeit in isolated and relatively limited groups. By the same token, heterodox beliefs could evolve which might, and did in some cases, evolve into major challenges to the imperial authority. The local and ecumenical councils tried to grapple with some of the causes for heresy: the lack of clerical discipline or supervision in far-flung regions; the ignorance of some of the lower clergy as well as of the ordinary populace; or the arrival of immigrant population groups with different views or different understanding of the basic elements of Christianity. Thus the Church was constantly active in this respect, often on a very low-key basis. But occasionally it had to confront a major heretical movement, in which the state would almost without exception be closely involved; it was, after all, the emperor's responsibility to defend and expand Orthodoxy. Such was the case, for example, with Paulicianism in eastern Asia Minor in the middle of the ninth century. Paulicianism (named probably after one of its early exponents, Paul of Samosata) was by the ninth century a mixture of dualist and neo-Manichaean elements, although its early history, from the later seventh century, suggests a more orthodox original doctrine. It had probably evolved much earlier. But only in the ninth century, when it appears to have become especially popular and powerful in the regions around Tephrike (modern Divriği in eastern Turkey), did the government take note of it, and begin to put pressure upon its members, and then actively to persecute it. The result was the military mobilization of the Paulicians under a series of very able commanders, an alliance with the Caliphate in the 870s, and a full scale war, waged by the emperor Basil I, which led eventually to its destruction.

Throughout the later seventh, eighth and into the ninth centuries the government had followed a policy of moving populations – sometimes in huge numbers – from parts of Asia Minor to the Balkans, especially southern Thrace, in order to repopulate that devastated region. People with Paulician beliefs numbered among these, and by the later eleventh century had influenced the evolution of a local heretical tendency, primarily among the Slavic populations of Bulgaria and the western Balkans. Known as Bogomilism – possibly after one of its early founders, the priest Bogomil – it shared the dualist heritage of the Paulicians, appearing in Bulgaria during the tenth century. Although fiercely persecuted by the emperors, especially by Alexios I, and eradicated from Constantinople, it spread throughout the Balkans and represented a major strand in the religious culture of the region. By the thirteenth century it had adherents in Asia Minor, and it exercised also an important influence over the development of the Cathar movement in southern France.

As well as these major heretical movements, the Church had to combat many much less significant heterodox beliefs. It also had to contend with Judaism, a religion with which Christianity had from its very beginnings an ambiguous relationship, the more so since the Jews, by failing to acknowledge the Messiah, had lost their status as the Chosen People, which had now transferred to the Romans. In general, until the sixth century, Jews were officially tolerated, although often treated with considerable prejudice. From the reign of Justinian, however, they became increasingly isolated within the Roman world. This process was greatly exacerbated by the results of the Persian and then the Islamic conquests, for which the Jews were partially – and quite irrationally – held to be responsible, a development which reflects the introversion and defensiveness with which East Roman culture seems to have responded to the catastrophic losses and defeats of the seventh century. Thereafter Jews were prohibited from a wide range of public activities as well as participation in the state in any form, were regularly persecuted, and frequently blamed for whatever ills befell the empire. They were not alone in this, since various heretical groups were usually listed alongside them, but they were regularly singled out for ill-treatment. In all these examples, the close relationship between secular and spiritual authority is evident, for it was, of course, only through the armed might of the state that the Orthodoxy of the day could be properly and effectively enforced or defended, at least within the empire's borders.

Church administration

Bishops typified the growing importance of the Church both spiritually and institutionally within the empire. Bishops were by the sixth century recognized as key members of city governing councils. They were, as managers of Church lands in their sees, major controllers of economic resources; a position they maintained throughout the history of the empire and beyond. Such was the wealth accumulated by the Church by the later sixth century that one estimate has suggested that the resources it consumed to maintain its charitable institutions, its clergy and episcopate, its public ceremonial and its public buildings were greater even than those of the state (excluding the army, of course). This wealth was mostly in land, although substantial amounts were invested in gold and silver or in buildings. The Church derived a large income from rents from its numerous estates, Church lands and property, whose importance was clearly understood; the canons, or laws, of the general council held at Constantinople in 692, known as the Quinisextum, included prescriptions about bishops staying in areas subject to hostile attacks in order to look after their flocks.

Charitable foundations were a major focus for the Church's philanthropic activities, but they had to be supported, and were usually funded by the rents from large estates. Orphanages, hospitals and almshouses were built and maintained, some by private persons after they had decided to endow their lands, sometimes by the Church itself. The importance of the Church in the state is reflected in the establishment by the emperors of various imperial charitable houses, illustrating the ideological importance of such commitments. Vast amounts of land were given to the Church over the centuries, sometimes in large bequests from wealthy persons, just as often in the form of tiny parcels of land willed to the Church by the less well-off. Church land could not be alienated – once devoted to God, always devoted to God – so that the accumulation could only grow. In fact, the use of emphyteutic leases, by which life-long and often hereditary lease contracts were agreed, meant that land frequently did fall outside Church control and supervision.

Church administration followed the secular organizational pattern of the late Roman Empire. Below the patriarch were metropolitan bishops, autocephalous archbishops, and bishops. The first was the senior cleric in each province, and was personally appointed by the Patriarch. Bishops were elected by provincial synods which all bishops attended, and until the sixth century the ordinary clergy and congregation of the region also had some influence, at least in nominating candidates. The bishop was the highest-ranking Church official in his region, with both the regular clergy as well as any monastic communities present under his authority. Bishops were leaders of their communities spiritually and politically. Many bishops had been martyred during the great persecutions of the later third and early fourth century, and the position of bishop was one to which considerable esteem was attached, but of which expectations were accordingly high. Bishops were based in cities, and insofar as the bishops' jurisdiction extended over the *territorium* of his city, the ecclesiastical administration of the empire preserved the late Roman secular administrative pattern of the Roman world well beyond the period of urban transformation which stretches from the later sixth into the ninth century. The task of the bishop was threefold: seek out and combat heresy; ensure that orthodoxy prevailed; and impose and apply Church law. As we have already noted, he was also the chief manager of Church lands, giver of charity to the poor and needy, as well as the leading ecclesiastical authority and judge in his district. He presided over the Church courts regarding clerical mores and correctness, and he arbitrated in cases involving conflicts between laypersons and the Church. Indeed, from the early seventh century the clergy had an especially-privileged legal status, to prevent their being mistreated at the hands of secular authorities. Bishops were generally, although by no means exclusively, drawn from the more privileged and the best-educated sections of society, and as such they shared all the vices as well as the virtues of ordinary mortals.

While responsible for the physical as well as spiritual welfare of their flock, bishops tended also to share the views of the privileged elite from which they were drawn, so that those based in the provinces in particular have left letters bewailing their fate, relegated as they felt themselves to be to regions of cultural darkness and barbarism. Of course, such images are often deliberately overdrawn for effect, and many bishops and senior clergy in the provinces were thoroughly committed to the care of their congregations. There certainly were corrupt and dishonest clergy, but there is little clear evidence of the degree of these problems. A major concern of the Church throughout the empire, and as aspect in which bishops played a fundamental role, was in public welfare: bishops were responsible within their sees for the organization of charitable activities, in particular the relief of the poor. Such activities depended, naturally, on the commitment and involvement of individuals, so that there is no uniformity of practice across the empire. Many bishops did very little, in contrast to those of whom we read in the sources who

Church of Sts Sergius and Bacchus, sixth-century, Constantinople.

funded the construction of alms-houses, hospitals, refuges for lepers, and so on. On the other hand, bishops and senior clergy might also be actively involved in politics, both secular and ecclesiastical. Bishops were often asked to speak out for particular individuals, or for certain groups in their jurisdiction: the poor peasants suffering from heavy taxation, for example, at one extreme, or the imperial official seeking redress from the emperor for political victimization. The extent to which bishops were successful depended largely on their contacts – their own network of connections at court and in the government – as well as on their ability to present the case convincingly, and on the context and personalities concerned. Senior clergy – bishops especially – had the right to exercise *parrhesia*, 'freedom of expression', which they often did, particular in respect of powerful secular figures – emperors, imperial officials and so on – on behalf of their flock or in order to speak out against what they perceived as unorthodox beliefs or behaviour. This often got them into trouble, especially where a patriarch, for example, attempted to oppose a strong-willed or determined emperor in respect of some issue of state affairs or high Church politics.

Surprisingly, perhaps, the Church only gradually established itself and its moral code as the arbiters of social and family practices such as marriage, leaving this ground to the traditional Roman civil law and the courts of provincial or central governors, at least until the later eleventh century. Traditional Roman law sometimes came into conflict with Christian canon law. An example of this is that the laws governing matrimony were Roman, and allowed the dissolution of the marriage as long as both parties agreed (with all the complexities arising from the property settlement), but the Church was most unhappy with this, for canon law prescribed that marriage could only be dissolved in the case of adultery. Yet it was only in 1084 that the emperor Alexios I conceded complete jurisdiction in such matters to the Church courts, even though the civil courts had long since recognized the difficulties in dealing with such issues, and tried to reach a compromise in many cases.

On the whole, the clergy of the Byzantine Church did not involve themselves in secular civil – and certainly not military – matters (in contrast to the western clergy who shocked Byzantine commentators by their active participation in fighting during the First Crusade). Regulations and customs prohibiting fighting, even to defend or protect their congregation or churches, seem to have been closely adhered to, and several sources describe the punishment of clergy who transgressed these rules, even with the best of intentions. But they were involved in the day-to-day politics of their world, indeed they could hardly avoid being so. As spiritual leaders of their communities, as representatives of the Church, and as managers of sometimes substantial resources in land, their views were always important. They possessed an intimate knowledge of local conditions, had good contacts with the leading members of society in their sees, and were often (by no means always) in touch with popular opinion. In times of political turmoil, the role of bishops was crucial, since it was they who might give a lead to a particular faction, and they were in any case expected to judge the rights and wrongs of such matters. Bishops could not ignore such affairs, and since they were invariably drawn into political events, they frequently suffered the consequences, especially if they chose the wrong side. The political significance of senior provincial as well as metropolitan clergy was recognized by the emperors, which explains their interest in the selection and appointment to such posts, since bishops could often lend crucial support to a particular emperor's policies. Emperors were always interested, therefore, in the appointment of bishops and metropolitans, and conflict over such appointments reflects the realities of imperial and provincial politics: for example, during the iconoclastic period, in which the support of the vast majority of the bishops for the imperial cause was probably a major factor in the stability of the rule of the emperors from Leo III to Leo IV; or during the slow recovery of imperial territory in western Anatolia during the first half of the twelfth century, when the support of the local clergy was a crucial element in the process of consolidation of recovered lands and the re-establishment of an effective administration. By the same token, senior clergy often acted effectively as imperial officials, representing the government or an emperor on foreign missions and embassies, getting involved in international politics, taking decisions independently and on the spur of the moment to deal with unforeseen situations, and so on.

In one respect, the political influence of the clergy did change. From the fourth century, there had been a resident synod at Constantinople, presided over by the patriarch, dealing with affairs of ecclesiastical discipline, dogma and liturgical matters, and made up of the bishops resident around Constantinople or visiting it from more distant sees. From the ninth century, its membership was limited to senior bishops (metropolitans and those with autocephalous sees) and patriarchal officials, but from the 1070s it grew dramatically as refugee bishops from the Seljuk occupation of much of Asia Minor progressed, and accordingly seems to have become much more influential in both ecclesiastical and, more significantly, in imperial politics. This development parallels the growing importance of canon law in relation to civil law, which can be observed over the same period, a development which was to become increasingly pronounced during the later centuries of Byzantine history. At the same time, the increasing autonomy of provincial towns, during the eleventh and twelfth centuries, from the capital and its elite, and the fragmentation of the empire's territory from the thirteenth century, meant that the bishops were more than ever foci of both political and social as well as moral authority. The Church courts came to play an ever greater role in the administration of justice and in the everyday affairs of the ordinary population. The influence and the moral and political status and authority of the Church in the provinces was thereby considerably enhanced, encouraging greater feelings of local pride and autonomy, as well as the readiness of provincial elites to question the actions and motives of the court or the elements which dominated it.

Emperors and patriarchs: spiritual authority, secular power

The close association of secular and ecclesiastical politics is most obvious in respect of the relations between emperors and their patriarchs. Emperors took a keen interest in the appointment of a patriarch, and it was very rarely that anyone became patriarch without imperial support, or survived for long if they did. In the period from the sixth to the fifteenth century more than 30% of all patriarchs were forced to resign or were deposed from office when they clashed with an emperor over some matter or other. Relations between patriarchs and emperors had two aspects, however: on the one hand – as a close affiliate of the ruler – patriarchs were in a position to influence imperial policy and play a key role in court politics. They were responsible, after the early seventh century, for coronations as well as other major events involving the imperial household, such as weddings, baptisms and funerals. On the other hand, outside this 'personal' relationship, patriarchs were in a powerful position to influence Church and public opinion for or against a particular ruler, so it was essential that the candidate chosen should be known to the emperor and trusted by him. Where this was not the case, tensions between the two often led to major political clashes involving much more than the imperial household or the population of Constantinople. Most major clashes occurred over doctrinal matters, although the line between doctrinal and personal was often difficult to see. The question of the emperor Leo VI's fourth marriage, for example, involved both a major doctrinal issue as well as a problem of local imperial politics, and was especially important in respect of patriarchal authority.

Throughout the history of the empire the relationship between emperor and patriarch remained fraught with tension. On the one hand, emperors were regarded as the defenders of Orthodoxy, and as such they invested considerable sums in building and decorating churches and endowing monasteries as symbols of their piety, as well as, in many cases, developing an advanced knowledge and understanding of the finer aspects of Christian theology. They also intervened directly in matters of strictly theological import; an aspect of their authority inscribed in the definition and assumptions about their role. This frequently led to clashes between emperors and patriarchs, on occasion the deposition of a patriarch, and the polarization of opinion within the Church. The emperor Justinian had attempted a general definition of this relationship in the sixth century, in which the Church and the clergy were defined by their role as pastoral and spiritual guardians of the Christian community, but within which the emperor's position, while not above the law, was nevertheless seen as the embodiment of the law, since he was chosen and appointed by God. The application of these concepts in reality was problematic. In 543, for example, Justinian issued an edict condemning three 'pro-Nestorian' texts ascribed to the writers Theodore of Mopsuestia, Theodore and Ibas of Edessa. The intention was thereby to conciliate the monophysites and to make the Roman Pope, Vigilius, accept the result. But while Vigilius initially bowed to imperial pressure, the Western clergy led by its bishops disowned Vigilius. In 553, an ecumenical council at Constantinople, at which the Western Church was heavily outnumbered, condemned both the 'Three Chapters', as they became known, and the Roman Pope. But the strength of ecclesiastical opinion eventually compelled Justinian to compromise, and his effort to bully the Church as a whole failed.

In situations where serious conflict within the Church or, at least, within the empire and between different elements of the Church, developed the spiritual power appears on the whole to have had the greater success, although this often involves taking a very long-term view. In the 640s, for example, and in his attempts to enforce the Monothelete policy (see Chapter 2 above), the emperor Constans II and his advisers had both Pope Martin and the main leader of the anti-Monothelete movement, Maximus, arrested and tried. But importantly, they were tried on charges of treason, accused of slandering the emperor and betraying imperial security to rebels or to outside enemies. The evidence of the trial and interrogation records, which have been partially preserved in an admittedly biased account compiled by Maximus' supporters, makes it clear that the emperor wanted recognition of his authority and acceptance of his decisions above all – the niceties of the theological issue were, in fact, of secondary importance. The imperial government won the struggle by effectively cutting out the leadership of the opposition. But this was at the expense of alienating the Western Church once more, and unity was only restored when, following Constans' death in Sicily in 668, his son and successor, Constantine IV, summoned the sixth ecumenical council of the Church at Constantinople in 680 and abandoned Monotheletism. Its only strong adherents thereafter remained the Christian communities of what is now the Lebanon and the region of Antioch, who have survived in the form of the Maronite Church to this day.

A similar situation, but with very much graver and long-lived consequences, as well as major theological results, can be observed in the earliest phase of iconoclasm. Whatever the reasons which encouraged him, in the late 720s the emperor Leo III imposed a public ban on the use of holy images in certain contexts; a policy which was supported by much of the clergy, or – at least – seems not to have been very actively opposed. But there was some opposition, resulting in 730 in the abdication of the patriarch Germanos (although only much later sources attribute this to his opposition to imperial iconoclasm) and the appointment thereafter of a series of patriarchs chosen by the emperors Leo and his son Constantine V for their willingness to accept and support the imperial policy. When the empress Eirene planned a change in this policy, she was careful to work through her own appointee, the former layman Tarasios, whose diplomatic skills and ability to persuade permitted a relatively smooth transition to the acceptance once more of icons, and who was responsible for the planning and the procedures followed at the seventh ecumenical council, held at Nicaea (after a failed initial attempt the year before in Constantinople) in 787. With a somewhat different background and different stimuli, the emperor Leo V reintroduced imperial iconoclasm in 815, and again it was the choice of patriarch which facilitated the implementation and pursuit of the policy. In the end, of course, imperial iconoclasm aroused little mass support and was supplanted relatively easily in the 840s. It was chiefly the iconophile writers, hagiographers and apologists in the period 787-815 and after 842 who made such a meal of it, branding the iconoclastic emperors as satanic tools and heretics, and in the process lionizing what opposition (especially among some monastic circles) there had been.

The story is similar in later centuries. But while the emperors might sometimes lose the struggle in the longer term, it was they who determined what counted as Orthodoxy at the time, and it was in the meanwhile individual patriarchs who suffered if they objected or challenged this. This was even more clearly the case in purely political matters, in which theology and dogma played no role at all. On his accession in 867, Basil I deposed the learned patriarch Photios because the latter's rapid rise – from lay status to the position of head of the imperial Church – had alienated both Rome and a substantial section of the Byzantine clergy. Although Photios recovered his position after the death of Basil's first choice, Photios' arch-rival Ignatios, he was deposed again by Basil's successor Leo VI in 886, and exiled, not only because Leo feared Photios' influence and possible opposition, but also because Photios began to elaborate the theory of the patriarchal position in the direction of raising his status in the hierarchical relationship God-emperor-patriarch at the expense of that of the emperor; a direct challenge to one aspect of the imperial authority. The eleventh-century patriarch Michael Keroularios, who was in part responsible for the success of the coup d'état which brought the soldier-emperor Isaac I Komnenos to the throne in 1057, soon found himself deposed by his protégé when he acted too independently of the emperor's will. A similar fate awaited the talented patriarch John Bekkos in 1282, an able diplomat and Church politician who served the emperor Michael VIII very ably. But upon Michael's death he was immediately removed from office, since he represented the unionist faction at court – those who wished to join the Byzantine and Western Churches together – and was outmanoeuvred at this crucial moment by those who opposed his ecclesiastical views.

Yet Photios' attempt to rewrite the theory of the relationship between emperor and patriarch reflects a marked shift in the nature of this relationship after the end of iconoclasm, at least in respect of issues of morality, since – from the time of the patriarch Tarasios – patriarchs appear more frequently to have intervened in matters of personal imperial lifestyle, most clearly in issues around imperial marriages and divorce. It is true that the patriarch Sergius had challenged the validity of Heraclius' marriage to his niece Martina, but the emperor had been able to persuade him to withdraw his objections. In contrast, Tarasios challenged Constantine VI's second marriage, on the grounds that he had divorced his first wife, Maria of Amnia, in order to marry his mistress Theodote. But Constantine threatened to reintroduce an iconoclastic policy and the patriarch remained silent. Although Tarasios lost this battle, the confrontation foreshadowed more difficult clashes to come. The patriarch Ignatios, who accused the Caesar Bardas (uncle of the emperor Michael) of adultery, was forced to resign rather than remain silent; the patriarch Nicholas I challenged the legitimacy of the emperor Leo's fourth marriage, and although he was deposed, his return to power permitted him to vindicate his opposition. In the 960s the patriarch

Polyeuktos fiercely denounced the emperor Nikephoros II's suggestion that soldiers who died fighting non-Christians should be treated as martyrs, with the result that the emperor had to abandon the idea; while the same patriarch also insisted – successfully – that John I Tzimiskes should depose and banish his mistress, the empress and wife of the murdered Nikephoros, for her complicity in the plot, before the new emperor could be crowned. Indeed, John had openly to beg forgiveness and act out his penance before the patriarch Polyeuktos before the latter would consent to crown him and give him legitimacy.

Emperors were more often successful in their conflicts with patriarchs than vice versa: in the ninth and tenth centuries alone four patriarchs – Ignatios, Photios, Nicholas I and Euthymios – were deposed when they refused to accept the imperial line, yet all four are recognized as outstanding churchmen and theologians in their own way. But the ambiguous relationship between emperors and patriarchs – varying from friendly support to open opposition – is summed up in the act of penance which an emperor might on occasion volunteer – or be required – to perform, to atone for his sins and other transgressions. And although emperors usually won the day when looked at from the short-term point of view, there were plenty of occasions when patriarchs were able to mobilize sufficient and effective opposition to prevent an emperor having his own way, as several of the examples already cited show.

A final point worth noting, and one that becomes particularly apparent towards the end of the empire's existence, is the fact that the relationship between Church and state was an evolving one, if only because the territory actually controlled by each changed over the centuries. In the period up to the middle of the seventh century the five patriarchates, although challenged by the existence of various regional oppositional movements such as monophysitism, had administered between them the whole Orthodox world. After the loss of the three eastern patriarchates, Constantinople controlled effectively only those lands controlled by the imperial government. Yet from the 860s the Orthodox world began to expand, first with the conversion of Bulgaria, then the central and western Balkans and then, from the end of the tenth century, with the conversion of the Rus'. The patriarchate of Constantinople did not administer these lands directly, of course, but it always retained an ideological hegemony, even in the last days of the empire. The result was a certain imbalance in the relationship between emperor and patriarch, since the latter actually exercised authority over a much wider world, a more 'ecumenical' world than that of the political empire of East Rome. It is understandable, in this context, that patriarchs often felt they had authority, and indeed a duty, to pronounce in political as well as moral matters, since the whole Orthodox world looked to them, as much as to – or even rather than to – the emperor of the Romans, for spiritual and moral guidance. In practice, naturally, this depended very much on the actual political situation of the time: the emperors of the late fourteenth century could hardly command the political or moral respect which their predecessors in the late tenth century had possessed.

The situation of the patriarchate towards the end of the twelfth century provides a clear example of what happened when the Church failed to give a moral lead when people expected it to do so. Already under the emperors from Alexios I to Manuel I there had been a clear tendency for the ruler to assert a moral authority over the Church, partly in response to the dangers presented by heresy, and to intervene increasingly in its organizational affairs. After the coup which placed Andronikos Komnenos on the throne in 1182, the patriarch Theodosios Boradiotes was forced to resign, and was replaced by a supporter of the usurper who, ignoring canon law, permitted a marriage between Andronikos' illegitimate daughter and the illegitimate son of Manuel Komnenos (they were cousins, and their relationship fell within the prohibited degrees of affinity). For the next twenty years the patriarchal throne was the victim of imperial bullying, frequently over quite petty matters, and as a result lost enormously in moral authority. Only under the first emperors of Nicaea, after Constantinople itself had been lost, were the patriarchs able to reassert their moral authority as well as their political influence. In the context of popular fear and hostility directed at the West, and in particular at the idea that the Orthodox should subordinate their Church to Rome, this gave the Church – represented by the great mass of the ordinary clergy and bishops who were fiercely opposed to the union – a greatly enhanced role in the day-to-day politics of Byzantines; for it was the Church rather than the state to which people turned for leadership in such matters. Together with the increasing importance of provincial towns and their bishops, these factors contributed still further towards the gradual tilting of the balance in favour of the Church and away from the state.

Monasteries: the wilderness in the city

As well as the secular Church, with its vast lands, stock of buildings, and numerous clergy, monastic communities also played a significant role. Indeed, the majority of bishops was drawn from a monastic background, since this lent them a certain spiritual authority. It also reflected the fact that, since the lower clergy were often married with families (whereas bishops were supposed to be celibate and single) a monastic background provided a greater pool of potential recruits to the episcopate. Yet the monastic life represented a rather different set of values to those implicit in the functions and activities of a bishop. Monasticism in Byzantium represented the alternative both to the secular Church and to life in 'the world'. Its origins – in late third-century Egypt and in Syria and Palestine during the fourth century – lie in the particular conditions of that time, but it rapidly assumed a universal relevance for the late Roman world, and underwent a dramatic expansion during the period up to the sixth century. In spite of efforts on the part of the Church and the state – embodied in particular in the acts of the council of Chalcedon in 451, and repeated in Justinian's legislation – to exercise some control over monasticism, its diversity and its anti-authoritarianism and spiritual utopianism represented a source of independence from the established structures of Christian life. Later councils, including the Quinisext of 691, repeated or expanded on some or all of these regulations, but on the whole with little real effect.

Monasteries and monks, and the even less-readily controlled individual hermits and 'holy men' who separated themselves from society by dwelling in the countryside away from other human settlement – frequently choosing quite deliberately a region of wilderness or desert in order to emphasize their withdrawal – often exercised a spiritual and moral authority gained through their lifestyle and their struggle with the forces of evil, which the regular Church could not. But this means neither that monasteries turned their back on the world – quite the reverse – nor that all such individuals were either successful or indeed genuine. Indeed, we occasionally glimpse examples in the sources of 'holy men' who were more akin to magicians and sooth-sayers than to monks and fighters for the faith; men and women who are accused of sorcery and black magic. In fact, there seems to have existed a continuum of practice reflected in the activities of such individuals. At one extreme was the genuinely committed Christian hermit whose social and cultural marginalization gave him, or her, the sort of spiritual power and authority admired in the hagiographical literature. At the other extreme were those who were unable to attain this sort of spiritual purity but who indulged in various forms of more-or-less harmless magic and healing practices. But even the most illustrious holy men of the Byzantine world were involved in what can only be described as semi-magical practices: the eighth/ninth-century monk Ioannikios, a hero of the hagiographical tradition, is described quite innocently by his biographer as exercising power over wild animals and of making them follow his commands, acts which directly contravened certain canons of the Church. There are several other examples.

Monasteries, like the Church, could be endowed with and could own property, in land or other forms. Some monasteries became substantial landlords with considerable estates, and the efforts of the Church to retain some degree of control over monastic establishments gave the bishops of the regions where they were to be found an important role. It also led to tensions and conflict: the agreement of the local bishop was necessary in order to establish a monastery, and each such establishment owed the local episcopate a regular tax, called the *kanonikon*. Elections of abbots and their consecration was also the responsibility of the bishop, and arguments over both the payment of the episcopal tax and the choice of abbot were not infrequent. Monasteries attracted the attention and support of lay persons from all ranks in society, from emperors to the humblest peasant, who endowed them with land for the salvation of their souls – for which the monks would be bound to pray – and who sometimes retired there when they had had enough of the world. Many soldiers, particularly quite high-ranking officers from relatively well-off backgrounds, are known to have entered the monastic life at the end of their careers – perhaps because they had been involved in the taking of human life – sometimes establishing their own monastery which they then directed as abbot themselves. Indeed, entering a monastery was a popular way of 'retiring' in the Byzantine world.

Monasteries varied enormously. Some remained very small, with a complement of a few monks, and many such monasteries seem to have survived for only a generation or so. Others became immensely successful and very wealthy. The extent of monastic property at any given period cannot be calculated with any degree of accuracy, but it was certainly considerable – enough by the later tenth century to cause some anxiety to the government in respect of fiscal and manpower resources. The lifestyles associated with such establishments also varied, from the 'idiorrhythmic', in which individuals followed their own daily rhythm, eating and worshipping independently of one another with hardly any communal activities, to the cenobitic (from the Greek *koinos bios*, 'common life'), in which all followed the same communal timetable for worship, meals, work and meditation. Monastic centres flourished in Constantinople, in the Aegean region, in north-western

Monastery of Panteleemon, Mount Athos (the 'Holy Mountain').

Asia Minor, in parts of the Balkans, in Cappadocia and in the Pontus; the most famous, with its origins in the later ninth century, remains to this day a substantial focus of monastic activity, on the Chalkidiki peninsula to the east of Thessaloniki, at Mt. Athos, the 'Holy Mountain'. But it is easy to overestimate and to exaggerate the size of such communities. While the number of monks may at times have been considerable, the empire was never overwhelmed by them: on the contrary, and as noted already, many joined monasteries only upon their retirement, while there are examples known of those who, having joined, later, left to take up a secular career once more. Just as importantly, the variety of types of monastery and the variation in the activities and lives of the monks diluted the overall effect of 'monasticism' in the Byzantine world. Monasticism was not a monolithic structure, but rather a very diverse range of communities and ways of living, and it was this very diversity which contributed to the particularity of Byzantine society and culture.

In many respects monks constituted an alternative source of spiritual authority, a type of authority which challenged implicitly the formally-endowed authority of the regular clergy and the Church. Such authority was won by men and women who demonstrated their piety and their spiritual worth by enduring hardships, physical and emotional, through which they were thought to gain a more direct and fuller access to God, and thus at the same time met the superstitious needs of ordinary people at all levels of society in respect of the difficulties and problems they confronted in their daily lives. The Church in the Byzantine world was never able to impose the sort of control and order upon the monastic life which the papacy developed, nor did it ever really seek to do so. On the contrary, access to the holy and to God in the East Roman world remained more widely available, so that the pluralism of spiritual authority shared by the Church, monasteries and individuals gifted with special authority created a much less readily controlled set of religious institutions. Monks thus figured prominently in the political as well as the religious life of the Byzantine world – although the two are hardly to be separated – acting as pressure groups, as representatives of popular as well as marginal opinion, as well as, at an individual level, as spiritual guides and advisers to persons of high as well as humble status.

This is especially the case after the end of the first period of iconoclasm when, rightly or wrongly (the later tradition was written from a very pro-monastic perspective, making it difficult to judge what really occurred), monks, and especially those of certain monasteries in and around the imperial capital, were hailed as the heroes of the anti-iconoclast opposition, who had led the struggle against heresy and wickedness. Thereafter we find monks intervening very often in matters of morality, and it is also interesting to note that many more patriarchs of the post-iconoclastic period came from a monastic background than had previously been the case. Some monks or holy men achieved indeed a considerable degree of openness when speaking with emperors and persons of similar rank, to the extent that they could influence imperial policy in ways which even a patriarch might find difficult. Such cases are not common, but the fact that they occur at all is important. At a humbler, day-to-day level, many high-ranking people had their own spiritual adviser – often a monk – to help with difficult decisions and provide guidance. Monks and monasteries played a central role in the cultural-ideological politics of the Byzantine world.

They also played a key role in controlling the forces of darkness and any mischievous elements which were thought to threaten the order of things. The world of the Byzantines, who were as superstitious as any other people, was inhabited not just by human beings and the rest of God's creatures, but also by a host of minor or major spirits, and people needed help in holding off or controlling such beings. This was done most effectively by those practised and experienced in such matters, who had themselves struggled against evil and overcome it. Those who followed a visibly ascetic life, whether they were monks or clergymen, had an obvious advantage in this respect, for they had tested themselves against the ideals preached by the Fathers of the Church in abjuring material things and the cares of the world for the sake of trying to attain as great a degree of spiritual purity (and hence of power to ward off evil) as possible.

Such persons could also act as spiritual advisers, and were hence essential links in the Byzantine world between the daily life of the ordinary subjects of the emperor, whatever their social and economic position, and the purity of soul to which all Christians were enjoined to aspire. Given the eschatological framework within which Byzantines were taught to understand the world – the second coming would follow the destruction of the Roman Empire – the importance of leading a life of piety and righteousness was crucial to one's ultimate fate. The vast majority of ordinary folk had neither the time nor the inclination for a life of chastity, fasting and spiritual purification, and so monks and monasteries took on an especial significance as centres of piety and orthodox belief, defending, so to speak, the reputation and guarding the morals of society as a whole. Indeed, written advice to the faithful stresses that the path of the ascetic was only for those who were thoroughly committed to things of the spirit and who had no earthly encumbrances – such as children and similar responsibilities – and that observing the basic rules of orthodox piety (prayer, communion, attending church, following a Christian way of life and moral code as interpreted and laid down by the Church) would suffice to permit one to pass through the gates of Heaven. But this attitude also explains in part the vehement response of some monks to imperial or patriarchal policies which were felt to stray away from the strictly orthodox, while it also serves to clarify the reactions of ordinary people on occasion in this respect. It likewise explains why monks, or those who had developed a reputation (through especially pious behaviour) for being able to offer advice in spiritual and moral affairs, were generally held in such esteem. There is some evidence (although usually from hagiographical contexts designed to maximize the deeds of the hero of the story) of cynicism and hostility, especially when those claiming to be holy men behaved in socially unacceptable ways. But these exceptions tend merely to reinforce the privileged position the ascetic occupied in the popular mind.

The demanding prescriptions for leading a pious Christian life laid down by the Church Fathers, and repeated by churchmen and monks thereafter, were meant to apply to all. In fact, as we have said, this was impractical for many reasons. In contrast to the busy world of secular life, monastic communities provided an appropriate environment for quiet contemplation, prayer and all the other tasks associated with the effort to approach a state of purification sufficient to permit one to commune with the divinity, to pray successfully for divine intercession in the affairs of humanity (and just as importantly, in the affairs of the orthodox, God-protected empire of the Romans, the Chosen People). As such, they were the objects of particular attention and admiration (but also, when they were perceived to be failing to meet these standards, of particular reprobation and criticism!). They were also taken for granted as an entirely necessary element of society, for without the support of those who struggled to master their own passions, neither the demonic forces which threatened constantly to overturn the orderly and harmonious nature of God's creation, nor the forces of darkness which threatened the Christian world on earth could be adequately warded off and defeated. Prayer was thus as important an aspect of the empire's defences as the maintenance of an army, and however pragmatic and devoted to warfare or fighting the empire's enemies, many soldiers and leading officers always remained conscious of the need for divine support, however much certain elements of the middle and later Byzantine elite gloried in their soldierly prowess. Byzantine armies always prayed before battle. As a late sixth-century text puts it:

> we urge upon the general that his most important concern be the love of God and justice; building on these, he should strive to win the favour of God, without which it is impossible to carry out any plan, however well devised it may seem, or to overcome any enemy, however weak he may be thought.

The forms which Byzantine spirituality and asceticism took varied across time and even across regions: those who chose such a path had been from the beginning of the monastic tradition especially drawn to deserted and barren districts, for there they could find the isolation in which to concentrate on their spiritual struggle. Monasteries originated as, and were meant to imitate as far as possible, such an environment, hence the emphasis on quiet, prayer, self-sufficiency and labour. But there was a broad spectrum of monastic

Left and right: The fifth-century monastery of St John, Stoudion, Constantinople.

organizations, ranging from the quite luxurious conditions written into the *typika* (or 'rules') of urban monastic houses endowed by wealthy aristocrats for their retirement, for example, to relatively poor and geographically isolated establishments.

By the same token, styles and fashions in spiritual devotion also varied and evolved. The period from the fourth to sixth centuries in particular seems to have witnessed a great growth in the importance of individual holy men, hermits and monks who by various ascetic means had attained a certain divinely-endowed spiritual power, reflecting the cultural and social needs of the time. Such individuals acted as guides not only in matters of the soul but also in secular affairs, in many respects like the oracles of the ancient world. The Church was worried by the threat which the unsupervised spiritual authority of such men and women posed to its own authority, as well as to orthodox belief, and in the following centuries tried, as we have already noted from the example of the canons of the council of 692, to exercise some control over their activities. While hermits and holy men continued to play an important role in the ensuing period, as the flourishing hagiographical literature of the ninth and tenth centuries suggests, they come also to be more closely associated with monastic communities.

For the most committed, the means of achieving spiritual purity, and more especially of experiencing the divine presence directly, involved contemplative prayer, and the idea that such direct experience could be achieved was present from the earliest days of Christianity. A number of theologians in the period up to the fifth and sixth centuries had theorized this relationship, but the popularity of such mystical contemplation seems to have varied considerably over time and according to circumstances. In the eleventh century Symeon the Theologian, building on the doctrine of these thinkers, argued that divine activity could be experienced both through the spirit and through the senses, a perspective which lay at the heart of the hesychastic movement of the fourteenth century on Mt Athos. Here, the idea was developed that such experiences were open to all, provided that the right means was employed to attain them. Paying less attention to traditional forms of meditation, it was argued that deep concentration and repetitive prayer, accompanied by special breathing techniques, could open the consciousness to visionary experiences; a development which contrasted strongly with traditional modes of spiritual devotion. This divided the Church as well as lay society (see Chapter 2), and the debate became closely entwined with the political issues of the day. Although hesychasm came to the fore for only a short period, it left its mark very clearly on the history of Orthodox spirituality, and the tradition of mysticism it entailed continued to play an important role after the Ottoman conquest.

The challenge of the West

Although relations between Rome and Constantinople had from the beginning been strained, and although this tension occasionally led to major breaks between the two Churches, the disagreements which arose were as much a reflection of, or a reaction to, the close political association in the Byzantine world between emperor and patriarch, and between imperial and ecclesiastical policy, as they were of real theological or doctrinal differences. Thus on several occasions members of the eastern clergy or monastic community appealed directly to Rome against decisions or policies followed in the East, because those policies reflected too closely imperial politics at a particular moment. The independence and the integrity of the Church was felt to be compromised, and it was on such grounds that the monastic opposition to compromise with former iconoclast clergy led to papal involvement, during the patriarchates of both Tarasios and Nikephoros, following the seventh ecumenical council in 787. But such situations also led to pope or patriarch on occasion condemning one another or their clergy, as during the attempts made by both Rome and Constantinople to bring the Slavs and Bulgars into the Church during the middle decades of the ninth century. Indeed, the enraged reaction of Nicholas I to the Byzantine success in bringing the Bulgars into the Constantinopolitan orbit exemplifies the problem.

Apart from the divisions caused by, first, monotheletism, and later by iconoclasm (although it is worth noting that the papacy refrained from condemning the iconoclast emperors Leo III and Constantine V until towards the end of the latter's reign) there were only two major conflicts before the Fourth Crusade. The first, the so-called 'Photian schism', followed the forced resignation of the patriarch Ignatios in 858, which had occurred due to the hostility of the Caesar Bardas (uncle of the reigning emperor Michael III). Photios, a learned and experienced imperial official, was quickly ordained and elected patriarch, and proceeded to install his supporters to key Church positions. Ignatios and his supporters enlisted the (initially reluctant) support of pope Nicholas I, who was able to use the situation, in combination with a number of relatively minor doctrinal differences or misunderstandings, to his advantage, intervening in Eastern Church politics and justifying the papacy's claim to a superior status within Christendom. However, when, on his accession in 867, the emperor Basil I removed Photios and restored Ignatios, things did not improve, since Ignatios was equally hostile to papal claims. Reconciliation finally took place at the council of Constantinople in 879.

The second (much more serious) break took place in the 1050s, and involved both political and doctrinal issues. At the beginning of the sixth century the words 'filioque' were added to the Chalcedonian creed in the Frankish lands, in an attempt to clarify the fact that the Holy Spirit proceeded from both Father and Son. Frankish churchmen used it during their efforts to convert the Bulgarians in the ninth century, and the patriarch Photios later wrote a detailed treatise condemning it. Eventually, at the council of 879, the Roman legates accepted its redundancy and it was withdrawn. But it appears to have been reintroduced by the early eleventh century, and it formed the basis of disagreement between the two Churches in the 1050s, although other matters of clerical discipline and liturgical practice were also involved. An attempt to reconcile the two failed in 1054, when the stubbornness of both the pope's legate, Cardinal Humbert, and the patriarch, Michael Keroularios, led to mutual anathemas – formal pronouncements of condemnation – being proclaimed. The two Churches remained estranged thereafter, in spite of a gradual lessening of the tension during the reign of Alexios I.

These differences were not simply differences over doctrine, nor conflicts over ecclesiastical primacy. On the contrary, they reflected also deep cultural differences and an increasing divergence between the Greek eastern Mediterranean and south Balkan world, and the Latin-dominated lands of central and Western Europe. Cultural alienation and misunderstandings are already apparent in the ninth and tenth centuries, first in the absurd claims made by the patriarch Photios (but writing in the name of the emperor Michael III) to pope Nicholas I about Byzantine political and cultural superiority, and in the pope's learned but damning response; second in the contempt and anger for the 'Greeks' displayed by the envoy of the German emperor Otto, Liutprand of Cremona, when he visited the court of Nikephoros II Phokas in the 960s. The situation became much worse as Western economic strength and political and military aggression began to be a serious problem for the Byzantine empire in the later eleventh century, with the Normans on the one hand and the German emperors on the other posing serious threats to Byzantine possessions in the Balkans, and with the growing challenge to Byzantine maritime power from Italian merchant cities such as Venice and Genoa. The Crusading movement, Western prejudices about Greek perfidy and effeteness, and the expansion of the Seljuk emirates in Asia Minor, transformed alienation and suspicion into open conflict. The capture of Constantinople in 1204 and the establishment of a Latin empire finalized the split, for the Latin patriarchate was not recognized by the Orthodox populations of the Byzantine or formerly-Byzantine regions: instead, the patriarch Michael Autoreianos, elected in Nicaea in 1208, was recognized as the true patriarch of the Constantinopolitan Church.

The rapidly expanding power of the Turks, especially once the Ottoman Sultanate had become established, together with the political and economic collapse and fragmentation of the Byzantine state, made reconciliation a matter of urgency, since otherwise the West tended to view the Byzantines as schismatics or, worse, heretics, and would offer no support. Negotiations for a union of the Churches continued throughout the fourteenth and fifteenth centuries, but at the councils of Lyons (in 1274) and Ferrara-Florence (1439) no agreement on many issues could be reached, even though in both cases the emperor of the time (Michael VIII and John VIII respectively) were willing to bow to western principles in order to obtain military and financial assistance. But the majority of the clergy and the population of the empire was utterly opposed to such concessions, and no real progress was ever made (nor was any western help ever forthcoming). The frustrations felt with regard to the attitudes and demands of the West are evident in the words of the *Megas Doux* (Grand Duke) Loukas Notaras, a leading minister of the last emperor Constantine XI, who is reported to have said in 1451: 'better to see the turban of the Turk ruling in the City than the Latin mitre'. Notaras had been active in the negotiations with the Western Church, and in fact was executed two years later, with his family, on the orders of Mehmet II after the city had fallen. It is probably an exaggeration to claim that all Byzantines felt as Notaras did, but the degree of alienation which his words reflect is clear.

Yet paradoxically the decline of the secular state meant a concomitant rise in the authority and prestige of the Church: as we have seen, by the end of the thirteenth century the patriarch held sway over a vastly larger territory than the emperor. And it was to the Byzantine Church and its clergy, and more particularly to the patriarchate in Constantinople, that the Ottomans turned when, having finally taken the city, they needed to devise a formula for ruling peacefully the Orthodox populations of the Balkan and Aegean regions. The differences in outlook and mentality which had become so apparent between East and West were part of an evolving cultural context, in which the economic and social developments outlined in Chapter 5 played an equally important role. The result was an increasing cultural isolationism in respect of Byzantine political attitudes, and an increasing rejection of alternatives coupled to a degree of fatalism with regard to the Church and to Orthodoxy, which made striving for anything but the impossible – unconditional Western support, a revival of Byzantine military might, and the turning back of the Ottoman advance – quite pointless. The fragmented rump of empire was left in political terms with nothing but an ideology which no longer corresponded to reality. Yet in day-to-day respects, Byzantine peasants, merchants and churchmen had to get on with life, so that when the end of the empire had become a reality, the Ottomans found that the 'Greeks', in spite of their ideological hostility, quickly settled down to a routine which was barely different from that to which they had been accustomed. The patriarch, and the Orthodox Church, were now the means through which Ottoman rule could be both tolerated and administered.

7 Power, art and tradition in Byzantium

Patterns of power

The evolution of the Byzantine state was determined, as we have now seen, by many interlinking factors, and in response to the question, 'Why did it develop in this particular direction?' different historians will supply different answers, depending upon their own areas of expertise, their own particular approach to their subject, their own implicit 'philosophy' of history, and so on. Indeed, as with most of the important questions about the human past, there is no single, all-embracing answer which will address all the concerns of those who have questions to ask.

One way to understand the history of the empire is to look at the issue of resources and power, in other words, what were the resources of the state and society as a whole, how were they exploited and controlled, and by whom, and how were the products of those resources distributed across the social formation as a whole at different times? How much of the wealth produced in the different sectors of the economy – agrarian, pastoral, commercial – could be taken in the form of rent and tax or indirectly, in skills, services and labour? Some of the elements towards answering this sort of question have already been given. But if we stand back for a moment and consider the history of the empire as a totality, observing how these particular relationships changed and altered over the period from the fourth to the fifteenth century, then we can hazard some answers which will go towards making sense of the empire's development. To begin with the question of resources. We have seen what form these took: in agricultural and pastoral produce; in ores and other raw materials; in manpower; and in skills and knowledge. The crucial issue for the central government was maintaining enough control over those resources to ensure its own continued existence – the structural evolution of taxation and the apparatus of fiscal exploitation can be best approached from this perspective, and, from this standpoint, the history of the empire as a political entity can be summed up in terms of the ways through which this aim was achieved. In particular, this means a discussion of the fact that, throughout its long history, the central government had always to compete with others – the senatorial landowning elite, the middle and later Byzantine aristocracy, foreign merchants – over these resources, which were, of course, finite. The importance of that tension reveals itself very clearly in the internal political history of the empire, and the instrumental means by which one set of interests or another within the leading elements of East Roman society gained or lost its predominance are reflected in the history of both fiscal policies and civil conflict.

Looking at the conflicts which thus arose offers particularly useful insights into the ways in which the Byzantine state actually worked, and under what conditions centralized state power and authority is liable to break down. In modern industrialized societies, for example, taxation is the means whereby the state redistributes surplus value – which has already been produced and distributed across society – among both the owners or controllers of productive resources in land and labour power, on the one hand, and those who sell their labour power in return for a wage/salary, on the other. In pre-modern societies, in contrast, surplus appropriation can take place only through rent or tax, in their various forms: the processes involved necessarily reflect the direct contact between state or dominant elite and tax- or rent-payers. In both cases, the nature of the social and economic tensions between those who do the appropriating and those who do the producing is determined by two features: by competition over the distribution of resources between the potentially antagonistic elements in this equation; and by the forms taken by tax and rent, through which surplus is appropriated in the first place.

Both state centres and ruling elites in pre-modern formations thus have an equally powerful vested interest in the maintenance of those social and economic relations to which they owe their position. The state (as embodied in a central or ruling establishment) must appropriate surplus itself, or ensure that an adequate portion of such surplus is passed on to it, to be certain of survival. But there has historically always been a tendency for the functionaries entrusted with these duties to evolve, however gradually, their own independent power base, thus representing a competitor with the state for resources. The relationship between the ruler or ruling elite and those who actually appropriate surplus on their behalf is in consequence always contradictory and potentially antagonistic because, as already indicated, dominant socio-economic groups and states function at the same level of primary appropriation, since there is no real difference (except in scale and administrative organization) between the extraction of tax and that of rent, whatever the form it takes. The 'antagonism' was, of course, a structural antagonism, that need not necessarily be expressed through any awareness on the part of the individuals or groups in question. Furthermore, this relationship is generally not a simple one-to-one equation: the state may be embodied in a particular power elite, which may or may not originate from a dominant social class or aristocracy, for example, so that a whole complex of interwoven social, economic and political vested interests is involved. But the ability of the state to extract surplus depends ultimately upon its power to limit the economic and political strength of such potentially competing groups. The only real way to achieve this has been to create, or attempt to create, a totally loyal (because totally dependent) administrative group; a bureaucracy which is identified entirely with the interests of the central establishment. Byzantine emperors were enabled to achieve this, for a while (although they may not have had this intention) by the circumstances peculiar to the second half of the seventh century. But as we have seen, in the longer term this structured relationship was central both to the failure of the Byzantine state to resist economic challenges from elsewhere, as well as to the success of the Italian commercial republics in respect of their own social and economic organization.

But the history of the structures of the state – taxation, military organization, justice, the palatine administration, and so forth – represent only one aspect of a more complex whole, and we must not forget that the individuals, who in groups or by themselves acted as agents in this scheme of things, also functioned within a field of cultural activities, through which they expressed themselves in language and through which they established and defended their own individual identities as members of a wider society. Literature and visual representation of all types, religious and secular buildings, all contributed to the perceived environment inhabited by the subjects of the Byzantine emperor, as well as of the emperor himself.

Patterns of representation

Literature and the visual arts, including functional structures such as buildings, also tell us a great deal about what makes a culture 'tick'. On the one hand, the nature of the investment of wealth in cultural artefacts such as icons or churches, the relationship between those who commissioned such works, whether individuals or institutions, and those who produced them, throws light on the distribution of wealth and the ways in which it was consumed or displayed, and thus on issues of social status, ideology and so forth. On the other hand, changes in these relationships, whether from one region to another, or in time from one century to the next, tell us something of the movement of the society as a whole, about changes or shifts in values and perceptions, and about how people's understanding of their world, and their place in it, was constructed and given voice. Thus the significant transformation in both the form and content of literary activity from the sixth into the seventh and eighth centuries, for example, provides important information about the nature of the cultural changes the empire was facing, the values and priorities of people at the time, and the relationship between cultural resources and political and military events.

Two related phenomena illustrate the change: first, the dramatic reduction in all forms of secular literary activity, in particular historical and chronicle writing and verse; second, the almost complete dominance of writing of a theological nature, from collections of miracles and saint's lives to complex theological and dogmatic tracts. Some historical writing did continue, but it was only at the end of the eighth and during the early ninth century that the genre begins to flourish once more. During the second phase of the iconoclastic controversy, from 815 until the 840s, there occurred a great flourishing of hagiography as the victors in the dispute celebrated their heroes (although the iconoclasts also wrote saints' lives); more importantly, the revival in secular literature reflected a conscious attempt among the educated to make sense of the past and make connections with the glorious age of Justinian. The anti-iconoclastic theologians, along with many other literate people at this time, rationalized the past in constructing their narratives of what happened. They made sense of what they knew or what they could hypothesize had happened through the lens of their own common-sense assumptions about the past and about the values and morality of their own culture. This view of the past was, in a sense, ahistorical. It suggested that since the fundamental modes of Christian behaviour and practice had been established in the time of the Fathers of the Church (just as the fundamental institutions of the state had been established by Constantine and reaffirmed by Justinian), change away from these practices (or what was assumed to have been such practices, as they had evolved by the ninth century) was a deviation from the true faith and, therefore, heretical. Thus if it was accepted that holy images had always been

John the Baptist, Pammakaristos church (Fethiye Camii), fourteenth century.

venerated in the form defined by the Seventh Ecumenical Council (and the sessions of the council went to great lengths to show that this was indeed the case), the policies of the Isaurian emperors were clearly heretical and a deviation from the norm. Any explanation that could throw light on why this deviation had occurred was therefore plausible, so that Jewish and Islamic influence, diabolic intervention and similar causes were ascribed as motivating the emperors and their evil henchmen. These rulers could thus be made responsible not only for the schism in the Church, but they could also be blamed for the 'disappearance' of classical education and a whole range of other evils.

This process of interpretation was cumulative, however, and reflected a many-faceted development, through which different elements within Byzantine society in the ninth century – including both emperors and their advisers – could justify their own actions and explain any weaknesses or failings in their own policies or the actions of their forbears. Much of the activity was concerned with copying and thus saving for posterity older texts of every imaginable genre, which had been written at a much earlier date and which were in danger of destruction. Such a perspective had a powerful influence on the sort of literature that was selected, of course, as well as on what was commissioned anew – historical accounts of recent times as well as the more distant past, in particular – as well as on the things the educated chose to write about. The development of a new, minuscule style of cursive writing, which meant that composing and copying could be carried out much more quickly than hitherto, served as an important stimulus to this.

As the empire's political situation stabilized, so a more diverse culture began to evolve, as various genres of late Roman and Hellenistic literature were revived, albeit in a clearly Byzantine form, while 'classical' motifs in visual art also made their appearance. And

Fourteenth-century frescoes, Church of the Chora (Kariye Camii).

together with this revival of learning and literature there evolved also a heightened consciousness of the differences between the educated and literate and those who were not; a consciousness that was represented especially strongly within the bureaucratic and ecclesiastical establishment at Constantinople. The educated writers of the ninth century were only beginning to grapple with this heritage and to make it their own again. By the middle of the eleventh century the revival of interest in classical literature and style was characteristic of the Byzantine social elite. The diglossy which had haunted the Greek-speaking world from the first century BC – by which the spoken demotic Greek of ordinary everyday life was distinguished from a literary and somewhat artificial and archaizing form of the language – was reinforced by this process, of course. An accurate use of archaic Attic Greek when writing, combined with a thorough knowledge of classical mythology and rhetorical methods as well as the established canon of Christian writers, was the hallmark of the educated Byzantine, through which she or he was differentiated from the functionally literate clerk or village priest as well as the illiterate mass of the population. Choice of theme and topic reflected not just the writer's educational attainment and classical knowledge, however, but also a strategy for reinforcing the point of the topic about which the author was writing. The deliberate exploitation by historians and chroniclers of material from ancient texts, often incorporated almost verbatim, was part of this picture, for the selection of material was dictated also by what was considered

157

appropriate as much as by what actually happened. Choice of language in speaking or in writing thus became a matter of cultural politics. It is no coincidence that the highly educated composer of a group of twelfth-century, Constantinople-set satirical poems, Theodore Prodromos, chose to set his verse down in a demotic form of the language, rather than in the classical form with which he was thoroughly familiar.

But political expansion, military success and the confidence engendered by the empire's dominant position in the east Mediterranean region in the first half of the eleventh century also led to an increasing cultural arrogance about Byzantine superiority, in which the culture and character of non-Byzantines were treated with an increasing element of contempt. This is not universally so, but it is clear enough in a substantial amount of the writing of the period. This is especially true of attitudes towards the 'Latins'. Until the ninth and early tenth centuries, and in spite of the power of the Frankish empire, there had been no serious rivals either to Byzantine ideological claims or to Byzantine cultural achievements. But as the tenth century drew on it became clear that the medieval West was in fact a region of great economic, social and above all military dynamism; a dynamism which the Byzantines had to confront in the eleventh century in the form of the Normans in particular, but equally, in terms of both economic and political power, in the shape of the Italian merchant cities. Stereotypes of the barbarous westerner became common. As the political and military success of these 'barbarians' began to be seen as a serious threat to imperial power, and as Western cultural attitudes challenged the assumptions of the Greek-speaking Byzantine elite and their values, so fear gave such caricatures an added edge. Traditional suspicion of western liturgical and other religious practices, of the papacy and its claims now combined to blind most Byzantines to the political realities of 'Latin' power and potential and to encourage a xenophobia and hostility which was, through the direct confrontation of these two halves of the Christian world in the events of the Crusades, to lead to massive and irreversible mutual misunderstandings and hatred. The sack of Constantinople and the fourth crusade were symptoms as well as results of these developments.

Other aspects of cultural production were similarly affected by the passage of time and the changing milieu, including visual imagery. The decorative programmes in churches as well as in illustrated manuscripts, while employing biblical as well as historical themes, are often clearly, if indirectly or allusively, related to contemporary attitudes to the recent political history of the East Roman world. This has been shown to be the case, for example, with the illustration of a number of psalters during the ninth century, which reflected the political programmes of those who commissioned them, such as the patriarch Photios. Byzantines were fully aware of the function and purpose of the monuments they produced: it was the end result that was important, either to increase the standing of the patron or creator of a work, or in addition, in the case of a religious artefact such as a church or an icon, to glorify God. 'Art' thus had no meaning outside the cultural context within which it could be understood. It possessed no market value in the modern sense: when an emperor built a new church, he was not simply glorifying God. He also increased his own prestige, demonstrated his orthodoxy, made connections with the (more glorious) past, and reaffirmed his authority. In building a fortress or repairing the walls of a city he did much the same, even where clearly secular buildings were concerned.

*Sixth-century sculpted pier, church of
St Polyeuktos, Constantinople.*

Byzantine art was both original and conservative, insofar as older or ancient items were prized for their antiquity and exploited as paradigms for the creation of new works. The apparently 'classicizing' moments in Byzantine cultural history, especially in terms of visual media, thus represent a continuous reference to the past which became especially apparent at those moments when sufficient resources and skill were invested in artefacts to bring out this attribute, so that the term 'renaissance', as frequently applied to such moments, better describes the availability of resources than the types of representation themselves, which had always been accessible, but dependent upon the availability of skilled craftsmanship.

Crucial to all artistic creation was the notion of authority. A representation, and especially one associated with religion, had to be authentic and conform to the canons of Orthodoxy. The result was a growth in the dependence of many images, for example, both large- and small-scale, on earlier works and, after the council of 787, the growth of an increasing number of conventions in respect of pose, dress and so forth where figures were concerned, as well as particular architectural structures which form the frame and background to many images. There is good evidence that from at least the fifth century, model-books and iconographical guides, containing a repertoire of figural types, existed and served as the basis for the transmission of standardized representations. As a fixed corpus of iconographical motifs evolved, employed in the assertion of the message of Orthodoxy, so the possibility of producing something outside the bounds of this corpus declined, and secular representation, found in the medieval West, for example, as well as

159

Fragment of eleventh-century sculpture, Constantinople.

in the Islamic world, is marginalized. The watershed for much of this is represented by the seventh ecumenical council held at Nicaea in 787, when questions of authority as well as authenticity were central to the arguments of both iconoclasts and iconophiles. The result was that (although the evidence for the eighth and much of the seventh centuries is rather thin) an earlier broad and less constrained range of representational themes and styles is subjected to an increasing number of prescriptive limitations, further reinforced by the role of the patron of a particular creation, whose views also needed to be followed.

Art also had a teaching role: images in particular were seen as a form of 'silent writing', giving understanding of the basic tenets of Christianity as well as access to the divine. By the end of the iconoclastic controversy, the issue of the relationship between image and prototype still remained to be resolved, although the debate engendered by the introduction of imperial iconoclasm represented an important step forward in this respect. But sacred images seem always to have been understood to offer the possibility for the supplicant to receive intercession through prayer to the person represented, and thus to strengthen the bond between that figure and the reality which the image was assumed to embody. Indeed, it is important to recognize that Byzantines viewed art as itself a version

160

Dome of the eleventh-century Hosios Loukas church.

of reality, able to present to the eye those elements which were normally not perceived, by penetrating to the essence – and beyond the mere appearance – of what was represented. Modern notions of aesthetics and naturalism are thus not always relevant to understanding how and why Byzantine art functioned in the ways it did, even though it is certainly the case that, from the eleventh century especially, classicizing notions of three-dimensionality became increasingly important.

In spite of the increasing number of models and exemplars which were intended to provide Byzantine artists with a guide and a framework, stylistic change thus remained an important feature of the evolution of the art of Byzantine culture, reflecting both the dominant themes in the theological debates of the times and the desire to produce more sophisticated renderings of complex issues of Christology and dogma, as well as the individual input of particular painters or artists. This is true of the tenth and eleventh centuries, when an emphasis on theological clarity and accessibility stimulated an increasingly frontal and symmetrical mode of figural representation. New themes appeared in response to developments in the liturgy, so that representations of liturgical feasts which evoked both the person for whom the feast was celebrated and the feast itself were developed, in which images representing events associated with Holy Week (the week before Easter) were especially important. An increased emphasis on the life of Christ and on the forms through which the eucharist could be represented is also evident. These developments were stimulated not just by developments internal to the Church. The nature of patronage and sponsorship played a key role, and – as the more fragmented political structures of the empire after 1204 brought about a more diverse and far less centralized pattern of distribution of wealth as well as political authority – so there evolved a much greater diversity of artistic patronage. The Palaeologan period, especially in the fourteenth and fifteenth centuries, produced as a by-product a very clear regionalization of style and quality, as the provinces of the empire became increasingly independent, socially and culturally, of Constantinople. It also meant that western styles and themes also began to appear, so that a far greater variety of styles and themes characterizes the artistic production, in all media, of the last two centuries of Byzantium.

The analysis of modes of representation, which reflected both the patterns of belief of the culture and one of the means through which it attempted to make sense of its physical as well as its spiritual environment, can thus provide vital clues to the ways in which it responded to shifts in its environment at a given moment or across a period of time. Representation also keys in to the social and economic contexts within which it is effective, and while this relationship is only rarely direct in terms of visual representation, the literary perception – or rather the literary interpretation of perception – offers, on occasion, much more direct access to patterns of thought and attitudes. The cultural arrogance and bigotry stimulated by the imperialism of the later tenth and early eleventh centuries, particularly marked in the literature and letters of the time, provides a clear instance. The elitist emphasis on classicizing forms of writing, which marked out the cultural elite of the empire in the fourteenth and fifteenth centuries, provides another; while the anti-classicizing reaction embodied in the hesychastic movement, with its emphasis on piety and an anti-rationalist, emotional interpretation of the world, reflects a 'populist' reaction against this elitism.

Both literary and visual imagery worked through the medium of narrative, either by invoking a narrative which is implicit in what is represented – for example, a scene taken from the Bible – and thus leading the observer to a particular conclusion, with all the moral adjuncts which accompany it; or by creating an account, for example through a historical narrative, which served either to warn against or to affirm a particular sort of action. In either case, the subject matter is often tied into the concerns or anxieties of a particular historical moment. This was certainly the case with the subjects and themes of literature during the seventh century and again during the period of iconoclasm; it is also true of the twelfth century, when it is quite clear that some literary activities also reflected the broader social and cultural picture. The acerbic social satire produced by the writer Theodore Prodromos, for example, reflected the rise during the eleventh century of a new element in middle Byzantine urban society: a group of professional writers of quite humble background, whose expectations were never met by the social realities of their lives, and whose frustration and anger was directed both at representatives of the old elite – people who happened to write because that was what members of their class were expected to do, rather than because they needed to earn a living from it – and at those who had encouraged them to take up their profession. The very fact of the shift in emphasis and expansion of the genre which Theodore's writings reflect says a great deal about patterns of social life in Constantinople at the time.

The last ancient society

The continued existence of the centralized bureaucratic state, in however altered a form, across the period from the sixth and seventh centuries to the fourteenth and fifteenth centuries, however much its appearance changed over such a length of time, is a remarkable story of adaptability and flexibility. With its roots ultimately in the Roman republic, and consciously aware of its Roman imperial heritage, the Byzantine empire is in truth the last of the ancient empires to survive beyond the great transformative movements of the period from the fifth to the seventh centuries. In particular, its history illustrates the ways in which a political ideological system such as that of the Christian Eastern Roman Empire possessed the capacity to respond to the very difficult and constantly evolving circumstances in which it found itself. From within the context of the particular social, economic and cultural conditions prevailing, this system of beliefs was able subtly to shift the angle from which the world was perceived, understood and hence acted upon, by focusing on aspects of the 'symbolic universe' – the 'thought-world' of the Christian East Roman world – which were better suited to bear new interpretations and alternative ways of thinking about the changed conditions in which people found themselves. However, in its final years, and in spite of the intellectual dynamism shown by Plethon or Palamas, no corresponding explanation emerged for the massive divergence between the political realities of the rapidly dwindling Byzantine state and the ideological pretensions to which it was the heir.

Yet through much of its history, the Byzantine symbolic universe was able to absorb the challenges thrown up by the transformed circumstances of its existence, and indeed, in the end, outgrow and outlast even the state which had nurtured it. This flexibility was founded on a solid footing. Their identity as Roman and Orthodox, together with the Hellenistic and classical Greek cultural heritage in literature in particular which Byzantines cherished as a key symbol of their cultural identity, provided them with a certainty which nothing could shake. And this was true, even if educated Byzantines in the ninth and tenth centuries spent a great deal of time pondering the questions raised by their recent history and searching for the historical roots they needed in order to furnish themselves with a clear image of the purpose of the events that had affected them.

This does not mean that there were not many difficulties which had to be overcome or addressed, as the debates in theological and popular circles over divine intervention and causation – or over the role of sacred images – demonstrate. In the last years of the empire's existence, similarly a time of soul-searching about the cause of the empire's eclipse and the means of arresting the decline, there took place equally fascinating debates about the nature of political order and the state – taking their cue in part from works of Plato, such as the *Republic* – as well as about the relationship between good government and character, or the proposed union of the Eastern and Western Churches. It is perhaps the case that in times of real crisis, when people are confronted with really transformative possibilities in their own lifetime or the near future, such discussions flourish, since the pressing questions of survival or submergence demand both explanations and solutions. The fourteenth and fifteenth centuries, on the one hand, and the seventh and first part of the eighth centuries, on the other, provide examples of such moments, although it should not be thought that Byzantine cultural and intellectual history was the less lively and interesting in other periods. On the contrary, the whole oeuvre of the copyists of the ninth and tenth centuries, who saved much classical and later Roman material, as well as of the encyclopaedists and historians of the tenth century, bear witness to the liveliness of the activity of that period of internal stability, military confidence and political expansionism.

It is a paradox that the relative social flexibility and openness of Byzantine society is founded in its late Roman social and political order, for it contrasts in this respect very strongly with the medieval West. Here, a group of successor states and principalities had sprung up on Roman ground, intermixing and integrating quite rapidly with the original elites, on the one hand, and more gradually with the mass of the ordinary indigenous population. The social relations which eventually evolved out of this produced by the twelfth century a society that was increasingly rigidly hierarchized, in which movement from one social level to another was achieved with great difficulty, if at all. In contrast, in the Byzantine world it was possible (as we have noted) to move from very humble status to that of mighty lord; and although the possibilities varied across time and according to the situation and, especially, the situation and power of the magnate elite, there are examples of several such characters throughout the period.

The paradoxes within Byzantine culture exist at several levels. But nowhere are they so obvious, perhaps, as in Byzantine attitudes to warfare, for in theory and in the oldest traditions of the Church, Christians should not shed blood. In fact, already by the third and fourth century a compromise situation had been reached, whereby the shedding of blood in defence of Orthodoxy and the Christian Roman Empire was justified, if regretted. While war was condemned, the virtues of peace were extolled and fighting was to be avoided at all costs. Medieval East Roman society was nevertheless the inheritor of the military traditions and organization as well as of the militaristic ideology of the pre-Christian Roman Empire at its height. Through the blending of Christian ideals with a remarkably tenacious refusal to give in to its external foes, late Roman Christian Byzantium evolved a remarkable culture, which could both remain true to the concept of pacifism and yet maintain and justify an army. Byzantine emperors and their advisers were no strangers to Realpolitik. Philanthropy was blended with practical and common-sense attitudes which, whatever the advice offered by the many handbooks and treatises on the subject, exploited both the pacific and the militaristic elements of the society. The culture of monasticism on the one hand and of the provincial soldiers and their leaders indicate the two extremes of the continuum. Retiring soldiers often entered a monastery as a means both of securing their future economically and physically, as well as of recovering spiritual well-being and working towards the remission of their sins, and there could hardly be a better illustration of the relationship between warmaking and the ideals of peace.

In many ways, the East Roman Empire, even in its last days, was a society organized for war. But it was hardly a warlike society, at least not in the eyes of many outsiders, especially the crusaders in the later eleventh and twelfth centuries, whose contempt for the effeteness and unwarlike nature of the 'Greeks' illustrates the chasm in attitudes and perceptions between these two halves of the post-Roman world. Thus, while the phraseology and vocabulary of warfare can be found throughout secular as well as religious literature, war and the taking of life continued to be regarded as evil, even by many of the soldiers who were so closely associated with it. The contradictions were ideologically reconciled because Byzantines believed they knew what to defend and why they were defending it, an issue which lies at the heart of the empire's success in surviving for so long. From the point of view of a 'cultural psychology', the strength of the imperial ideological system, with its vast array of potent symbols evoking the values of both the Roman and Christian Orthodox traditions, was crucial. Effective through a variety of forms through society as a whole, it reinforced the beliefs and values maintained by the literate cultural and political elite. It underlined the close relationship between the Church, as the guardian of the spiritual values and Orthodox belief of the East Roman world, and the emperors, and thus emphasized the ideological motivation to maintain the state in existence. As relayed through the imagery of the Church and as recalled by the Orthodox liturgy and by the various communal festivals of the Christian calendar, it was firmly rooted in the hearts and minds of the ordinary population. Thus in spite of fundamental differences in economic outlook and interests between exploited peasantry and middling landowners, magnates and bureaucrats, there remained common values across the whole social spectrum which reinforced a single East Roman, Christian identity which was perceived and felt to be fundamentally different from the surrounding cultures. Only as the state became increasingly fragmented and as more and more territory came under foreign rule did this change. This becomes especially apparent after 1204.

Identity was crucial to survival. Byzantine identities were shaped not in a vacuum, but in the context of both the relations between different elements within society, and of neighbouring cultures and peoples. There were two strains or tendencies in particular within Byzantine culture which made an especial contribution to the Byzantine identity, elements which had been combined, not always comfortably, through much of the empire's history, and which finally came into open opposition in the last century or so of the empire's existence. Hellenistic rationalism, and the classical literary and philosophical heritage which accompanied it, had always lived in uneasy co-existence with the religious anti-rationalism and piety of the 'fundamentalist' strain of Christianity. In the seventh century, as noted already, this conflict or tension had revealed itself in the debates over issues of causation and faith, resulting in an uneasy compromise. As we have seen, the empire had no rivals in the 'barbarian' West until the later tenth and eleventh centuries; while in the East the Islamic Caliphate replaced the Sassanid Persian empire as one of the two 'great lights in the firmament', as the patriarch Nicholas I (901-907, 911-925) put it in a letter to the emir of Crete. The difference between the two was that while the latter was Muslim, it was also civilized; the West was a barbarous region. But when Western military and economic strength began to affect this comfortable view of things, the Byzantines coped only with difficulty. Already in the later ninth century Pope Nicholas I had humiliated the emperor and his advisers by demonstrating that they were relatively ignorant of their Roman heritage and its traditions, contributing at least in part to an imperially-sponsored revival of interest in Roman law, amongst other things. Western Christianity and its different ways, on the one hand, and the existence of Christian neighbours in the Balkans with whom the empire was often at war, on the other, made a simple identity of Roman Empire with (orthodox) Christianity difficult, if not impossible. Rival political formations which could effectively challenge Byzantine power on land and at sea, and the very public rejection by western powers of Byzantine claims to hegemony, heightened the tensions and brought home the contradictions in the imperial ideological claims to universal imperial authority. And as we have already seen, the simple fact was that after the ninth century the Orthodox Church exercised effective authority over a far wider territory than the Roman emperors themselves. As the empire shrank territorially and politically after 1204 this became even more marked.

The result was, beginning already in the eleventh to the twelfth century, a retreat into 'hellenism', the search for the Greek roots of East Roman culture. Yet ironically, this conceded just the point which had in the first place so outraged Byzantine sensibilities, when in the ninth century western rulers began to refer to the Byzantine emperor as ruler 'of the Greeks'. To an extent, the flowering of Greek literature and classicism, which marks the period from the twelfth century, signals a retreat towards a form of cultural isolationism through which Byzantines could continue to believe in their own superiority and uniqueness, in their right to be the Chosen People, and in their destiny as the true representatives of God's kingdom on earth, regardless of the political realities.

These tendencies, both in their metropolitan and their provincial forms, became even more marked as the empire shrank and fragmented. After 1204, the patronage of an imperial court disappeared, to be replaced by the much less generous support, for a more limited range of cultural activities, of the various small successor states, and even after the restoration of the empire in 1261, the provincialization of much cultural production as well as the reduction in expenditure is apparent. But by this time the realities of Byzantine politics and economic life and the formal ideology of the empire could no longer be comfortably matched. The empire became a small and dependent state, its rulers impoverished, its treasury empty, its defences dependent upon foreign goodwill or hired soldiers. At the same time, the power and authority of the Church which, of course, now exercised authority over more territory than the imperial government, grew in proportion as imperial authority declined. In the last century of the empire's life, indeed, it was often the Church, with its greater resources and greater authority, which paid for or maintained defensive structures and the soldiers to man them. And as the Byzantine state declined, so the retreat into a Greek and Orthodox identity independent of the earthly empire became an increasingly prominent feature of late Byzantine thought.

It was in this context that the clash of ideas took place between the Hellenistic rationalist tradition, so recently revitalized, and the hesychastic movement, with its anti-rationalist emphasis on personal sanctity, contemplation and the power of prayer. As we have seen in Chapter 6 above, there had long been a tradition of mysticism in the Eastern Church, in which it was open to any Christian to attain a momentary union with the divinity through meditation and spiritual devotion. This tradition had co-existed alongside the Hellenistic elements of Byzantine culture, and a substantial theological literature evolved around the issue of contemplation. But the advent of hesychasm, with its alien modes of posture and meditative practices, caused both concern and ridicule among many traditional thinkers (see Chapter 2 above). Hesychasm or – in its politicized form under the leadership and influence of Gregory Palamas – 'Palamism' nevertheless received the support of many intellectuals and also that of the claimant to the throne, John Kantakouzenos, so that it rapidly became implicated in the political strife and civil conflict between Kantakouzenos and Andronikos III and, after he had died in 1341, his son John V and the empress regent, Anne of Savoy. The two perspectives were embodied in the politics of the time, with the hesychasts able to dominate the imperial court during the period of civil war of the 1340s and to retain considerable authority thereafter. To what extent the hesychastic movement also reflected a response to the political decline of the empire and a flight from the concerns of a secular and religious tradition, which appeared to be doomed to extinction, is impossible to say. But the effects of this influence in cultural terms is evident through a real reduction in the study of the natural and physical sciences (mathematics, astronomy, music) as well as of history and classical literature, and a corresponding rise in the amount of virulent anti-Latin polemic. There continued to be scholars of this classical heritage, but in far fewer numbers and working in a more isolated cultural environment.

Yet an extreme version of the alternative, Hellenistic tradition also found its protagonists, most notably at Mistra in the Despotate of the Morea, in the person of George Gemistus Plethon. Plethon (which is the classical version of his Byzantine Greek name, Gemistos [meaning 'complete' or 'full'], which he adopted to emphasize his philosophical position) moved to the opposite extreme by rejecting Christianity and proposing a Hellenic religion. In this, the moral precepts of Plato would predominate, and in an ideal state – ruled by a philosopher-king and guided by the rule of law, modelled on Plato's *Laws*, – it would provide the Greeks (and here Plethon consciously recalled what he perceived as the unbroken continuity of Greek culture in the Peloponnese) with a new future. Although he had some disciples and supporters – later persecuted by the Church – his more extreme ideas were never taken up, while his more moderate notions on reforming the state could not have worked in view of the inevitable opposition they aroused from the landowning and ecclesiastical elite.

The appearance of these two variant aspects of the Byzantine tradition nicely illustrate the ways in which Byzantines tried to come to terms with the dramatic changes their society was undergoing in its final years. It is ironic that, in the end, the last Byzantines, who increasingly had begun to call themselves *Hellenes* (Greeks), rather than *Romaioi* (Romans), turned their back on the Roman part of their heritage in order to maintain their delusion of superiority and to preserve the force of the imperial ideology. They sought to preserve their identity through a quest for a lost Hellenic – a classical Greek – identity, on the one hand, or a mystical spiritualism which largely ignored the realities of contemporary politics, on the other. Political leaders retreated into literary and artistic pursuits and interests. From the point of view of Hellenic culture and imperial ideology, it was the Church which became the heir to the Roman Empire in the East.

Although the secular state of Byzantium disappeared, the culture which it had nurtured and represented for so long continued to exist through the study of patristic and Byzantine theological literature within the Orthodox world, particularly in monastic contexts; and in the study of the classics and history, especially in Italy, to which many learned Byzantines removed prior to or shortly after the fall of Constantinople in 1453. The influence of Byzantine learning in all fields, as well as of the classical tradition in Byzantine painting, was fundamental to the shaping of the Italian Renaissance thereafter. And even within the new Ottoman world, Greek historians – notably Doukas, Sphrantzes, Kritoboulos and Chalkokondyles – were able to chronicle the last years of the empire, some espousing a pro-Ottoman perspective, others remaining studiously neutral in their account of the disappearance of what had been the foremost power in the east Mediterranean and Balkan region. This historiographical inheritance along with many other facets of Byzantine civilization, was then transmitted to the European Enlightenment scholars of the seventeenth and eighteenth centuries, and so on to our own time. But it is an inheritance that concerns not simply the transmission of a culture and its forms to our own forbears. It has had a direct impact both on Western European responses to the history of the Balkans and the Levant up to the present day, and it has even more directly (through the school syllabus, the structures and traditions of the modern Orthodox Church, the political agendas of politicians from the later eighteenth century into the twenty-first century) affected the political and cultural evolution of Greece, Turkey and their neighbours. Neither the history of the Greek state and its relations with Turkey, nor that of the south and central Balkan lands, can be properly understood without an appreciation of the determining influences of the Byzantine past.

Conclusion

Byzantium holds an abiding attraction for those interested in the history of the western world, and not only because it stood at the crossroads of East and West and served as a bridge between cultures which had evolved in very different directions. It has also come to symbolize a romantic lost medieval Christian world, which was both 'oriental' in its ways and yet 'occidental' in its cultural significance. It represented for many later observers a bastion of Christianity against Islam. It was also a source of politically-relevant – indeed vital – information about the Ottomans who threatened Europe in the sixteenth and seventeenth centuries. In terms of literature and scholarship as well as politics, it was to Byzantine authors and texts that Renaissance scholars and leaders turned when they wanted to find out about this dangerous and powerful challenge to the Christian world. Later, they likewise directed their attention to Byzantine writers, in the context of increasing national self-awareness, as interest grew in the pre-Renaissance and early medieval antecedents of their own lands: in Italy in particular, for example, during the sixteenth and seventeenth centuries, when the value of both Procopius and Agathias was 'discovered'. And although it was both the Islamic world as well as Byzantium which served to transmit the classical heritage to the Renaissance and Enlightenment West, there is no doubt that it was through collections of Byzantine manuscripts and books, moved through various owners or dealers as both gifts and sales, that many texts were preserved, edited and recovered for further study, thus influencing directly the evolution and content of modern classical scholarship.

But in addition, it is important to emphasize that through a complex process of selection of texts and motifs, this classical heritage was reworked and came also indirectly to influence the cultural capital and the moral programme of the ruling elites of the great imperial powers, particularly Great Britain, during the eighteenth and especially the nineteenth and early twentieth centuries. Indeed, it still plays a powerful role. Yet Byzantium continues to carry a negative stigma associated with complex political intrigue and machinations, with corruption and weakness: values which reflect not only the rationalist views of the Enlightenment, but also the racial and cultural prejudices of the crusaders, whose suspicions of this people, whom they considered to be both wealthy as well as effete, cunning and treacherous, were mirrored in the Byzantines' own prejudice and ignorance of the West. The present volume has, I hope, shown that neither romanticism nor caricature are helpful in understanding this dynamic medieval society and culture, indeed, only a careful analysis of its various strands can help to clarify the later course of the history of the lands once ruled by East Rome, especially the Balkans and, in respect of cultural antecedents and claims, of the modern Greek state.

The supposedly static nature of Byzantine culture and society, which was the impression transmitted by much of the popularizing historiography about the empire until not too long ago, has been shown to be a serious misconception. In part, this misconception arises from the fact that the Byzantine presentation of their civilization to the outside world – through literature, art and above all through ritual and ceremonial, as both observed by contemporaries and as transmitted through written sources – has been so successful. It was intended to give the impression of a stately, harmonious and orderly society, in which divinely-ordained hierarchy and order were the rule, and where nothing could contrast more clearly with the chaotic, disorderly outside world: the world of barbarian and foreigner (the two terms meant the same thing for many Byzantines, even at the end of the empire's existence). Beneath this surface of stability and orderliness, however, we can find a lively, evolving and constantly changing society, with many different facets to attract the attention and interest of the observer. The peasant, the bureaucrat, the aristocrat, the merchant, the priest, the monk and the soldier have all left their traces in one form or another, both in respect of the written evidence about their activities and identities, but also in the archaeological and material cultural record, in constructions such as fortresses and roads, for example, as well as in smaller artefacts such as items of textile, ceramic and metalwork. It is from this broad assemblage of data that we can endow the Byzantine world, however partially and imperfectly, with some life, and from which we may perceive something of the liveliness and complexity of this medieval culture; a culture which, through its state administration and its ideological and symbolic structures, above all provides an invaluable link with the world of the late Roman Empire.

Byzantium is best taken on its own terms, neither as the precursor of anything, nor as the successor to something greater: the Roman Empire. Its complex and efficient administrative apparatus, its armies, its equally complex and dynamic ideological system, the thought-world or symbolic universe through which it understood itself, and through which it also represented itself to outsiders: these can only properly be appreciated as parts of a living and evolving social and cultural whole, and only then can its impact on later generations and on the physical space which it once occupied and marked be delineated. This short volume is intended as an introduction to a complex social and cultural formation and, as I noted in the Introduction, I have touched on many aspects only very sketchily. But through those facets I have dealt with, I have nevertheless tried to give an impression of the ways in which the Byzantine state evolved, the sorts of natural and human factors which determined how it could evolve, and the ways in which the complex elements which constitute this medieval society and political formation fit together. I hope at the very least that I will have encouraged the reader to pursue the subject in more detail.

Notes

[1] W.E.H. Lecky, *A History of European Morals from Augustus to Charlemagne*, 2 vols. (London 1869) II, 13f.

[2] Anatolia, from Greek *Anatole*, 'the east', literally, 'the rising of the sun'.

[3] Levant, derived from Fr. lever, 'to raise', with reference to the rising sun, and hence, the east.

[4] Balkan, Turkish for 'range of wooded mountains'.

[5] For a good overview of the Roman road system in Asia Minor, see the map edited by W.M. Calder, G.E. Bean, *A Classical map of Asia Minor* (London: British Institute of Archaeology at Ankara, 1958).

[6] See Chapter 5, below, for this question.

[7] The Lusignans were counts of Poitou in central France. Guy of Lusignan became king of the crusader kingdom of Jerusalem in 1186 when he married Sibyl, the daughter of king Amalric I. Having been captured by Saladin, he was released and made regent of Cyprus by Richard I of England in 1192. Guy died in 1194, whereupon his brother, Aimery, became king of Cyprus. The family ruled the island until 1489.

Glossary

Annona Military rations issued from taxation collected in kind; Gk. *synone*

Apotheke A state depository for various goods and materials; in the 7th-9th centuries the warehouse, and the district to which it pertained, under the control of a *kommerkiarios*

Arianism Christian tendency which viewed Christ as man alone. Condemned as heretical at council of Nicaea, 325

Archontes Holders of imperial titles or offices; provincial landholding elite dominating towns

Augustus Senior emperor of a group, either a college of rulers (e.g. the tetrarchy) or within a single family

Autokrator Greek equivalent of the Latin *imperator*, emperor, used especially after the 7th century to emphasise the emperor's autonomous and God-granted rule

Basileus Formal title of the Byzantine emperor from the 7th century

Book of the Eparch a regulatory guide issued by the office of the governor of Constantinople in the late 9th or early 10th century

Caesar During the tetrarchy, a subordinate ruler under the authority of the *Augustus*; thereafter used of a junior emperor, and from the 7th century also the highest court dignity, normally limited to the emperor's sons, but exceptionally granted to another.

Capitatio-iugatio A formula relating land to labour power for the assessment of taxation, 4th-7th centuries

Chorion A village; in technical usage, a fiscal unit

Civitas Gk. *Polis*, 'city', understood as a self-governing unit with its own territory and administration; the basic fiscal administrative district into the 7th century

Clarissimus Lowest grade of senatorial rank

Codex Justinianus Codification of Roman law produced at the beginning of the reign of Justinian I, and the basis for all later Byzantine law

Colonus Peasant tenant cultivator; some *coloni* were bound to the land they farmed, others retained their freedom of movement

Comitatenses Soldiers/units of the field armies under their *magistri militum*, 4th-7th centuries (cf. *limitanei*)

Curia/curiales Town council and councillors, governing body of a city

Cursus publicus The public postal, transport and relay system

Demes Chariot-racing fan clubs, sometimes acting as foci of political/religious violence or protest

Despotes High imperial title in the later Byzantine period, generally preserved for members of the ruling dynasty; or designation for the ruler of a semi-independent imperial territory

Diocese Lat. *dioecesa*, Gk. *Dioikesis*, an administrative unit consisting of several provinces; from the 4th century the episcopal administrative unit of the Church

Dioiketes Fiscal administrator responsible for the land-tax, usually in a single diocese, from the 7th century

Donatism Rigorist Christian sect chiefly in North Africa, which challenged the validity of sacraments issued by those who compromised with the pre-Christian imperial administration. Condemned on several occasions from the 4th century, it appears to have survived into the 7th century

Dromos Greek term for *cursus publicus*

Dynatos literally, a 'powerful person', so described because of his position in the military or administrative establishment

Dux In later Roman period, commander of a military unit; commander of a unit of *limitanei*, or garrison troops; in the middle and later Byzantine period the title *doux* re-introduced as a high military rank

Ecloga 'Selections' from Roman law, interpreted in the light of its own time and codified as a handbook of Roman law during the reign of Leo III (717-741). The basic Byzantine law-book until the time of the emperor Basil I (867-886)

Emphyteutic lease Lease by which the tenant paid a fixed rent (in kind or cash), the terms of which were transferrable and were often held in perpetuity and hereditarily

Eunuch Castrated male who could occupy most positions in the imperial system; some offices were, at least in theory, restricted to eunuchs or non-eunuchs alone. Eunuchs often received special preference since they were legally barred from imperial office and were therefore regarded as trustworthy subordinates by the emperors

Excubitores Small palace bodyguard recruited from Isaurian mountain people by the emperor Leo I. During the 7th century they became a show troop, but the unit was revived as a larger active elite regiment under Constantine V in the 760s, as the *exkoubita*. It disappears during the later 11th century

Foederati 'Federates', from the later 4th century barbarian troops recruited on the basis of a treaty by which they and their families were allowed to move onto imperial territory and share the land and its income with the indigenous population and landlords. During the 6th century the term came to mean units of non-Roman mercenaries (although Romans could also join) brigaded together; and during the 7th century the whole corps was posted to Asia Minor, probably Lycaonia, where they formed a subdivision or *tourma* of the *Anatolikon* theme. The term disappears after the early 12th century.

Follis Low value copper coin worth 40 *nummi*: there were 288 to the gold *solidus* or *nomisma*

Gasmouloi In the later empire, originally persons of mixed Greek and Latin race, paid as mercenaries

Genikon (sekreton) The general treasury and main fiscal department of government after the 7th century

Gloriosus Gk. *endoxos*, high-ranking senatorial title introduced by Justinian

Hesychasm Late Byzantine mystical approach to prayer and meditation, especially popular in monastic circles

Hexagram Silver coin introduced by Heraclius, lit. 'six grams', twelve to a *nomisma*. Although issued in large quanities under Heraclius and Constans II, its use dwindled until production ceased in the early 8th century

Homoiousios 'Of like substance', i.e. of similar, but not the same, essence. A key term in the Christological controversies of the period up to the 7th century

Homoousios 'Consubstantial', i.e. of the same essence, another basic term in the Christological debates of the 4th-7th centuries

Hyperpyron The highest value gold coin from the reform of Alexios I Komnenos

Iconoclasm Rejection of the honouring of sacred images, which was regarded as a form of idolatry. Condemned as a heresy at the council of Nicaea in 787, and again in 843

Illustris Until the middle of the 6th century the highest grade of senatorial rank

Kapnikon Tax on 'hearths' or households, introduced probably during the later seventh or 8th century

Kastron 'Fortress', but after the 7th century also used to mean 'town' or 'city'

Kastrophylax 'Castle guardian', governor of a fortress

Katepano Military officer in command of independent unit and/or district (8th-12th centuries); imperial provincial/regional governor (after the 13th century)

Kephale Provincial military and civil governor, in charge of a *katepanikion*, a military-administrative district, in the 14th-15th centuries

Kleisoura Small frontier command; district along/behind the frontier (esp. later 8th-10th centuries)

Kommerkiarioi Fiscal officials responsible for state-supervised commerce and the taxes thereon. During the 7th and 8th centuries had a much expanded role in the fiscal system and the supplying of the armies; from the middle of the 8th century reverted to chiefly commercial functions.

Limitanei Provincial garrison troops in the later Roman period

Logariastes Chief fiscal officer following the reforms of Alexios I

Logothetes Fiscal official, lit. 'accountant'; from the 7th century all the main fiscal bureaux were placed under such officials, who were often very high-ranking

Logothetes ton agelon 'Logothete of the herds', in charge of imperial stud ranches in the provinces of Asia and Phrygia, and successor of the older *praepositus gregum*

Magister militum Divisional military commander, replaced by the *strategos* after *c*.660

Magister Officiorum 'Master of offices', leading civil minister and close associate of the emperors in the later Roman period

Magnificus High-ranking senatorial grade introduced by Justinian

Metochion a subordinate or daughter monastery under the authority of a larger or more powerful monastic house

Miliaresion Lat. *milliarensis*, a silver coin worth one twelfth of a *solidus/nomisma*. Originally struck at 72 to the pound, from the seventh-eleventh centuries used of the basic silver coin, struck at varying rates from 144 to 108

to the pound, especially of the reformed silver coin introduced under Leo III. Production ceased under Alexios I, but the term continued in use as a money of account

Monophysitism Doctrine of the 'single nature': Christian tendency rejecting the two natures, both human and divine, of Christ, believing instead that the divine subsumed the human nature after the incarnation. Condemned as heretical at council of Chalcedon in 451, but remained the majority creed in large parts of Syria and Egypt, and of the Syrian and Coptic churches today

Monoenergism A compromise formula developed by the patriarch Sergius, by which the issue of the two natures was made secondary to the notion that they were united in a single divine energy. Rejected by all parties within a few years of its being proposed, and condemned as heretical at the sixth ecumenical council in 681

Monotheletism A second attempt at compromise proposed by Sergius and supported by the emperor Heraclius, by which the key issue was acceptance of the notion of a single divine will, within which natures and energy were subsumed. Imposed during the reign of Constans II, but condemned and rejected at the council of 681

Nestorianism 5th-century Christian heresy in which the divine and human aspects of Christ were seen not as unified in a single person, but operating in conjunction. Nestorians were accused of teaching two persons in Christ, God and man, and thus two distinct sons, human and divine. Condemned in 431 at the council of Ephesus, the Nestorians left the empire and established their own Church in Persia in 486. Nestorianism established a firm foothold in Persia and spread across northern India and central Asia as far as China. It survives today, especially in northern Iraq, as the Assyrian Orthodox Church.

Nomisma Lat. *solidus*, the gold coin introduced by Constantine I which remained the basis for the Byzantine precious metal coinage until the Latin conquest in 1204. Weighing 4.5g, it was reckoned at 24 *keratia*, a unit of account (carat), and its fractions were 12 silver *hexagrams* or *milliaresia* and 288 copper *folleis*. From the middle of the 11th century increasingly depreciated, it was reformed by Alexios I, and more commonly known thereafter as the *nomisma hyperpyron* or simply *hyperpyron*

Paroikos Peasant tenant on private or state land, paying rent as well as tax. Byzantine equivalent of *colonus*

Paulicians A dualist sect of the 7th-9th centuries. During the mid-9th-century they took over much of eastern Anatolia and fought the empire with the support of the Caliphate. They were crushed by Basil I

Polis see *Civitas*

Praetorian Prefecture The largest administrative unit of the empire from the time of Constantine I, under a praetorian prefect (originally a commander of the praetorian guard). Each prefecture was divided into dioceses, then provinces, and had its own fiscal administrative and judicial structure

Praktikon Document drawn up by fiscal officials listing obligations of tenants on an estate or estates

Prokathemenos Town/fortress governor of the Comnene period

Pronoia Attribution of fiscal revenues, usually to a soldier in return for military service. Appears first on a limited basis in the 12th century; eventually included lifelong and heritable grants

Prosalentai Oarsmen in the imperial ships who appear to have been given lands in certain coastal regions and islands to support their service

Protonotarios Chief fiscal administrator of a theme from *c.*820 to mid-11th century

Res privata Imperial treasury, originating in emperor's private finances. Subsumed during the 7th century into the department of imperial estates

Sacred largesses Government fiscal department originating in the imperial household, responsible for bullion and coinage until the seventh century

Sakellarios Senior fiscal officer with oversight over other fiscal departments after the 7th century. Originally in charge of emperor's personal treasury or 'purse' (*sacellum*)

Scholae In the period from Constantine I until the later 5th century a crack cavalry unit; by the later 5th a show force. The units were reformed and became once more elite

regiments under Constantine V, forming until the 11th century the core of the imperial field armies

Spectabilis Second-rank senatorial grade

Strateia (1) State service of any sort (2) Service in the army (3) The obligation to support a soldier/a property whose tenant/owner was subject to such an obligation

Strategos A general; in Byzantine times usually the governor of a military district or *thema*, and commander of its soldiers

Stratiotes A soldier; by derivation from the 10th century a holder of 'military' land, subject to the obligation to support a soldier

Stratiotikon

logothesion Fiscal department which dealt with recruitment, muster-rolls and military pay from the 7th century

Tagmata (1) Elite field units recruited by Constantine V. They formed the core of imperial field armies until the eleventh century; (2) any full-time mercenary unit – used especially of foreign mercenary troops in the 10th-12th centuries

Territory Lat. *territorium*, the region pertaining to and administered from a city

Tetrarchy Lit., 'rule of four', the system invented by Diocletian to provide for better administrative and military governance of the empire. It broke down, however, over the period from 305-310

Thelematarioi 'volunteers', soldiers/watchmen who served on the basis of grants of land given by the emperors, in the region of Constantinople

Thema A 'theme', from the middle of the 7th century (1) the district across which soldiers were quartered, and from which they were recruited; (2) an administrative unit; (3) the army based in such a region

Theotokos Literally, 'God-bearer', epithet applied to the Virgin Mary

Typikon Document setting out the rules and regulations for the administration of a monastic community

Tzakones (or *Lakones*) From the southern Peloponnese, they served as light-armed troops

Varangians Mercenary unit first recruited during the reign of Basil II, consisting of Russian and Scandinavian adventurers and mercenaries

Appendix 1
Emperors of the Eastern Roman empire

Constantine I	324-337	Romanos I Lakapenos	920-944
Constantius II	337-361	Romanos II	959-963
Julian	361-363	Nikephoros II Phokas	963-969
Jovian	363-364	John I Tzimiskes	969-976
Valens	364-378	Basil II	976-1025
Theodosius I	379-395	Constantine VIII	1025-1028
Arcadius	395-408	Romanos III Argyros	1028-1034
Theodosius II	408-450	Michael IV the Paphlagonian	1034-1041
Marcian	450-457	Michael V Kalaphates	1041-1042
Leo I	457-474	Zoe and Theodora	1042
Leo II	474	Constantine IX Monomachos	1042-1055
Zeno	474-475	Theodora (again)	1055-1056
Basiliscus	475-476	Michael VI Stratiotikos	1056-1057
Zeno (restored)	476-491	Isaac I Komnenos	1057-1059
Anastasius I	491-518	Constantine X Doukas	1059-1067
Justin I	518-527	Eudokia	1067
Justinian I	527-565	Romanos IV Diogenes	1068-1071
Tiberius II Constantine	578-582	Eudokia (again)	1071
Maurice	582-602	Michael VII Doukas	1071-1078
Phokas	602-610	Nikephoros III Botaneiates	1078-1081
Heraclius	610-641	Alexios I Komnenos	1081-1118
Constantine III and Heraclonas	641	John II Komnenos	1118-1143
Constans II	641-668	Manuel I Komnenos	1143-1180
Constantine IV	668-685	Alexios II Komnenos	1180-1183
Justinian II	685-695	Andronikos I Komnenos	1183-1185
Leontios	695-698	Isaac II Angelos	1185-1195
Tiberios III	698-705	Alexios III Angelos	1195-1203
Justinian II (restored)	705-711	Isaac II (restored) and	
Philippikos Bardanes	711-713	Alexios IV Angelos	1203-1204
Anastasios II	713-715	Alexios V Mourtzouphlos	1204
Theodosios III	715-717	Constantine (XI) Laskaris	1204 (Nicaea)
Leo III	717-741	Theodore I Laskaris	1204-1222 (Nic.)
Constantine V	741-775	John III Doukas Vatatzes	1222-1254 (Nic.)
Artabasdos	741-742	Theodore II Laskaris	1254-1258 (Nic.)
Leo IV	775-780	John IV Laskaris	1258-1261 (Nic.)
Constantine VI	780-797	Michael VIII Palaiologos	1259-1282
Eirene	797-802	Andronikos II Palaiologos	1282-1328
Nikephoros I	802-811	Michael IX Palaiologos	1294-1320
Staurakios	811	Andronikos III Palaiologos	1328-1341
Michael I	811-813	John V Palaiologos	1341-1391
Leo V	813-820	John VI Kantakouzenos	1341-1354
Michael II	820-829	Andronikos IV Palaiologos	1376-1379
Theophilos	829-842	John VII Palaiologos	1390
Michael III	842-867	Manuel II Palaiologos	1391-1425
Basil I	867-886	John VIII Palaiologos	1425-1448
Leo VI	886-912	Constantine XI (XII)	
Alexander	912-913	Palaiologos	1448-1453
Constantine VII	913-959		

Appendix 2
Chronological chart

284-305 Diocletian and the tetrarchy

306-37 Constantine I (sole ruler from 324)

311 Edict of toleration issued by Galerius

312 Constantine's victory at the Milvian bridge

313 Edict of toleration issued by Constantine and Licinius

325 Council of Nicaea and condemnation of Arianism (first ecumenical council)

330 Consecration of Constantinople

337 Baptism and death of Constantine I

361-3 Julian the Apostate leads pagan reaction and attempts to limit the influence of Christianity

364 Jovian dies: empire divided between Valentinian I (West) and Valens (East)

378 Defeat and death of Valens at hands of Visigoths at battle of Adrianople

381 First council of Constantinople (second ecumenical council): re-affirms rejection of Arianism; asserts right of Constantinopolitan patriarchate to take precedence after Rome

395 Death of Theodosius I and division of empire into eastern and western parts again

410 Visigoths sack Rome

413 Construction of Theodosian land walls of Constantinople

429-533 Vandal kingdom in North Africa

431 Council of Ephesus, rejection of Nestorianism (third ecumenical council)

449 Council of Ephesus ('robber council')

450/451 Council of Chalcedon, defeat of Monophysitism (fourth ecumenical council)

450 Attila and Huns defeated at Chalons

455 Sack of Rome by Vandals

476 Deposition of Romulus Augustulus by master of soldiers, Odoacer. End of the Western Roman empire

488 Ostrogoths under Theoderic march into Italy

493-526 Theoderic rules Ostrogothic kingdom of Italy

507-711 Kingdom of Visigoths in Spain

529 Justinian closes Academy of Athens; Codex Justinianus completed

532 'Nika' riot in Constantinople

533-4 Belisarius reconquers Africa (pacification completed in 540s); Pandects or Digest completed

534 Belisarius begins reconquest of Italy (war lasts until 553)

537 Dedication of the new Church of the Holy Wisdom (Hagia Sophia) in Constantinople

540 Persian king Chosroes I takes Antioch in Syria

542+ Plague in the Byzantine world

550+ Avars establish hegemony over Slavs north of Black Sea and Danube

552 Narses defeats Totila and last Ostrogothic resistance in Italy

553 Second council of Constantinople (fifth ecumenical council): Three Chapters condemned, concessions to Monophysites.

553+ Reconquest of South-East Spain from Visigoths

558 Treaty with Avars and agreement to pay 'subsidies'

562 'Fifty-year peace' signed with Persia

568+ Lombards driven westward from Danube, invade Italy.

565-591 Wars with Persia

566+ Slavs begin to infiltrate across Danube frontier; pressure on frontier fortresses from Avars

572 Lombards besiege Ravenna

577 Major invasion of Balkans led by Avars

584, 586 Avaro-Slav attacks on Thessaloniki

591-602 Gradual success in pushing Avars back across Danube

602 Maurice overthrown, Phokas proclaimed emperor

603 War with Persia; situation in Balkans deteriorates

610 Phokas overthrown by Heraclius, son of exarch of Africa at Carthage

611-620s Central and northern Balkans lost

614-619 Persians occupy Syria, Palestine and Egypt

622 Mohammed leaves Mecca for Medina (the 'Hijra')

622-627 Heraclius campaigns in East against Persians

626 Combined Avaro-Slav and Persian siege of Constantinople fails

626-628 Heraclius defeats Persian forces in East

629 Peace with Persia

634+ Arabs begin raids into Palestine

634-646 Arab conquest and occupation of Syria, Palestine, Mesopotamia, Egypt (636 – battle of Gabitha/Yarmuk)

638 *Ekthesis* of Heraclius: attempt to reconcile Monophysites and Chalcedonians

644+ Beginning of long-term raids and plundering expeditions against Byzantine Asia Minor

648 *Typos* of Constans II. Imperial enforcement of Monotheletism

649 Lateran synod in Rome; Maximus Confessor and pope Martin reject imperial Monotheletism

653 Martin and Maximus arrested by exarch Theodore Calliopas and sent to Constantinople

655 Martin and Maximus found guilty of treason and exiled. Sea battle of Phoenix, Byzantines defeated

662 Constans II leads expedition through Balkans into Italy, takes up residence in Sicily

668 Constans assassinated; Mizizios proclaimed emperor in Sicily, but defeated by forces loyal to Constantine IV

674-8 Arab blockade and yearly sieges of Constantinople. First recorded use of 'liquid fire' (Greek fire), to destroy Arab fleet

679-80 Arrival of Bulgars on Danube; defeat of Byzantine forces under Constantine IV

680-1 Third council of Constantinople (sixth ecumenical council). Monotheletism rejected

685-92 Truce between caliphate and Byzantium (Arab civil war)

691-2 Quinisext or Trullan council at Constantinople. Canons partly rejected by papacy

693 Byzantine defeat at Sebastoupolis

698 Carthage falls to Arabs; final loss of Africa

717-8 Siege of Constantinople; Leo, general of Anatolikon, seizes power, crowned as Leo III

726 Volcanic eruption on Thera/Santorini, leading Leo to adopt iconoclastic ideas

730 Patriarch Germanus resigns; probable beginning of public policy of iconoclasm

739/740 Leo and Constantine defeat Arab column at Akroinon

739 Earthquake hits Constantinople

741 Artabasdos, Leo's son-in-law, rebels against Constantine V and seizes Constantinople

743/4 Artabasdos defeated

746+ Plague in Constantinople

750 Abbasid revolution, removal of Umayyads from power, capital of Caliphate moved to Baghdad.

751-2 Constantine V begins publicly preaching in favour of iconoclasm

754 Iconoclast council of Hiereia (claims to be seventh ecumenical council)

750s-770s Constantine launches major expeditions against Bulgars and Arabs

786 Eirene attempts to hold seventh ecumenical council in Constantinople. Council abandoned due to opposition of iconoclast soldiers

787 Second council of Nicaea (seventh ecumenical council). Iconoclasm rejected and condemned

792 Byzantines under Constantine VI defeated by Bulgars at Markellai

797 Constantine VI deposed by mother Eirene; blinded and dies

800 Coronation of Charlemagne by pope in St. Peters, Rome

802 Eirene deposed by chief finance minister Nikephoros (Nikephoros I)

811 Nikephoros defeated and killed by forces under Khan Krum after initially successful campaign in Bulgaria

813 Bulgar victories over Byzantine forces

815 Leo V convenes synod at Constantinople; iconoclasm reintroduced as official policy

821-3 Rebellion of Thomas 'the Slav'

824+ Beginning of Arab conquest of Sicily and of Crete

826 Theodore of Stoudion dies

838 Arab invasion of Asia Minor; siege and sack of Amorion

843 Council held in Constantinople to re-affirm acts of seventh ecumenical council. Empress regent Theodora and chief courtiers restore images; end of official iconoclasm

850s Missionary activity in Bulgaria

860 Rus' (Viking) attack on Constantinople; mission to Chazars of St. Cyril

863 Major Byzantine victory over Arabs at Poson in Anatolia

864 Conversion of Bulgar Khan and leaders

869-70 Council convoked by Basil I at Constantinople to settle Photian schism: Photios deposed, Ignatios, his predecessor, re-instated. Bulgaria placed under Constantinopolitan ecclesiastical jurisdiction (contrary to papal demands)

879-880 Acts of council of 869-870 annulled, Photios re-instated. Recognized in Rome, schism ended

900+ Final loss of Sicily; Bulgar expansionism under Tsar Symeon; war with Byzantines

917 Bulgar victory at river Achelo

920 Local council of Constantinopolitan Church held in Constantinople to settle schism caused by the fourth marriage of Leo VI ('Tetragamy'), reconciling Nicholas I and his supporters, who condemned the marriage, with the patriarch Euthymios, who had condoned it.

922 Peace with Bulgars

923-44 Byzantine conquests and eastward expansion led by general John Kourkouas

960-1 Recovery of Crete under general Nikephoros Phokas

963+ Major Byzantine offensives in East, creation of new frontier regions

965 Nikephoros II captures Tarsus and Cyprus

969 Nikephoros II captures Aleppo and Antioch

969-76 Reign of John I Tzimiskes. Continuation of eastern expansion; defeat of Bulgars with help of Rus' allies under Svyatoslav; defeat of Rus' at Silistra (971)

975 John I invades Palestine, takes several towns and fortresses, but withdraws

989 Conversion of Vladimir of Kiev to Christianity

985+ Bulgar resistance in western Balkans leads to growth of first Bulgarian empire under Tsar Samuel

990-1019 Basil II crushes Bulgar resistance; Bulgaria re-incorporated into empire, Danube new frontier in North

1022 Armenian territories annexed to empire

1034-41 Michael IV takes first steps in debasement of gold currency

1054 Schism with papacy

1055 Seljuks take Baghdad; Norman power in southern Italy expanding

1071 Romanos IV defeated and captured at Mantzikert by Seljuks; beginning of Turk occupation of central Anatolia; Normans take Bari

1070+ Major Pecheneg advances into Balkans; civl war within empire

1081 Alexios Komnenos rebels, defeats Nikephoros III and is crowned emperor

1081-5 Norman invasion of western Balkan provinces

1082-4 Commercial privileges granted to Venice

1091 Seljuk-Pecheneg siege of Constantinople; defeat of Pechenegs

1092 Coinage reform carried out by Alexios I

1094 Synod held at Blachernae to decide the issue of Leo of Chalcedon, a hard line opponent of the Church's decision to melt down ecclesiastical treasures to aid the imperial treasury. Deposed by the permanent synod in 1086, this council reinstated him after he was reconciled to the official Church position.

1097+ First crusade; Seljuks defeated

1098/9 Jerusalem captured; Latin principalities and Kingdom of Jerusalem established in Palestine and Syria

1108 Alexios defeats Normans under Bohemund

1111 Commercial privileges granted to Pisa

1130s Alliance with German empire against Normans of S. Italy

1138-1142 Byzantine confrontation with Crusader principality of Antioch

1143-1180 Manuel I Komnenos: pro-western politics become major factor in Byzantine foreign policy

1146-1148 Second crusade

1153 Treaty of Constanz between Frederick I (Barbarossa) and papacy against Byzantium

1155-7 Successful imperial campaign in Italy; commercial and political negotiations with Genoa

1156-7 Council of Constantinople: teachings of the patriarch elect, Panteugenos, condemned

1158-9 Imperial forces march against Antioch

1160+ Successful imperial political involvement in Italy against German imperial interests; Manuel defeats Hungarians and Serbs in Balkans and reaffirms imperial pre-eminence

1166-7 Local Constantinopolitan council meets to discuss Christological issues arising from discussions with western theologians

1169-70 Commercial treaties with Pisa and Genoa

1171+ Byzantine-Venetian hostilities increase

1175-6 Manuel plans crusade in East

1176 Defeat of imperial forces under Manuel by Seljuk Sultan Kilidj Aslan at Myriokephalon

1180 Manuel dies; strong anti-western sentiments in Constantinople

1182 Massacre of westerners, especially Italian merchants and their dependents, in Constantinople

1185 Normans sack Thessaloniki; Andronikos Komnenos deposed

1186+ Rebellion in Bulgaria, defeat of local Byzantine troops, establishment of second Bulgarian empire

1187 Defeat of third crusade at battle of Horns of Hattin; Jerusalem retaken by Saladin

1192 Treaties with Genoa and Pisa

1203-4 Fourth crusade, with Venetian financial and naval support, marches against Constantinople. After the capture and sack of the city in 1204, the Latin empire is established, along with several principalities and other territories under Latin or Venetian rule

1204-5 Successor states in Nicaea, Epirus and Trebizond established

1205 Latin emperor Baldwin I defeated by Bulgars

1259 Michael VIII succeeds to throne in empire of Nicaea; Nicaean army defeats combined Latin and Epirot army at battle of Pelagonia. Fortress-town of Mistra handed over to Byzantines (Nicaea)

1261 During absence of main Latin army Nicaean forces enter and seize Constantinople

1265 Pope invites Charles of Anjou, brother of Louis IX of France, to support him militarily against Manfred of Sicily and the Hohenstaufen power in Italy

1266 Manfred of Sicily defeated at battle of Benevento by Charles of Anjou; Angevin plans, supported by papacy, evolve to invade and conquer the Byzantine empire

1274 Gregory X summons second council of Lyons; representatives of Byzantine Church present; union of the Churches agreed, under threat of papally-approved invasion led by Charles of Anjou. Union not accepted in the Byzantine empire

1282 'Sicilian vespers'; death of Charles of Anjou and end of his plans to invade Byzantium

1285 Council of Constantinople ('second synod of Blachernae'): discusses and rejects pro-western interpretation of the Trinity as enunciated by the patriarch John XI Bekkos. Also rejects decisions of Council of Lyons (1274)

1280-1337 Ottomans take nearly all remaining Byzantine possessions in Asia Minor (Ephesus 1328, Brusa 1326)

1303 Andronikos II hires Catalan company as mercenary troop

1321-1328 Civil war between Andronikos II and Andronikos III

1329 Turks take Nicaea

1331-55 Stefan Dušan Kral (King) of Serbia

1337 Turks take Nicomedia

1341 Synod in Constantinople to discuss the issues raised by the traditionalist Orthodox views (defended by Barlaam of Calabria) and those who supported Hesychasm (Gregory Palamas). The hesychast faction won a clear victory and Barlaam left Constantinople

1341-7 Civil war between John V (supported by Serbs) and John VI Kantakouzenos (with Turkish help)

1341-50 Commune hostile to aristocracy rules Thessaloniki

1346 Stefan Dušan crowned emperor of the Serbs and Greeks

1340+ Height of Serbian empire under Stefan Dušan

1347 Black Death reaches Constantinople; local council at Constantinople confirms decisions of council held in 1341

1351 Synod in Constantinople approves Palamism (hesychasm) in detailed discussion of its theological arguments

1354-5 Civil war between John VI and John V (backed by Genoa). Ottomans employed as allies establish themselves in Gallipoli and Thrace

1355 John VI abdicates and enters a monastery. John V proposes union of Churches to Pope

1365 Ottomans take Adrianople, which becomes their capital

1366 John V visits Hungary seeking support against Ottoman threat

1371 Ottomans defeat Serbs in battle

1373 John V forced to submit to Ottoman Sultan Murat I; John's son Andronikos IV rebels but is defeated

1376-9 Civil war in Byzantium: Andronikos IV rebels against John V, who is supported by his younger son Manuel

1379 John V restored with Turkish and Venetian support

1388 Bulgarians defeated by Ottomans

1389 Battle of Kosovo: Serbs forced to withdraw by Ottomans, Serb empire ends. Accession of Bayezit I

1393 Turks capture Thessaly. Battle of Trnovo, Bulgarian empire destroyed

1396 Sigismund of Hungary organises crusade against Ottoman threat, but is utterly defeated at Nicopolis

1397-1402 Bayezit I besieges Constantinople, but army withdrawn when Turks defeated by Timur at battle of Ankara (1402)

1399-1402 Manuel II tours Europe to elicit military and financial support (December 1400, guest of Henry IV in London)

1422 Murat II lays siege to Constantinople

1423 Governor of Thessaloniki (a brother of John VIII) hands the city over to the Venetians

1430 Thessaloniki retaken by Ottomans; populace and Venetian garrison massacred

1439 Council of Ferrara moves to Florence; union of Churches formally agreed by emperor John VIII, present at council

1444 Hungarians and western crusaders, led by Vladislav of Hungary and Poland, defeated at battle of Varna. Vladislav killed in battle

1448 John VIII dies; his brother Constantine, Despot of the Morea, succeeds as Constantine XI, with coronation at Mistra in 1449

1451 Mehmet II becomes Sultan

1452 Union of Churches proclaimed at Constantinople

1453 Mehmet II lays siege to Constantinople. May 29th: Janissaries break through defences and permit main Ottoman army to enter city. Constantine XI, the last emperor, died in the fighting, and his body was never identified.

1460 Mistra falls to the Turks

1461 Trebizond falls to the Turks

Appendix 3
Further reading

It is unfortunately the case that a great deal of the modern literature on the Byzantine world is not in English – German, French, Greek and Russian predominate. This means that large numbers of works, both general surveys of Byzantine culture as well as detailed studies of particular aspects of Byzantine history, civilisation or institutions is not accessible to those who cannot read these languages. In the following I have tried to present a good cross-section of modern studies in English which cover the aspects I have touched upon in this volume, and which will provide more detailed accounts of the many issues I have dealt with only superficially. I have included a small number of non-English publications for the opening chapters, which may serve as a guide to some of this literature for those who wish to pursue it. For the latter, good current biibliographies and reviews of work in progress can be found in several of the specialist journals, such as: *Byzantion* (Brussels); *Byzantinische Zeitschrift* (Cologne); *Byzantinoslavica* (Prague); *Revue des Études Byzantines* (Paris).

Introduction

Norman H. Baynes and H. St.L.B. Moss, eds., *Byzantium: an introduction to East Roman civilization* (Oxford 1969)

Robert Browning, *The Byzantine empire* (Washington D.C. 1980/1992)

Guglielmo Cavallo, ed., *The Byzantines* (Chicago 1997)

Deno J. Geanakoplos, *Byzantium. Church, society, and civilization seen through contemporary eyes* (Chicago 1984) (a useful collection of sources in translation)

Alexander Kazhdan with Giles Constable, *People and Power in Byzantium: an introduction to modern Byzantine studies* (Washington D.C. 1982)

Cyril Mango, *Byzantium: the empire of New Rome* (London 1980/1994)

George Ostrogorsky, *A history of the Byzantine state*, trans. J. Hussey (Oxford 1968) (somewhat out-of-date, but not yet replaced)

Speros Vryonis, Jr., *Byzantium and Europe* (London 1967)

Philip D. Whitting, ed., *Byzantium: an introduction* (Oxford 1971/1981)

Alexander Kazhdan, ed., *The Oxford dictionary of Byzantium*, 3 vols. (New York-Oxford 1991)

Chapter 1: The transformation of the Roman world c. 300-741

J.W. Barker, *Justinian and the later Roman empire* (Madison, Wisconsin 1966)

P.S. Barnwell, *Emperors, prefects and kings. The Roman West 395-565* (London 1992)

P.R.L. Brown, *The world of late antiquity* (London 1971)

J.B. Bury, *A history of the later Roman empire from Arcadius to Irene (395 A.D. to 800 A.D.)* (London 1889/Amsterdam 1966)

The Cambridge History of Islam, vol. 1: *The central Islamic lands*; vol. 2: *The further Islamic lands, Islamic society and civilisation*, P.M. Holt, A.K.S. Lambton, B. Lewis, eds. (Cambridge 1970)

Av. Cameron, P. Garnsey, eds., *The Cambridge ancient history*, XIII: *The late empire, A.D. 337-425* (Cambridge 1998)

Averil Cameron, *The Mediterranean world in late antiquity A.D. 395-600* (London 1993)

R. Collins, *Early medieval Europe 300-1000* (London 1991)

T. Cornell, J. Matthews, *Atlas of the Roman world* (Oxford 1982)

P. Crone, *Slaves on horses. The evolution of the Islamic polity* (Cambridge 1980)

P. Crone, M. Cook, *Hagarism. The making of the Islamic world* (Cambridge 1977)

F.M. Donner, *The early Arabic Conquests* (Princeton 1981)

J.F. Haldon, *Byzantium in the seventh century: the transformation of a culture* (Cambridge 1990)

M.G.S. Hodgson, *The venture of Islam. Conscience and history in a world civilization*, 3 vols. (Chicago 1974)

A.H.M. Jones, *The later Roman empire: a social, economic and administrative survey*, 3 vols. and maps (Oxford 1964)

W.E. Kaegi, *Byzantium and the early Islamic conquests* (Cambridge 1992)

W.E. Kaegi, *Byzantium and the decline of Rome* (Princeton NJ 1968)

D. Kagan, *The end of the Roman empire. Decline or transformation?* (Lexington, Mass. 1978)

H. Kennedy, *The Prophet and the age of the Caliphates: the Islamic Near East from the sixth to the eleventh century* (London 1986)

R. Krautheimer, *Three Christian capitals, topography and politics* (Berkeley 1983)

S. Mazzarino, *The end of the ancient world*, trans. G. Homes (London 1966)

M. McCormick, *Eternal victory. Triumphal rulership in late antiquity, Byzantium and the early medieval West* (Cambridge 1986)

G. Ostrogorsky, *A history of the Byzantine state*, Eng. trans. J. Hussey (Oxford 1968)

M.A. Shaban, *Islamic history, AD 600-750 (AH 132). A New Interpretation* (Cambridge 1971)

E.A. Thompson, *Romans and barbarians: the decline of the western empire* (Madison, Wisconsin 1982)

J. Vogt, *The decline of Rome: the metamorphosis of ancient civilization* (London 1967)

F.W. Walbank, *The awful revolution: the decline of the Roman empire in the West* (Liverpool 1969)

M. Whittow, *The making of Orthodox Byzantium, 600-1025* (London 1996)

C.J. Wickham, *Early medieval Italy* (London 1981)

C.J. Wickham, 'The other transition: from the ancient world to feudalism', *Past and Present* 103 (1984) 3-36

Chapter 2: A medieval empire c. 741-1453

M. Angold, *The Byzantine empire 1025-1204. A political history* (London 1984)

M. Angold, *A Byzantine government in exile: government and society under the Laskarids of Nicaea (1204-1261)* (Oxford 1975)

M. Angold, *Church and society in Byzantium under the Comneni, 1081-1261* (Cambridge 1995)

M.C. Bartusis, *The late Byzantine army. Arms and society, 1204-1453* (Philadelphia 1992)

C.M. Brand, *Byzantium confronts the West, 1180-1204* (Harvard 1968)

J.B. Bury, *A history of the later Roman empire from Arcadius to Irene (395 A.D. to 800 A.D.)* (London 1889/Amsterdam 1966)

R. Browning, *The Byzantine empire* (Washington D.C. 1992)

L. Brubaker, ed., *Byzantium in the ninth century: dead or alive?* (Aldershot 1998)

The Cambridge medieval history, IV: *The Byzantine empire*, 2 parts, revised ed. J.M. Hussey (Cambridge 1966)

R. Collins, *Early medieval Europe 300-1000* (London 1991)

S. Franklin, J. Shepard (eds)., *Byzantine diplomacy* (Aldershot, 1992)

S. Franklin, J. Shepard, *The emergence of Rus, 750-1200* (London 1996)

S. Gero, *Byzantine iconoclasm During the Reign of Leo III with particular attention to the oriental sources* (CSCO subsidia, 41. Louvain 1973)

S. Gero, *Byzantine iconoclasm during the reign of Constantine V with particular attention to the oriental sources* (CSCO subsidia, 52. Louvain 1977)

J.F. Haldon, *Warfare, state and society in the Byzantine world, 565-1204* (London 1999)

A. Harvey, *Economic expansion in the Byzantine empire 900-1200* (Cambridge 1989)

J. Herrin, *The formation of Christendom* (Princeton 1987)

W.E. Kaegi, Jr., *Byzantine military unrest 471-843: an interpretation* (Amsterdam 1981)

H. Kennedy, *The early Abbasid Caliphate: a political history* (London 1981)

R.-J. Lilie, *Byzantium and the Crusader states 1096-1204*, trans. J.C. Morris, J.E. Ridings (Oxford 1993)

M. McCormick, 'Byzantium and the West' in R. McKitterick, ed., *New Cambridge Medieval History* (1995) 349-80; a general overview focussed on the eighth and ninth centuries.

P. Magdalino, *The empire of Manuel I Komnenos, 1143-1180* (Cambridge 1993)

C. Mango, *Byzantium: the empire of New Rome* (London 1980/1994)

D.M. Nicol, *Byzantium and Venice* (Cambridge 1988)

D.M. Nicol, *The Despotate of Epiros, 1267-1479* (Cambridge 1984)

D.M. Nicol, *The last centuries of Byzantium, 1261-1453* (London 1972)

D.M. Nicol, *The end of the Byzantine empire* (London 1979)

D. Obolensky, *The Byzantine commonwealth. Eastern Europe 500-1453* (London 1971)

G. Ostrogorsky, *A history of the Byzantine state*, Eng. trans. J. Hussey (Oxford 1968)

S. Runciman, *A history of the first Bulgarian empire* (London 1930)

B. Spuler, *The Muslim world, I: the age of the Caliphs; II: the Mongol period*, trans. F.R.C. Bagley (Leiden 1960)

A. Toynbee, *Constantine Porphyrogenitus and his world* (London 1973)

Sp. Vryonis, jr., *The decline of medieval Hellenism in Asia Minor and the process of Islamization from the eleventh through the fifteenth century* (Berkeley-Los Angeles-London 1971)

M. Whittow, *The making of Orthodox Byzantium, 600-1025* (London 1996)

C.J. Wickham, *Early medieval Italy* (London 1981)

Chapter 3: The peoples and lands of Byzantium

a. Physical geography, communications, land use

Atlas of the Arab world and the Middle East ed. C.F. Beckingham (London/NY 1960)

A.A.M. Bryer, 'Byzantine Agricultural Implements: the Evidence of Medieval Illusrations of Hesiod's *Works and Days*', *Annual of the British School at Athens* 81 (1986) 45-80

C. Cahen, *Pre-Ottoman Turkey: a general survey of the material and spiritual culture c.1071-1330* (London 1968)

M. Cary, *The geographic background of Greek and Roman histsory* (Oxford 1949)

F.W. Carter, ed., *An historical geography of the Balkans* (London-NY-San Francisco 1977)

H.L. Cooke, H.W. Hazard, *Atlas of Islamic history* (Princeton[3] 1954)

A.W. Dunn, 'The Exploitation and Control of Woodland and Scrubland in the Byzantine World', *BMGS* 16 (1992) 235-298

J.C. Edmondson, 'Mining in the later Roman empire and beyond', *JRS* 79 (1989) 84-102

M.F. Hendy, *Studies in the Byzantine monetary economy c.300-1450* (Cambridge 1985)

R.P. Lindner, *Nomads and Ottomans in medieval Anatolia* (Bloomington, Indiana 1983)

R.S. Lopez, 'The Evolution of Land Transport in the Middle Ages', *Past and Present* 9 (1957-58) 17-29

V.J. Parry, M.E. Yapp, eds., *War, technology and society in the Middle East* (NY 1977)

P. Pattenden, 'The Byzantine Early Warning System', *Byzantion* 53 (1983) 258-99

N.J.G. Pounds, *An historical geography of Europe, 450 BC-AD 1330* (Cambridge 1973)

R. Roolvink et al., *Historical atlas of the Muslim peoples* (Amsterdam 1957)

J.C. Russell, *Late ancient and medieval population* (Philadelphia 1958)

W.M. Ramsay, *The historical geography of Asia Minor*, Royal Geographical Society, Supplementary Papers IV (London 1890/Amsterdam 1962)

Sp. Vryonis, 'The question of the Byzantine mines', *Speculum* 37 (1962) 1-17

J.M. Wagstaff, *The evolution of the Middle Eastern landscapes* (Canterbury 1984)

J. L. Teall, 'The grain supply of the Byzantine empire, 330-1025', *DOP* 13 (1959) 87-139

M. Whittow, 'The strategic geography of the Near East', in *idem*, The *making of Orthodox Byzantium, 600-1025* (London 1996) 15-37

Excellent accounts of the climate, geography and communications of the central Byzantine lands can be found in the Admiralty geographical handbooks:

> *Greece*, I: *Physical geography, history, administration and peoples*, Naval Intelligence Division, Geographical Handbook Series, B.R. 516 (London 1944)
>
> *Greece*, II: *Economic geography, ports and communications*, Naval Intelligence Division, Geographical Handbook Series, B.R. 516A (London 1944)
>
> *Greece*, III: *Regional geography*, Naval Intelligence Division, Geographical Handbook Series, B.R. 516B (London 1945)
>
> *Turkey*, I, Naval Intelligence Division, Geographical Handbook Series, B.R. 507 (London 1942)
>
> *Turkey*, II, Naval Intelligence Division, Geographical Handbook Series, B.R. 507A (London 1943)
>
> Other volumes in the series, for Albania, Yugoslavia and Bulgaria are also accessible

b. Transport, livestock

B.S. Bachrach, 'Animals and warfare in early medieval Europe', in *L'Uomo di fronte al mondo animale nell'alto Medioevo* (Settimane di Studio del Centro Italiano di Studi sull'alto Medioevo 31. Spoleto 1983 [Spoleto, 1985]), pp. 707-51

R.W. Bulliet, *The Camel and the Wheel* (Cambridge, Mass. 1975)

C. Gladitz, *Horse breeding in the medieval world* (Dublin, 1997)

Ann Hyland, *Equus: the horse in the Roman world* (London, 1990)

A. Hyland, *The medieval warhorse: from Byzantium to the Crusades* (Stroud, ²1996)

R.S. Lopez, 'The evolution of land transport in the Midle Ages', *Past and Present* 9 (1957-1958) 17-29

W.B. Tegetmeir, *Horses, asses, mules and mule breeding* (Washington DC, 1897)

c. Some useful non-English works

M. Kaplan, *Les hommes et la terre à Byzance du VIe au XIe siècle* (Byzantina Sorbonensia 10) (Paris 1992), esp. ch. 1: 'Aperçu géographique', 5-24; ch. 2: 'L'agriculture byzantine: produits, techniques, résultats', 25-88

J. Koder, *Der Lebensraum der Byzantiner. Historisch-geographischer Abriß ihres mittelalterlichen Staates im östlichen Mittelmeerraum* (Graz-Wien-Köln 1984)

E. Malamut, *Sur la route des saints byzantins* (Paris 1993)

O. Maull, 'Der Einfluß geographischer Faktoren auf die Geschichte des byzantinischen Reiches', *Südostforschungen* 21 (1962) 1-21

A. Philippson, *Das byzantinische Reich als geographische Erscheinung* (Leiden 1939)

W.C. Schneider, 'Animal laborans. Das Arbeitstier und sein Einsatz im Transport und Verkehr der Spätantike und des frühen Mittelalters', in *L'Uomo di fronte al mondo animale nell'alto Medioevo* (Settimane di Studio del Centro Italiano di Studi sull'alto Medioevo 31. Spoleto 1983 [Spoleto, 1985]), pp. 457-578

For a more specialist approach, the series of detailed historical maps with commentaries and topographical-historical catalogues produced by the Austrian Academy are indispensable:

> J. Koder, F. Hild, *Tabula Imperii Byzantini* 1: *Hellas und Thessalia* (Denkschr. d. Österr. Akad. d Wiss., phil.-hist. Kl. 125. Vienna 1976)
>
> F.Hild, M. Restlé, *Tabula Imperii Byzantini 2: Kappadokien (Kappadokia, Charsianon, Sebasteia und*

Lykandos) (Denkschr. d. Österr. Akad. d Wiss., phil.-hist. Kl. 149. Vienna 1981)

P. Soustal, with J. Koder, *Tabula Imperii Byzantini 3: Nikopolis und Kephallenia* (Denkschr. d. Österr. Akad. d Wiss., phil.-hist. Kl. 150. Vienna 1981)

K. Belke (with M. Restle), *Tabula Imperii Byzantini 4: Galatien und Lykaonien* (Denkschr. d. Österr. Akad. d Wiss., phil.-hist. Kl. 172. Vienna 1984)

F. Hild, H. Hellenkamper, *Tabula Imperii Byzantini 5, 1/2: Kilikien und Isaurien* (Denkschr. d. Österr. Akad. d Wiss., phil.-hist. Kl. 215. Vienna 1990)

P. Soustal, *Tabula Imperii Byzantini 6: Thrakien (Thrakê, Rodopê und Haimimontos)* (Denkschr. d. Österr. Akad. d Wiss., phil.-hist. Kl. 221. Vienna 1991)

K. Belke, N. Mersich, *Tabula Imperii Byzantini 7: Phrygien und Pisidien* (Denkschr. d. Österr. Akad. d Wiss., phil.-hist. Kl. 211. Vienna 1990)

K. Belke, *Tabula Imperii Byzantini 9: Paphlagonien und Honorias* (Denkschr. d. Österr. Akad. d Wiss., phil.-hist. Kl. 249. Vienna 1996)

Volumes 8, 11 and 12 are to appear: *Tabula Imperii Byzantini 8: Lykien und Pamphylien,* 11: *Makedonien,* 12: *Marmarameer-Region (Bithynia, Hellespontos, Europê)*

Chapter 4: The Byzantine state

M. Angold, *A Byzantine government in exile: government and society under the Laskarids of Nicaea (1204-1261)* (Oxford 1975)

M.C. Bartusis, *The late Byzantine army. Arms and society, 1204-1453* (Philadelphia 1992)

C.M. Brand, 'Two Byzantine Treatises on Taxation', *Traditio* 25 (1969) 35-60

J.B. Bury, *A history of the later Roman empire from Arcadius to Irene (395 A.D. to 800 A.D.)* (London 1889/Amsterdam 1966)

J.B. Bury, *The imperial administrative system in the ninth century, with a revised text of the Kletorologion of Philotheos* (British Academy Supplemental Papers I) (London 1911)

Av. Cameron, ed., *States, resources and armies: papers of the third workshop on late Antiquity and early Islam* (Princeton 1995)

K.R. Dixon, P. Southern, *The late Roman army* (London 1996)

H. Elton, *Warfare in Roman Europe, AD 350-425* (Oxford 1996)

J.F. Haldon, *Byzantium in the seventh century: the transformation of a culture* (Cambridge 1990/1997)

J.F. Haldon, *State, army and society in Byzantium. Approaches to military, social and administrative history* (Aldershot 1995)

J.F. Haldon, *Warfare, state and society in the Byzantine world, 565-1204* (London 1999)

A. Harvey, *Economic expansion in the Byzantine empire 900-1200* (Cambridge 1989)

M.F. Hendy, *Studies in the Byzantine monetary economy, c.300-1450* (Cambridge 1985)

A.H.M. Jones, *The later Roman empire, 284-602: a Social, Economic and Administrative Survey*, 3 vols and maps (Oxford 1964)

M. Kaplan, *Les hommes et la terre à Byzance du VIe au XIe siècle. Propriété et exploitation du sol* (Paris 1992)

P. Lemerle, *The agrarian history of Byzantium from the origins to the twelfth century: the sources and the problems* (Galway 1979)

N. Oikonomidès, ed., *Byzantium at war* (Athens 1997)

G. Ostrogorsky, *History of the Byzantine state* (Oxford 1968)

A. Toynbee, *Constantine Porphyrogenitus and his world* (London 1973)

M. Whittow, *The Making of Orthodox Byzantium, 600-1025* (London 1996)

Chapter 5: Life in town and countryside

D.Z.de F. Abrahamse, *Hagiographic sources for Byzantine cities* (Ann Arbor, Michigan 1967)

D. Abulafia, *Italy, Sicily and the Mediterranean, 1100-1400* (London 1987)

M. Angold, 'The shaping of the medieval Byzantine "city"', *Byzantinische Forschungen* 10 (1985) 1-37

M. Angold, *The Byzantine empire 1025-1204: a political history* (London 1984)

M. Balard, 'The Genoese in the Aegean', in B. Arbel, B. Hamilton, D. Jacoby, eds, *Latins and Greeks in the eastern Mediterranean after 1204* (London 1989) 158-174

G.P. Brogiolo, B. Ward-Perkins, eds., *The idea and ideal of the town between late antiquity and the early middle ages* (Leiden 1999)

G. Duby, *The early growth of the European economy. Warriors and peasants from the seventh to the twelfth century* (London 1974)

A. Dunn, 'The transformation from *polis* to *kastron* in the Balkans (III-VII cc.): general and regional perspectives', *Byzantine and Modern Greek Studies* 18 (1994) 60-80

C. Foss, 'Late antique and Byzantine Ankara', *Dumbarton Oaks Papers* 31 (1977) 29-87

C. Foss, D. Winfield, *Byzantine fortifications. An introduction* (Pretoria 1986)

C. Foss, *Ephesus after antiquity: a late antique, Byzantine and Turkish city* (Cambridge 1979)

C. Foss, *Byzantine and Turkish Sardis* (Cambridge, Mass.-London 1976)]

C. Foss, 'Archaeology and the 'Twenty Cities' of Byzantine Asia', *American Journal of Archaeology* 81 (1977)

J.F. Haldon, *Byzantium in the seventh century: the transformation of a culture* (Cambridge 1990) (chapters on rural society, cities)

J. F. Haldon, W. Brandes, 'Towns, tax and transformation: state, cities and their hinterlands in the East Roman world, *c.*500-800', in N. Gauthier, ed., *Towns and their hinterlands between late antiquity and the early middle ages* (Leiden, 1999)

A. Harvey, *Economic expansion in the Byzantine Empire 900-1200* (Cambridge 1989)

M.F. Hendy, 'Byzantium, 1081-1204: the economy revisited, twenty years on', in *The economy, fiscal administration and coinage of Byzantium* (London 1989) III

R. Hohlfelder, ed., *City, town and countryside in the early Byzantine era* (New York 1982)

D. Jacoby, 'Silk in western Byzantium before the Fourth Crusade', *BZ* 84/85 (1991/2) 452-500

A.H.M. Jones, *The Greek city from Alexander to Justinian* (Oxford 1967)

A.H.M. Jones, 'The cities of the Roman Empire: political, administrative and judicial functions', *Recueils de la Société Jean Bodin* 6 (1954) 135-173 (repr. in idem, *The Roman economy: studies in ancient economic and administrative history* ed. P.A. Brunt [Oxford 1974] 1-34

A.H.M. Jones, *The later Roman Empire 284-602: a social, economic and administrative survey* (Oxford 1964) 716-719

J. Koder, 'The urban character of the early Byzantine empire: some reflections on a settlement geographical approach to the topic', in *Seventeenth International Byzantine Congress. Major Papers* (New York 1986) 155-187

Angeliki Laiou, 'The Byzantine economy in the Mediterranean trade system: thirteenth-fifteenth centuries', *DOP* 34-35 (1980-1981) 177-222

A. Laiou, 'The Greek merchant of the Palaeologan period: a collective portrait', *Praktika tês akademias Athênôn* (Athens 1982) 96-124

P. Lemerle, *The Agrarian History of Byzantium from the Origins to the Twelfth Century: the Sources and the Problems* (Galway 1979)

C. Mango, 'The development of Constantinople as an urban centre', in *Seventeenth International Byzantine Congress. Major Papers* (New York 1986) 118-136

C. Mango, *Studies on Constantinople* (Aldershot 1993)

C. Mango and G. Dagron, eds., *Constantinople and its hinterland* (Aldershot 1995)

M. Martin, 'The Venetians in the Byzantine empire before 1204', *BF* 13 (1988) 201-214

D.M. Nicol, *Byzantium and Venice* (Cambridge 1988).

J. Russell, 'Transformations in early Byzantine urban life: the contribution and limitations of archaeological evidence', in *Seventeenth International Byzantine Congress. Major Papers* (New York 1986) 137-154

M. Whittow, 'Ruling the late Roman and early Byzantine city: a continuous history', *Past and Present* 129 (Nov. 1990) 3-29

Chapter 6: Byzantine political society

M. Angold, ed., *The Byzantine aristocracy, IX to XIII centuries* (Oxford 1984)

M. Angold, 'Archons and dynasts: local aristocracies and the cities of the later Byzantine empire', in Angold, ed., *The Byzantine aristocracy*, 236-253

M. Angold, *The Byzantine empire 1025-1204. A political history* (London 1984)

T.S. Brown, *Gentlemen and officers. Imperial administration and aristocratic power in Byzantine Italy, A.D. 554-80* (Rome 1984)

J.B. Bury, *The imperial administrative system in the ninth century, with a revised text of the Kletorologion of Philotheos* (British Academy Supplemental Papers I) (London 1911)

Av. Cameron, *The Mediterranean world in late antiquity A.D. 395-600* (London 1993)

Cambridge medieval history, vol. iv, parts 1 and 2, revised edn. J.M. Hussey (Cambridge 1966)

J.F. Haldon, *Byzantium in the seventh century: the transformation of a culture* (Cambridge 1990/1997)

A. Harvey, *Economic expansion in the Byzantine empire 900-1200* (Cambridge 1989)

M.F. Hendy, 'Economy and state in late Roman and early Byzantium: an introduction', in M.F. Hendy, *The economy, fiscal administration and coinage of Byzantium* (Northampton 1989)

M.F. Hendy, 'Byzantium 1081-1204: an economic re-appraisal', *Transactions of the Royal Historical Society* 20 (1970) 31-52 (repr. in Hendy, *The economy, fiscal administration and coinage of Byzantium* III)

M.F. Hendy, *Studies in the Byzantine monetary economy, c.300-1450* (Cambridge 1985)

A.H.M. Jones, *The later Roman empire: a social, economic and administrative survey*, 3 vols. and maps (Oxford 1964)

A. Kazhdan, G. Constable, *People and power in Byzantium: an introduction to modern Byzantine studies* (Washington D.C. 1982)

A. Kazhdan, A. Epstein, *Change in Byzantine culture in the eleventh and twelfth centuries* (Berkeley-Los Angeles-London 1985)

A. Laiou, 'The Byzantine aristocracy in the Palaeologan period', *Viator* 4 (1973) 131-151

P. Magdalino, *The empire of Manuel I Komnenos, 1143-1180* (Cambridge 1993)

P. Magdalino, 'Honour among Romaioi: the framework of social values in the world of Digenes Akrites and Kekaumenos', *BMGS* 13 (1989) 183-218

C. Mango, *Byzantium: the empire of New Rome* (London 1980/1994)

M. McCormick, *Eternal victory. triumphal rulership in late antiquity, Byzantium and the early medieval West* (Cambridge 1986)

R. Morris, 'The Powerful and the poor in tenth-century Byzantium: law and reality', *Past and Present* 73 (1976) 3-27

G. Ostrogorsky, 'Observations on the aristocracy in Byzantium', *DOP* 25 (1971) 1-32

A. Toynbee, *Constantine Porphyrogenitus and his world* (London 1973)

Chapter 7: Church, state and belief

P. Alexander, *Religious and political history and thought in the Byzantine empire* (London 1978)

P. Alexander, 'The strength of empire and capital as seen through Byzantine eyes', *Speculum* 37 (1962) 339-357

P. Alexander, *The Patriarch Nicephorus of Constantinople. Ecclesiastical policy and image worship in the Byzantine empire* (Oxford 1958)

A.S. Atiya, *A history of Eastern Christianity* (London 1968)

M. Angold, *The Byzantine empire 1025-1204. A political history* (London 1984)

M. Angold, *Church and society in Byzantium under the Comneni, 1081-1261* (Cambridge 1995)

N.H. Baynes, 'Eusebius and the Christian empire', in N.H. Baynes, *Byzantine studies and other essays*, 168-172

P.R.L. Brown, *The world of late antiquity* (London 1971)

P.R.L. Brown, *The cult of the saints* (London 1981)

P. Brown, 'Eastern and Western Christendom in late antiquity: a parting of the ways', *Studies in Church History* 13 (1976) 1-24

P. Brown, 'The rise and function of the holy man in late antiquity', *Journal of Roman Studies* 61 (1971) 80-101

Av. Cameron, *The Mediterranean world in late antiquity A.D. 395-600* (London 1993)

Av. Cameron, *Christianity and the rhetoric of empire* (Berkeley 1991)

H. Chadwick, *The early Church* (Harmondsworth 1967)

H. Chadwick, *The role of the Christian bishop in ancient society* (Berkeley 1980)

P. Charanis, *Studies on the demography of the Byzantine empire* (London 1972)

P. Charanis, 'The transfer of population as a policy in the Byzantine empire', *Comparative Studies in Society and History* 3/2 (1961) 140-154 (repr. in Charanis, *Studies* III)

P. Charanis, 'The monk as an element of Byzantine society', *Dumbarton Oaks Papers* 25 (1971) 61-84

P. Charanis, 'The monastic properties and the state in the Byzantine empire', *Dumbarton Oaks Papers* 4 (1948), 53-118 (reprinted in his *Social, Economic and Political Life*, essay I)

D. Chitty, *The Desert a City* (Oxford 1966)

D.J. Constantelos, *Byzantine philanthropy and social welfare* (New Brunswick, N.J. 1968)

Cambridge medieval history, vol. iv, parts 1 and 2, revised edn. J.M. Hussey (Cambridge 1966)

G. Dix, *Jurisdiction in the early Church, episcopal and papal* (London 1975)

F. Dvornik, *Early Christian and Byzantine political philosophy*, 2 vols. (Washington D.C. 1966)

F. Dvornik, *The Photian Schism: history and legend* (Cambridge 1948)

G. Every, *The Byzantine Patriarchate (451-1204)* (London 1947)

C. Frazee, 'St Theodore of Stoudios and ninth-century monasticism in Constantinople', *Studia Monastica* 23 (1981) 27-58

W.H.C. Frend, *The rise of the Monophysite movement* (Cambridge 1972)

C. Galatariotou, 'Byzantine women's monastic communities: the evidence of the typika', *Jahrbuch der Österreichischen Byzantinistik* 38 (1988) 263-90

N. Garsoïan, *The Paulician heresy* (The Hague-Paris 1967)

S. Hackel, ed., *The Byzantine saint* (London 1981)

J.F. Haldon, *Byzantium in the seventh century: the transformation of a culture* (Cambridge 1990/1997)

P. Henry, 'What was the Iconoclast controversy about?', *Church History* 45 (1976) 16-31

J. Herrin, *The formation of Christendom* (Princeton 1987)

J.M. Hussey, *The Orthodox Church in the Byzantine empire* (Oxford 1986)

A. Kazhdan, G. Constable, *People and power in Byzantium: an introduction to modern Byzantine studies* (Washington D.C. 1982)

A. Kazhdan, A. Epstein, *Change in Byzantine culture in the eleventh and twelfth centuries* (Berkeley-Los Angeles-London 1985)

A.P. Kazhdan, 'Hermitic cenobitic and secular ideals in Byzantine hagiography of the ninth century', *Greek Orthodox Theological Review* 30, nr.4 (1985), 473-87

M. Loos, *Dualist heresy in the Middle Ages* (Prague 1974)

V. Lossky, *The mystical theology of the Eastern Church* (Cambridge 1957)

C. Mango, *Byzantium: the empire of New Rome* (London 1980/1994)

R. A. Markus, *From Augustine to Gregory the Great: history and Christianity in late antiquity* (London 1983)

R.A. Markus, *The end of ancient Christianity* (Cambridge 1990)

E.J. Martin, *A history of the Iconoclastic controversy* (London 1930)

M. McCormick, *Eternal victory. triumphal rulership in late antiquity, Byzantium and the early medieval West* (Cambridge 1986)

J. Meyendorff, *Byzantine theology: historical trends and doctrinal themes* (NY 1974)

R. Morris, *Monks and laymen in Byzantium, 843-1118* (Cambridge 1995)

R. Morris, ed., *Church and people in Byzantium* (Birmingham 1990)

D. Obolensky, *The Byzantine commonwealth. Eastern Europe 500-1453* (London 1971)

D. Obolensky, *The Bogomils* (Cambridge 1948)

J. Pelikan, *The Christian tradition*, 4 vols. (Chicago 1971-83)

K. Ringrose, *Saints, holy men and Byzantine society, 726-843* (Ann Arbor 1976)

S. Runciman, *The medieval Manichee. A study of the Christian dualist heresy* (Cambridge 1947)

A. Sharf, *Byzantine Jewry from Justinian to the Fourth Crusade* (London 1971)

J. Starr, *The Jews in the Byzantine Empire, 641-1204* (Athens 1939)

J. Starr, 'An Eastern Christian sect: the Athigganoi', *Harvard Theological review* 29 (1936) 93-106

Sp. Vryonis, jr., *The decline of medieval Hellenism in Asia Minor and the process of Islamization from the eleventh through the fifteenth century* (Berkeley-Los Angeles-London 1971)

C. Walter, *Art and ritual in the Byzantine Church* (London 1982)

P. Verghese, 'The Monothelite controversy – a historical survey', *Greek Orthodox Theological review* 13 (1968) 196-211

Chapter 8: Power, art and tradition in Byzantium

M. Angold, *Church and society in Byzantium under the Comneni, 1081-1261* (Cambridge 1995)

J. Beckwith, *The art of Constantinople* (London 1961)

C.M. Brand, *Byzantium confronts the West, 1180-1204* (Harvard 1968)

R. Browning, 'Literacy in the Byzantine world', *Byzantine and Modern Greek Studies* 4 (1978) 39-54

L. Brubaker, 'Perception and conception: art, theory and culture in ninth-century Byzantium', *Word and Image* 5/1 (1989) 19-32

The Cambridge medieval history, IV: *The Byzantine empire*, 2 parts, revised ed. J.M. Hussey (Cambridge 1966)

R. Cormack, ed., *The Byzantine eye: studies in art and patronage* (London 1989)

R. Cormack, *Writing in gold: Byzantine society and its icons* (Oxford 1985)

F. Dvornik, *Early Christian and Byzantine political philosophy*, 2 vols. (Washington D.C. 1966)

C.M. George, *George Gemistos Plethon: the last of the Hellenes* (Oxford 1986)

R.-J. Lilie, *Byzantium and the Crusader states 1096-1204*, trans. J.C. Morris, J.C. Ridings (Oxford 1993)

J. Lowden, 'Luxury and liturgy: the function of books', in R. Morris, ed., *Church and People in Byzantium* (Birmingham 1990) 263-280

P. Magdalino, *The empire of Manuel I Komnenos, 1143-1180* (Cambridge 1993)

H. Maguire, *Art and eloquence in Byzantium* (Princeton 1981)

H. Maguire, *The icons of their bodies. Saints and their images in Byzantium* (Princeton 1996)

C. Mango, *Byzantine architecture* (New York 1970/1976)

C. Mango, *The art of the Byzantine empire 312-1453* (Sources and documents in the history of art. Englewood Cliffs 1972)

C. Mango, *Byzantium: the empire of New Rome* (London 1980/1994)

M. Mullett, 'Writing in early medieval Byzantium', in R. McKitterick, ed., *The uses of literacy in early medieval Europe* (Cambridge 1990) 156-185

M. Mullett and R. Scott, eds, *Byzantium and the Classical Tradition* (Birmingham 1981)

D.M. Nicol, *The Despotate of Epiros, 1267-1479* (Cambridge 1984)

D.M. Nicol, *The last centuries of Byzantium, 1261-1453* (London 1972)

D.M. Nicol, *The end of the Byzantine empire* (London 1979)

D. Obolensky, *The Byzantine commonwealth. Eastern Europe 500-1453* (London 1971)

G. Ostrogorsky, *A history of the Byzantine state*, Eng. trans. J. Hussey (Oxford 1968)

L.D. Reynolds and N.G. Wilson, *Scribes & scholars: a guide to the transmission of Greek and Latin literature*, 2nd ed. (Oxford 1974)

L. Rodley, *Cave monasteries of Byzantine Cappadocia* (Cambridge 1985)

S. Runciman, *The last Byzantine renaissance* (Cambridge 1970)

I. Ševčenko, 'The search for the past in Byzantium around the year 800', *Dumbarton Oaks Papers* 46 (1992)

J. Shepard and S. Franklin, eds., *Byzantine Diplomacy* (Aldershot 1992)

C. Walter, *Art and ritual of the Byzantine Church* (London 1982)

K. Weitzmann, *The classical heritage in Byzantine and Near Eastern art* (London 1981)

N.G. Wilson, *Scholars of Byzantium* (Baltimore 1983)

List of illustrations

Key: ★ courtesy of A.A.M. Bryer; † courtesy of Leslie Brubaker; †† courtesy of the Barber Institute of Fine Arts, Birmingham. All other illustrations are from the author's collection.

Index: Individuals, peoples and places